Reproductions of Banality

# REPRODUCTIONS OF BANALITY

## Fascism, Literature,
## and French Intellectual Life

## Alice Yaeger Kaplan

### Foreword by Russell Berman

**Theory and History of Literature, volume 36**

**University of Minnesota Press, Minneapolis**

Published with assistance from the Margaret S.
Harding Memorial Endowment honoring the first
director of the University of Minnesota Press.

Published by the University of Minnesota Press
2037 University Avenue Southeast, Minneapolis, MN 55414
Published simultaneously in Canada
by Fitzhenry & Whiteside Limited, Markham.
Printed in the United States of America.

**Library of Congress Cataloging-in-Publication Data**

Kaplan, Alice Yaeger.
  Reproductions of banality.

  (Theory and history of literature ; v. 36)
  Bibliography: pp. 195-204
  Includes index.
  1. France—Intellectual life—20th century.
2. Fascism—France—History. 3. French literature—20th
century—History and criticism. I. Title. II. Series.
DC33.7.K37 1986     944.08     86-1428
ISBN 0-8166-1494-6
ISBN 0-8166-1495-4 (pbk.)

The first section of chapter 4 and chapter 6 are revised versions
of articles published originally in *Yale Italian Studies*, vol. 1,
no. 3 (1981):39-56 and *Modern Language Notes*, vol. 95, no.
4 (1980):864-83. An abbreviated version of chapter 7 has
appeared in *Substance*, no. 49 (1986):44-68. Selections from
previously unpublished writings by F.-T. Marinetti, copyright
© 1986 by Luce Marinetti Barbi, are used by arrangement with
Luce Marinetti Barbi.

The University of Minnesota
is an equal-opportunity
educator and employer.

# Contents

**Theory and History of Literature**
**Edited by Wlad Godzich and Jochen Schulte-Sasse**

# Acknowledgments

Financial aid from the North Carolina State Faculty Research and Professional Development Fund and the Penrose Fund of the American Philosophical Society allowed me to pursue full-time research on this book during the summers of 1982 and 1983. A grant from the American Council of Learned Societies allowed me to devote January through June of 1984 to writing; a grant for the summer of 1984 from the Columbia University Council for Research in the Humanities allowed me to complete the project, in August 1984. I am grateful to Joseph Halpern, Fredric Jameson, Louis Martz, Linda Orr, Ann Smock, and Joan Stewart, who have written letters of support for me on numerous occasions.

Jacques Guicharnaud, Joseph Halpern, Miriam Hansen, Fredric Jameson, Bernhard Kendler, Paolo Valesio, and Elie Wiesel read my doctoral dissertation. Thanks in part to their encouragement and suggestions, that document is by now a rather distant ancestor of the pages that follow. Bernard Wishy, too, will recognize how much I benefited from his page-by-page annotation of the dissertation manuscript. David Auerbach, Janet Beizer, Jay Cantor, Reed Dasenbrock, Denis Hollier, Charles Krance, Larry Kritzman, Linda Orr, Kristin Ross, Ann Smock, Barbara Spackman, Jean-Jacques Thomas, Alan Williams, Pattie Winspur, and Steven Winspur read and commented on later work. Again, Fredric Jameson has been of consistent support and inspiration.

Some of the most useful help I received was quite specific—an important question, a bibliographic lead, a book lent—and so I have thanked a number of people in individual notes to the text. Still, I must thank Janie Kritzman of the Barnard Women's Center for bibliographic wisdom, and Dario Cortez and

Yvonne Rollins for advice and information on grant writing. Nathaniel Wing invited me to present a paper, a version of which is incorporated into chapter 1, at the French Department of the Miami University in 1982. Michael Riffaterre invited me to present a paper, an expanded version of which appears as chapter 5, at the Columbia University Colloquium on the Poetics of Ideology in 1983. I profited greatly from those two occasions. I also feel lucky to have been able to discuss some of my ideas with the graduate students in my course on fascism in France—Betsy Bowman, Rena Miller, Phil Watts, Fereshteh Yadegar. Joseph Rio's fine research assistance has proved invaluable in the preparation of notes and references.

Jochen Schulte-Sasse has offered sound theoretical and editorial advice over a period of several years, introducing me to important new German theories of fascism and specifically to the work of Klaus Theweleit.

Finally, on a personal note, my affectionate thanks go to Peter Zorach and to David Auerbach, Kristin Ross, and Martha Williams.

That I have received so much support from so many people and institutions is surely the sign of an ongoing commitment within the intellectual community to the struggle against fascism. I bear full responsibility for any documentary and analytic shortcomings that remain in this book in spite of their help.

# Foreword
# The Wandering Z:
# Reflections on Kaplan's
# *Reproductions of Banality*
# *Russell Berman*

An orthographic bagatelle, a misspelling of two names, connects the inception of the postwar French discussion of intellectual fascism and the seminal investigation among German exiles in the United States of the descent of *Kultur* into barbarism. In "Qu'est-ce qu'un collaborateur?" of 1945, Sartre presents Robert Brasillach, who figures centrally in Alice Kaplan's study as a representative of the Parisian ideologues of a radical fascism, as "Brazillach," inscribing in his name his enthusiastic support for the Nazi German Occupation. This was perhaps no naive error but at least a significant lapsus if not a calculated effort to represent the collaborator as a traitor, as if the French intellectual could have greeted the Nazis only by surrendering his native identity and aiding an emphatically foreign power. In the wake of the liberation, Sartre's antifascist project appears to constitute itself on the basis of an initial premise that equates fascism and treason, a premise which automatically precluded inquiries into either a specifically French fascist lineage or a genuine attraction to the ideology of fascism on the part of intellectuals, especially those formed by the innovations of the early twentieth-century avant-garde. *Nomen est omen*: a "Brazillach" could only be a Nazi thug, and, even when masquerading as a Parisian film critic, his connections to France and to the French mind could only be nill. Yet an antifascism that defines itself by insisting on the inviolability of the national community is evidently implicated in the same discursive structure it purports to oppose, producing the image of a French *Volksgemeinschaft*. It thereby crippled subsequent efforts to come to terms with the real tragedy of France, the massive

acquiescence during the Occupation, occluded by the myth that the genuine resistance of a heroic minority had been the experience of the whole people.

Yet not only in its constitution of an organic national unity but also in the rhetorical gesture of abusing names did antifascism mirror the enemy it purported
to oppose. To denounce opponents in political or cultural life, Nazi propagan-
dists and *völkisch* ideologues in Germany regularly insisted on labeling them
with real or, with equal frequency, fictive names that were intended to sound
Jewish. By the late thirties in fact Jewish men were uniformly designated as "Israel," and Jewish women as "Sara." This rhetoric of specious nomenclature was
even extended into international politics with the derivation of "Roosevelt" from
"Rosenfeld," proving that American hostility to Hitler's Germany was ultimately
a consequence of a Jewish conspiracy initiated by the Elders of Zion.[1] "Brazillach" and "Rosenfeld": the name testifies to the enemy as ontological outsider,
fundamentally excluded from the homogenity of the people. The discursive
similarity can of course not be taken as evidence of a proximity of fascism and
antifascism — that would be absurd — but it does point to a structural weakness in
an antifascist politics that, imitating the strategy of its antagonists, locates the
danger outside of an otherwise untroubled national community, as if fascism had
no local roots, as if French fascism were in no way heir to a French tradition.
Ophuls's film *The Sorrow and the Pity* began to open up the premature closure
of these problems, and this volume can be read, at least in part, as an extension
of his project in a new terrain.

In the first years after 1945 little would seem to connect Sartre in Paris and
Thomas Mann in Pacific Palisades. As Sartre emerged as the representative
intellectual of postwar France by integrating philosophical thought with an emphatically political presence, Mann, who beyond any doubt had acted as the
leading anti-Hitler spokesman of the German exile, appeared to retreat into a
world of mandarin culture and hermetic prose, rejecting impassioned pleas for
him to return to Germany where he might have become the mentor of a new
generation of writers and most likely the conscience of a rudimentary political
culture. Equally little is shared by two of their texts, "Qu'est-ce qu'un collaborateur?" and *Doktor Faustus* (1947), little, that is to say, except for their
thematic inquiry into the complicity of intellectual culture in fascism and their
common orthographic idiosyncrasy, the mercurial z. Mann borrows the name
of the nineteenth-century music historian Hermann Kretzschmar to portray the
eccentric musicologist, Wendell Kretzschmar, whose lecture on Beethoven's
opus 111, one of the best-known passages of the novel, introduces the first and
clearest account of the dialectic of culture and barbarism, in other words, intellectuals and fascism. But the z that Sartre adds to metamorphosize the film
historian Brasillach into the Nazi Brazillach disappears in the simultaneous English version of Mann's novel, when Kretzschmar becomes Kretschmar. What
meaning does the z carry that is lost in translation — or liquidated? What compels

an immigrant to adapt the ethnic name to anglo-saxon spelling? The z disappears in the new world like the memory of the old country, like Bardèche's ghetto, gone up in smoke. Or what is the z in German culture which is so violently denied that the mere sight of the sign becomes intolerable?

The distortion in "Brazillach" explains the code; marked with a z, the musicologist, who expounds on culture, his special purview, is a Nazi, and the novel is designated as specifically political: as if the z in the name were like a J in the passport, but of course its opposite. The omission of the z in the English translation where Kretzschmar is reborn as Kretschmar shows how the European text (even if written in the United States) appears before the American public robbed of its political coloration that disappears in the melting pot of ideas.[2] To be sure, even this depoliticization was a political gesture, since at the moment of publication of Mann's dissection of the cultural genealogy of fascism, the antifascist coalition of the war had already given way to the hostilities of the Cold War, and this account of the Nazi roots in German culture – the meaning of the z – was displaced by a general discourse of totalitarianism. Kaplan draws attention to a similar displacement: when American agents tapped into an Italian radio broadcast of Ezra Pound, they mistook mentionings of Céline as references to Stalin.

Mann's narrator recounts how Adrian Leverkühn, the central figure of the novel, took particular note of Kretzschmar's historico-philosophical location of Beethoven's work within a history of the secularization of art. Once lodged within the objective structures of premodern society and religious cult, music achieved its own specific autonomy simultaneously with the emergence of the autonomous subjectivity of the bourgeois personality in the context of modernity as *Neuzeit*. What Max Weber would describe as the immanent rationalization of a differentiated value sphere, no longer dependent on the exigencies of political or ecclesiastical representation, permits a previously unknown development of a particular aesthetic substance as well as of the interiority of the individuated subject: the freedom of art and the freedom of the individual. Yet the formal structure of opus 111, which comes to an apparently premature conclusion at the end of the second movement, indicates the obsolescence of a limited bourgeois project of emancipation, a project that casts emancipation in terms of merely individual creativity. This line of thought anticipates the emergence, later in the novel, of the program for twelve-tone composition in which the composer, restricted by the dictate of seriality, surrenders all freedom or, as Leverkühn will insist, achieves a new and substantively superior freedom through adherence to a freely chosen order. In the debate following the Kretzschmar lecture, however, this trajectory appears as a speculation on the history of music, which once was embedded in liturgy and cult; which later became autonomous in the subjectivist culture of an emancipatory modernity; and which – this is the speculation – might transcend the limitations of bourgeois freedom in a future objective order and thereby cease to be only "culture." Such a regained objectivity need not imply a return to the Church but it would certainly effect a radical break with the privatized creativity that had reached its height in the aestheticism of the late nineteenth century.

Leverkühn's interlocutor, the humanist Serenus Zeitblom, is horrified by his friend's suggestion of an end to culture, which he understands as necessarily implying a regression to a precultural barbarism. The exchange concludes with Leverkühn's retort that barbarism is the opposite of culture only within the world-view of culture and that a sublation of the contradictions in culture could point to something different, something qualitatively new. The discussion itself is indicative of Mann's dialectical ambivalence regarding the legacy of modern art and the genesis of fascism. Although Mann regards aesthetic innovation as an indisputable imperative of the cultural sphere, the European avant-garde of the early twentieth century lodges its diverse innovative projects within a broad attack on the categories of bourgeois emancipation or at least against their deficient realization in the philistine societies of the nineteenth century. Furthermore, the fascist movements of Germany and Italy—and, as Kaplan demonstrates, in France as well—translate this aesthetic rhetoric into the political dimension as dictatorial terror, war, and genocide. This is not to say that the avant-garde intellectuals were the sole or even a major cause of the European catastrophe (just as today the neo-conservative contention that a new class of intellectuals has eroded the fiber of the Protestant ethic misses the socio-economic forces behind the legitimation crisis of contemporary capitalism). This connection does, however, insist on the complicity of intellectual culture, even at its best, in reactionary politics at its worst. Adorno's assertion that "the Absolute became absolute horror" means that German culture, the insistence on the autonomy of the spirit and the absolute idea of idealism, participated in a motion that culminated in Auschwitz.[3] An intellectual antifascism that recognizes the still urgent project of explaining Auschwitz and National Socialism cannot retreat to Zeitblom's position of angrily denouncing barbarism as merely barbaric, outside of culture, and therefore impervious to cultural scrutiny. For an antifascism that makes do with references to inexplicable catastrophe or unmotivated regression or the criminality of the mob has delineated a rhetorical borderline, constructing fascism as the absolute other, and denies itself the possibility of investigating intellectual lineages, perhaps even its own. Has it constructed a self-serving alibi?

"Brazillach" and "Kret(z)schmar"—the wandering z, homeless, crossing borders, never finding a genuine home: the orthographies work at counterpurposes, but the shifting terrain is the same. Sartre's z marks the French fascist as Nazi and an outsider and consequently obviates any further investigation into the native origins of fascism. Mann's z locates the Nazi potential in the center of the discourse of high culture, and its disappearance effects the denial of the past and the blockage of another antifascist project. In the case of France,

Kaplan undertakes the scandalous task of doing without the compulsive denunciation and denial in order to identify the proximity. A double agenda inspires her
investigation: to study a radical French fascism as French and not merely a German import of the "Brazillachs"; and to uncover the intellectual motivations as
intellectual, aesthetic, and cultural and not merely barbaric, monstrous, and
evil. She cites this tension in the title of her volume which draws the reader's
attention to two extraordinarily different but equally controversial accounts of
the genesis of fascism: Hannah Arendt's *Eichmann in Jerusalem: A Report on
the Banality of Evil* and Walter Benjamin's "The Work of Art in the Age of
Mechanical Reproduction."

Fascism and the Holocaust cast a shadow on postwar political culture that
makes dispassionate scholarship extremely difficult and even calls into question
the desirability of a value-free neutrality, blind to the dimensions of human
crime and human suffering. Forty years after the end of the war, cinematic
accounts like Reitz's *Heimat* or Lanzmann's *Shoah* still provoke emotionally
charged responses, just as even such a scholarly voice as that of Stanley Hoffmann becomes "unashamedly subjective" when addressing this material.[4] Kaplan
too makes no bones about her antifascist partisanship. Yet no reexamination of
the Nazi past has provoked more emotion and controversy than Arendt's report
on the Eichmann trial in Jerusalem and especially her designation of the "banality" of the defendant. Because of the crucial importance of the term, its precise
significance needs to be rescued from the misunderstandings that surround it.

Nothing could be further from Arendt's intentions than the suggestion that the
"banality of evil" denotes the triviality or normalcy of Eichmann's actions. On
the contrary, she repeatedly insists that it was the duty of the court to investigate
those actions and to determine the substance of their unique criminal character.
Although she criticizes the handling of the trial, its instrumentalization by Ben-
Gurion, the strategies of the prosecutor, and the logic of the court, she leaves
no doubt that she too considers Eichmann guilty, and, moreover, guilty of
crimes of an extraordinary status which she describes by differentiating among
various components of the Nazi persecution of the Jews. The Nuremberg laws
of 1935 introduced a systematic policy of discrimination, the legality of which
would have to be approached from within the tradition of German law. It lacks
the international character that necessarily accrues to a policy of expulsion that
compels individuals to enter the sovereign territory of foreign nations. Yet discussions of discrimination and expulsion both miss the core of Eichmann's activity which involved an effort to exterminate a nation completely and therefore
amounted to an attack on the diversity of humanity, a feature that Arendt regards
as central to the human condition.[5] Discrimination and expulsion were not unknown (if not the norm) in modern European history; systematic genocide (if
not unprecedented) represented a crime of a different order, and one of Arendt's
major critiques of the trial involves the reluctance of the judges to recognize this

particular status that would have necessitated the establishment of an international tribunal, rather than a court of the Jewish state, as the appropriate forum to pass judgment.

If the "banality of evil" does not designate the character of the crime, neither does it have the implication of commonality, i.e., a collective guilt or the indeed banal suggestion that everyone is an Eichmann. As far as the trial goes, Arendt's commentary depends on her insistence that the task in Jerusalem was to do justice, which in turn rested on perspicuous arguments both for the human possibility to do good or evil and for the human faculty to distinguish between the two. Her ultimately neo-Aristotelian conservatism turns out to be more radical than the contemporary moral relativism that has gained currency within the academic community. For the thrust of her political philosophy aims at recovering a political dimension of agonistic comity, in which diverse individuals realize freedom, beyond the economic necessity of the natural order, through the intersubjectivity of conflictual action. Of course she locates the model of this public sphere in the Greek polis and complains that its decline and the rise of mass society displace politics — the proper realm of freedom — with the conformism of mass society marked by the emergence of the social dimension as the universalization of economic exigency. Nevertheless, even if the modern world increasingly takes on the character of bureaucratic domination — absolutist "one-man-rule" has not been replaced by genuine democracy but by a totalitarian "no-man-rule" — a residual political potential constitutes a constant feature of the human condition. Hence her appreciation of the decentralized character of the original American republic as well as of the model of participatory democracy proposed by the New Left. Hence also her antipathy toward the pessimistic anthropology that suggests that free action is never possible, that following orders or conforming to structures is always inevitable, and that Eichmann therefore stands for us all. That sort of argument is of course tantamount to the objection raised by the defense that Eichmann was only a scapegoat: for Israel, for West Germany, or for the wartime allies. As Arendt emphasizes, the crucial issue before the court was that the individual defendant had indeed committed certain acts, deemed criminal, and that they had not been committed by the whole of humanity (even if they had been, the consequence, within Arendt's logic, would not be an obliteration of their criminal status but rather a universalization of crime). Conversely, because of her concern with the particular guilt of the accused, her term "banality of evil" can obviously not be taken to mean that the crimes were common acts that every individual had performed, could have performed, or, owing to a melancholy construction of human nature, could not escape from performing.

Writing to Heinrich Blücher on April 14, 1961, Arendt described her initial estimation of Eichmann after seeing him for the first time: "nicht einmal unheimlich," not even uncanny or sinister.[6] The defendant does not appear to be an evil monster (as the prosecutor Gideon Hausner would attempt to portray him); neither his demeanor nor his self-understanding seems to correspond to the heinous nature of his crime. Eichmann, at least in Arendt's portrayal, will avoid both a defense of his past and a denial of it, for he can simply not understand it and its magnitude, and this inability to think—what might be referred to as an absence of individual character—points toward the significance of banality, as it would eventually be formulated in the postscript to the book: "Eichmann was not Iago and not Macbeth, and nothing would have been farther from his mind than to determine with Richard III 'to prove a villain'. . . . He *merely*, to put the matter colloquially, *never realized what he was doing.*"[7] For Arendt, the issue remains the guilt of the individual accused; to the extent however, that she views Eichmann as a prototype, he is not everyman but rather the individual who, in bureaucratic society, surrenders individuality and thereby the ability to think, to make moral decisions, and to recognize the humanity of other individuals. Retreating from the dimension of human action, i.e., political encounters with the diversity of community, he transgresses against the community and becomes criminal. His evil is banal because it is predicated not on the decision to do bad but on the refusal to make any decisions at all, and to follow orders, and stifle the moral faculty of which justice presumes the individual capable. His banality is not a quality necessarily shared by everyone but rather the lack of quality and the lack of character that mark human behavior in societies where the valorization of conformism displaces individual autonomy.

For Arendt, this loss of autonomy and the political freedom of the public sphere entails a regression to the level of natural necessity in the guise of the "social" world. Perhaps more that any other motif, the desire for a nature as guarantor of unchanging order—and as the alternative to the metropolis as the locus of individuality and democracy—marks the various fascist literary imaginations: the German literature of blood and soil, Pound's invocations of the natural order of ancient China, and above all the cult of nature in Hamsun. Nature is the structure that precedes and predetermines individuality; subjectivity is merely a bourgeois illusion implicated in a liberal narrative of emancipation that Hamsun denounces from the standpoint of the constancy of power inherent in the sheer facticity of the earth and its seasonal cycles. Lowenthal's trenchant commentary underscores the status of nature within Hamsun's fascist project: "Uniformity of rhythm and tempo is sought in both the natural and human spheres; the passage of time brings recurrence, and not change. Nature's timetable replaces the timetable of history. . . . Whoever senses and accepts these rhythmic patterns as fundamental has full knowledge immediately and without rational effort. At the same time, the endless reproduction of natural phenomena, the cyclic order of nature, as opposed to the apparent disorder and happenstance of all individual and historical facts, testifies to the powerlessness of man. . . . Man must expect a life without meaning unless he obediently accepts as his own what may be called the law of nature. And the social counterpart to the law of natural rhythm is blind discipline."[8] Eichmann's surrendering human autonomy reduces his practice to the "blind discipline" of executing orders, the social corollary to the nature that Arendt relegates to the prepublic realm of economy. Lowenthal similarly identifies a naturalization of political activity as a characteristic of fascist authoritarianism, without however ontologizing the separation of economic privacy and public politics that Arendt derives from classical philosophy. In both cases, fascism—Hamsun or Eichmann—reduces politics to necessity, that appears simultaneously as banality and discipline. "Banality" is therefore not that which is shared by all of humanity, but the substance of the individual who, relinquishing humanity, only submits to discipline and necessity and is consequently "natural." More satisfactory than Arendt's arguments regarding the improverishment of politics in modern mass society as a consequence of quantitative expansion beyond the dimensions of the idealized polis, Kaplan's title points toward a clarificaton of this naturalization of human action in an age of "reproductions," i.e., Benjamin's thesis regarding the transformation of aesthetic production and reception in industrial society and the ramifications for radical political change in the era of communism and fascism.

However, Benjamin's claims regarding the relationship of advanced methods of artistic reproduction and the political dynamics of reception rely on anterior assumptions concerning nature, redemption, and art. For the young Benjamin, nature represents a fallen world of graceless silence, antithetical to the force of messianic redemption lodged in the language of divine provenance. Aesthetic objects constructed as imitations of nature therefore only reproduce the unredeemed state, and their reception consequently appears to take on an idolatrous character. This is in particular the case for bourgeois art and idealist aesthetics that foster a model of the symbolic work as an organic totality, toward which a contemplative reception within a secularized *Kunstreligion* is directed. Both the artist, compelled to imitate the teleology of nature and therefore to refrain from interrupting the logic of the work with fragmentation or commentary, and the passive recipient are condemned to a silence that excludes the redemptive moment of language.

This hostility toward the symbolic work as the image of fallen nature, particularly evident in the 1918 remarks on Adalbert Stifter and in the famous essay on Goethe's *Elective Affinities,* drew on metaphysical and theological commitments that lead Benjamin to a valorization of the allegorical character of the German *Trauerspiel.* Later, behind an emphatically marxist diction, they still structure the denunciation of the auratic work of art in the 1936 essay where technological progress, i.e., the ability to generate mass reproductions of works, performs the labor he had earlier reserved for criticism: the mortification of the work. Photography and cinema wrest aesthetic representation from the debilitating consequences of auratic uniqueness, and cultic traditionalism is replaced with a secular reception by the masses who become the agents of speech and criticism. The symbolic image no longer enervates the collective recipient, the vocalization of which permits it to enter history and politics: the politicization of aesthetics.

Despite this progressivist optimism, Benjamin locates a resistance to the process of deauraticization in the aestheticism of l'art pour l'art and in its political legacy, fascism. The suggestion that fascism undertakes an aestheticization of politics implies, in the context of the essay, that the categories of the traditional auratic work are transferred from the aesthetic sphere, where mechanical reproduction has rendered them obsolete, and transplanted into politics. Thus the genius reappears as the fascist leader, the contemplative recipient becomes the manipulated following, and beauty, once reserved for the autonomous work, is projected onto the battlefield. Fascism, as the aestheticization of politics, is therefore specifically modernist insofar as it participates in the demontage of autonomy aesthetics, but it preserves the substance of an earlier bourgeois culture, just as it preserves bourgeois property relations, by restructuring domination as an aesthetic object. The extended citation of Marinetti's paen to the beauty of war at the conclusion of the essay could be replaced with any number of Ernst Jünger's battlefield descriptions.

The reminiscences of Maurice Bardèche, included in the final chapter, confirm the estimation of the banal character of fascism; Kaplan provides a stand-in for the Eichmann who, as Arendt assures us, could not think. The elegant critic of literature and film refuses to comprehend that his political commitments such as his led to genocide and the destruction of the same Jewish community, the memory of which he purports to cherish with a sort of romantic nostalgia for the exotic. Of equal importance, however, is the judgment that Bardèche and Brasillach apparently shared on the end of the silent-film era: the introduction of the sound track and especially language destroyed the mythic character of the cinema which, in its earlier phase, exuded the power of the *chanson de geste* to evoke and strengthen the populist unity of the nation. The fascist film theoreticians contrast the organic—and organizing!—homogeneity of the silent image with the introduction of speech that dissolves the nation through individuation and criticism. No clearer corollary to Benjamin's aesthetics of mass reproduction could be imagined. Bardèche and Brasillach value the pure image, popularized aestheticism, in order to produce the fascist folk, while the iconoclast Benjamin applauds the shattering of the image in montage in order to call the masses (for him at this point the communist masses) to language. Fascism constructs the film as a mechanism of a preindividuated imaginary; Benjamin's cinema surpasses individuation by permitting for the first time a genuinely symbolic (now in the different sense of linguistic communication) collectivity.

This conflict between imaginary and symbolic orders marks off the quandary of the fascist intellectual. The full banality of "Brazillach" attempts to occupy the sophisticated aestheticism of Kretzschmar in order to carry out reactionary politics with modernist art. The art of mechanical reproduction is appropriated as the vehicle to prevent individuation and developmental subjectivity and to produce the nation as the infinite reproduction of the same; the fascist paradigm of iteration and eternal return corresponds to the project of Kretzschmar's student, serial composition. Like aesthetic modernism, fascism thrives on a denunciation of nineteenth-century bourgeois culture and appropriates avant-garde forms, although it constantly asserts its own return to archaic origins. The contradiction remains unresolved. In *Voyage au bout de la nuit*, Céline's Bardamu, despairing at the imminent death of the young innocent Bébert, seeks help but finds succor in neither the medical establishment nor in the counsel of the literary legacy. Science and art, the bourgeois institutionalizations of culture, are never adequate to life, but Bardamu has no solution, and Céline ultimately has none either, except the three-point ellipsis. Yet the dissatisfaction with inherited cultural forms remains potent even without a rational alternative, and an irrational one is chosen instead: fascism and anti-Semitism.

To the extent that fascism signifies a specific unresolved tension between imaginary and symbolic orders, the Jew was by no means an arbitrary victim. Cipher of the old religion, he stood in for the older world against which fascism as the movement of youth rebelled; hence the standard fascist caricature of the Jew as aged. Cipher of the law and the book, he bears the brunt of the aestheticist preservation of the image impervious to conceptual scrutiny and outside the venue of any legal rationality. Perpetual patriarch, he draws on himself the wrath of the matriarchal moment of vitalist desire in the presymbolic "oceanic feeling" of fascism. The fear of the spoken word, disembodied in the radio and disruptive in the cinema, thrives on these aspects and produces anti-Semitism as the logical concretization of a paralogic fascism. Mechanical reproduction permits an aesthetic practice emanicipated from the auratic image, but the compulsive fixation on the image and the associated fear of language, signs of a blocked oedipal maturation, turn into a search for origins and an extermination of the different as nonoriginal, as outside the sacred image: mass murder as the answer to mass media.

Image or language, imaginary or symbolic, gentile or Jew: these levels are collapsed in the tradition of regenerative aesthetics that finds its first emphatic articulation in Wagner's essays, especially "Judaism in Music" of 1850. The force of the argument depends on a rhetorical distinction between the particularity of visual perception and the threatening universality of linguistic abstraction. The choice to begin with the assertion of an "instinctive dislike" for Jews, repeated in the dramatic opening scene of George Montandon's *Comment reconnaître le Juif?* (1940), conveys a priority of visible facts over any general discourse of emancipation. For Wagner, one recoils at the appearance of Jews, for his Jews are ontologically antithetical to appearance. He consequently shifts the terrain to an aural realm, the only one in which Jews, as the carriers of language, can operate, but in which the eternal wanderers, without origin, still lack a genuine native speech; the strangers can only imitate. A parenthetical comment, added in 1869, reveals the religious-historical source of these constructions: "Since this essay was written, the Jews have succeeded in taking over not only the theater but also the playwright's characters. A famous Jewish 'character actor' has done away with the poetic figures in Shakespeare, Schiller, and so on, and has substituted creatures of his own effect-laden and tendentious imagination. One's impression is as though the Savior had been cut out of a painting of the Crucifixion, and replaced by a Jewish demagogue. This falsifying of our theatrical art is now complete, and this is why nowadays Shakespeare and Company are spoken of only in terms of their limited suitability for the stage."[9] The image of Christ supplanted by Jewish speech, which, as demagoguery, is associated with the democratic politics Wagner increasingly came to fear: the people of the book, prohibited by the decalogue from a cult of graven images, operate in a linguistic realm of perpetual mediation that endangers the auratic uniqueness of visual representation and the corporeal presence of the eucharist. Wagner seizes upon major components of traditional Christian anti-Semitism, while replacing the religious substance with an aesthetic project which returns eternally within the discourse of revolutionary fascism: "But the Jew has stood quite apart from . . . community, alone with his Jehovah in a dispersed and barren stock, incapable of real evolution, just as his own Hebraic language has been handed down as something dead."[10] As the carrier of the law, the Jew represents the state and conceptual rationality, from the strictures of which only a recovery of genuine origins, preserved in the prelinguistic imaginary, can emancipate the nation. Fascism promises to overthrow the law and resurrect a primitive community by obliterating symbolic abstraction and the liberal state.

Benjamin's account of an aestheticization of politics consequently appears as a civilizational regression to graven images of the deity, as in Riefenstahl's representation of Hitler's descent from the clouds in *Triumph of the Will*. The corollary is the fear of Jewish speech in the fascist critique of the radio of the Popular Front, the immaterial voice infecting the national homogeneity with foreign accents, as Kaplan describes with reference to Rebatet. Unlike the elite conservatism of the Action Française and Maurras, radical fascism inverts the antipathy toward technology as a force of modernization into a fascination with technology as a vehicle of regeneration. Thus Rebatet's attack on the Jewish radio becomes the basis for a program for a fascist radio, just as Wagner, denouncing the Jewish preference for language and sound over visual representation, appropriates music as the cohesive power in the retotalization afforded by the *Gesamtkunstwerk*. Both Rebatet and Wagner operate within an aural medium — Kaplan speaks of "telephonocentrism" — and apparently imitate the very objects of their anti-Semitic diatribes. This fascist mimesis of the Jew as a moment in its own imagination is echoed in the title of the journal, *Je Suis Partout*, for no one was ever more ubiquitous than the Jew for whom Montandon ascertains "une moindre franchise d'origine" and whose universality threatens the particularity of national identity.[11] Yet the advocates of that particularity as the project of revolutionary fascism mimic universality in order to retract its emancipatory substance, just as Rebatet occupies the air waves, the domain of the enemy's articulations, in order to obviate communication. From Hitler to Father Coughlin, the radio is the field in which the fascist demagogue (imitating and inverting Wagner's "Jewish demagogue") appropriates the modern mass media as part of the resistance to modernity. Is this the self-deception of fascism, unable to perceive its own contradictions? To preserve culture, it becomes barbaric; to oppose modernization, it seizes technology. Arendt reports how Eichmann, in his final words at the gallows, first asserted his standard Nazi disbelief in an afterlife and then promised those present that *we shall all meet again. Such is the fate of all men.*"[12]

The fascist claim to be everywhere, which repeats the transgression ascribed to the homeless Jew, remains ideological insofar as it obscures the political weakness of the Parisian radicals, enamored with the Germans who never give them real power but only manipulate them as a threat to the conservatives of Vichy.[13] Asserting that they are *partout*, they denounce the universality of a progressive humanism but can never realize that they are ultimately nowhere at all. It is a utopian fascism in the etymological sense of not in any place, devoid of the materiality of presence: Arendt's rule of nonentities, banality as a political program. Neither their efforts to appropriate technology nor their anti-Semitism leads to the construction of a successful identity. The violence of sacrifice does not produce a genuine community but only the compulsive eradication of individuals.

The individual who is eradicated is the Jew as patriarch, and extermination is implicated in a retreat from patriarchal law (Blum and the Third Republic) that is a constituent of the autonomous identity, so enviously detested by fascism. A brilliant connection links the fascist critique of patriarchy to the matriarchal moment of the oceanic feeling that accompanies the technology of the mass media and the rejection of the written culture of the nineteenth-century bourgeoisie. There is no programmatic anti-feminism behind this argument. Instead, Kaplan locates the root of a civilizational discontent that endowed the Parisian radicals with the power of a utopian seduction to which they themselves constantly succumbed. The oedipal conflict with the father is never resolved through maturation (as Erik Erikson demonstrated long ago in the case of Hitler) but perpetually deferred in a valorization of the presymbolic infantilism of an imaginary order without mediation, a constant disruption of identity by semiotic ruptures, in the sense of Kristeva.[14] Hence Rebatet's need to seize the radio as a rebellion against speech, Céline's destruction of syntax in order to write, and Brasillach's fascination with film, the countertext to the law. What Bardèche presents as philosemitic reminiscences of the traditional Jewish quarter are in fact the opposite, floorplans of Auschwitz. To preserve identity, identity is destroyed, but the sacrificial equation, the compulsive neurosis of fascism, never succeeds. The fascination with the populist community remains an image, imagination, deception, the constantly broken *promesse de bonheur*. It is here that the provocation of Kaplan's study is to be sought: aesthetic modernization in the age of mechanical reproduction incites cultural intellectuals to an anti-intellectual heroism that never escapes banality as the refusal of speech, while this banality culminates in a tragedy that leaves us speechless.

## Notes

1. Cf. "Roosevelt Rules America," *World-Service (Welt-Dienst)* No. V/22 (November 15, 1938), p. 3. *World-Service* was a Nazi press service with a viciously anti-Semitic character. It was published in Erfurt in several languages. Kaplan describes the link to Céline and Montandon.

2. A telling error in the critical literature confirms this conjecture regarding the significance of the letter. In a seminal study of the novel, Gunilla Bergsten misspells the name of the real historian as "Kretschmar," which leads the translator to suggest that Mann's inclusion of the z "underlines the reference to Nietzsche" (Bergsten, *Thomas Mann's Doctor Faustus: The Sources and Structures of the Novel* [Chicago and London: University of Chicago Press, 1969], p. 27). The connection is repeated in Patrick Carnegy's *Faust as Musician: A Study of Thomas Mann's Novel Doctor Faustus* (London: Chatto and Windus, 1973), p. 14. While this evidence does not explain the abbreviated version of the name in Lowe-Porter's English translation, it does demonstrate clearly that the z in Kretzschmar was read (or misread) as the carrier of a cultural allusion, which, given the current associations of Nietzsche with Nazi ideology, signified a political connection as well.

3. Theodor W. Adorno, "Auf die Frage: Was ist deutsch," *Gesammelte Schriften* 10/2, ed. Rolf Tiedemann (Frankfurt: Suhrkamp, 1977), p. 695.

4. Stanley Hoffmann, *Decline or Renewal? France Since the 1930s* (New York: Viking Press, 1974), p. x.

5. Hannah Arendt, *Eichmann in Jerusalem: A Report on the Banality of Evil* (New York: Penguin Books, 1979), pp. 268–69; Hannah Arendt, *The Human Condition* (Chicago: University of Chicago Press, 1958), p. 8.

6. Elisabeth Young-Bruehl, *Hannah Arendt: For Love of the World* (New Haven: Yale University Press, 1982), p. 329.

7. Arendt, *Eichmann in Jerusalem*, p. 287.

8. Leo Lowenthal, *Literature and the Image of Man* (Boston: Beacon Press, 1957), p. 202.

9. Richard Wagner, *Stories and Essays,* ed. Charles Osborne (London: Peter Owen, 1973), p. 23.

10. Ibid., pp. 27–28.

11. George Montandon, *Comment reconnaître le Juif?* (Paris: Nouvelles éditions françaises, 1940), p. 19.

12. Arendt, *Eichmann in Jerusalem*, p. 252.

13. Hoffmann, *Decline or Renewal?*, pp. 36–37.

14. Erik Homburger Erikson, "Hitler's Imagery and German Youth," *Psychiatry* 5 (1942), 475-493.

# Translations and Documentation

I have quoted in English, using an occasional key foreign word in brackets to clarify a nuance. In cases where, to my knowledge, good translations exist (as is the case for Céline and for some of the criticism), I've quoted from them and listed them in the references. Otherwise the translations are my own. The pages given in the notes correspond to the editions noted in full in the references. In chapters where textual variants are part of my analysis, I have listed each relevant edition in the references; I refer to these in the notes by their date.

# Fascism: Etymologies and Political Usage

*bhasqo* — *Indo-European root underlying a series of words meaning to bind:* **bund** *(German),* **bundle** *(English),* **fasces** *(Latin).*

*fasces* — *Latin. Rods or branches wrapped around an ax. Carried by Latin "lictors" (executioners) as a show of power. By extension: (1) to cede the* **fasces***, to acknowledge authority; (2) an assembly or crowd.*

*fascinum* — *Latin. Amulet in the shape of a phallus, hung around children's necks to guard against evil; a phallic deity displayed in various rites; connotates bewitchment or, in modern usage,* **fascination***. A false etymology, rejected by serious philologists but often reasserted by alliterative association, as in Sontag's "Fascinating Fascism".*[1] *Note a received idea suggested by the ersatz fascinum/fasces connection: that people are seduced and fascinated by the leader; that the language of fascism is a fascinating one.*

*fascia* — *English/French. In architecture: the bands decorating a column. In medicine: tissue supporting and binding the muscles. In astronomy: belts around a planet.*

*fascine* — *English. Bundle of wood; figuratively, a bundle of citations.*

*faisceaux* — *French, plural. Bundles of wood, bound guns, converging railroad tracks, electromagnetic waves.*

*faix* — *French. Physical or moral burden, fetus.*

*fascicule* — *English. Small volume of pages.*[2]

Citing Sicilian gangs such as the *fasci dei Lavoratore* and *fasci Siciliani*, the Oxford English Dictionary (Supplement) and Encyclopedia Britannica mark the reemergence of a political connotation for *fasces* in the 1890s.

An obscure French gangster-aristocrat named the Marquis de Morès may have had some knowledge of these groups when, in 1894, he published his "doctrine du faisceau," an anti-Semitic populism that moved him to organize racist leagues in the Paris suburb of La Villette. *It is in France, then, that a "faisceau" bound by racism is first organized.*

The Marquis de Morès's organization, unrecorded in the major dictionary etymologies of fascism, was recently unearthed by a scholar interested in the specifically French intellectual origins of fascism.[3] In a growing body of scholarship in which the "origins" of and, by implication, the intellectual responsibility for modern racism are constantly at issue, that discovery has obvious emblematic importance.

However, the first well-known twentieth-century groups to use the name were Italian interventionists (*fasci interventista rivoluzionario, fasci d'azione internazionalista*, and so on) organized in 1914 in support of Italy's entrance into World War I. Again, at the level of received ideas, the first modern fascist movement was undoubtedly the Italian one. Mussolini's *fasci di combattimento*, founded in 1919 as a splinter group of the Italian Socialist party, was established in power in 1922 with the Roman *fasces* (*fascio*, in Italian) as its symbol. By 1925, when Frenchman Georges Valois founded *Le Faisceau*, a rebel splinter group of Action Française, the name was conceived and understood as a tip of the hat to Italian politics. Valois dreamed of a French "March on Paris" modeled after Mussolini's March on Rome. Although his rhetoric was full of references to roots, national blood flow, and a revitalized antibourgeois state directed by an elite of war heroes, it was not explicitly racist.

Marcel Bucard founded a short-lived *Francisme* movement in France in 1933. He called on both German Nazi and Italian Fascist parties for inspiration. Later French groups, which grew out of post-World War I veteran leagues, took initialed names. These included de la Rocque's PSF (Parti Social Français), Doriot's PPF (Parti Populaire Français), Déat's RNP (Rassemblement National Populaire); only the last name owed something to the physical notion of binding.[4]

A final adjectival use of *fascism* remains extremely popular to this day: **fascist**—a loose condemnatory epithet signifying hatred on the part of the speaker, usually for political reasons; as in the American interjection "You fascist pig!" or its French equivalent "facho!"

## Notes

1. Susan Sontag, "Fascinating Fascism," pp. 73–108.

2. Dictionaries consulted: Alois Walde, ed., *Vergleichendes Wörterbuch der Indogermanischen Sprachen*, vol. 2, p. 135; Lewis and Short, *Harper's Latin*; *The Oxford English Dictionary, Supplement to the Oxford English Dictionary*; *Trésor de la Langue française: Dictionnaire de la langue du 19ème et du 20ème siècle (1789–1960)*. The last-named work, admirably thorough and ambitious,

carefully defines fascism with reference to the work of both marxist critic Nicolas Poulantzas and right-wing philosopher (and one-time fascist "fellow traveler") Thierry Maulnier.

3. In Zeev Sternhell, *La Droite révolutionnaire*, pp. 180–84, 197–220; see also the discussion in Jeffrey Mehlman, "Of Literature and Terror: Blanchot at *Combat*," in *Legacies*, p. 7. Mehlman analyzes the fictional role given Morès in Bernanos's *La Grande Peur des bien-pensants*. For discussions of the French tradition of racist thinking, see George Mosse's *Toward the Final Solution* and Bernard-Henri Lévy's inflammatory *L'Idéologie française*.

4. For discussions of the swastika, see Dominique Pelassy's Saussurian analysis of National Socialism in *Le Signe nazi*.

# Reproductions of Banality

# Chapter 1
# Theoretical Voices

In order to characterize French fascism — a phenomenon that existed in splinter groups, marginal theories, and eccentric imaginations rather than in government — I must first define the utopian aspect of fascism in general. My concerns in this chapter are therefore fascism's appeal to European intellectuals in the years preceding the Second World War and the problems of critics who have confronted it.

Fascism was conceived by its enthusiasts as a new form of revolt, competitive with marxism; a revolt of human consciousness against a so-called undramatic liberalism, against the alienation of the individual from government. They imagined fascism as a revolt that would affect the arts as much as the military, that would render a notion like "drama" as valid a criterion of political life as any economic term. Against the distance between the state and the people, they hoped for immediacy; against alienation and fragmentation, they hoped for unity of experience. They thought of themselves as an elite at one with the people. They claimed the energy of youth and the prerogatives of ancient wisdom. Their fascism involved a new poetic language, an immediate vocal presence, an entirely new way of writing and speaking about the state and the world.

In what cultural context did these surprising utopian expectations about fascism occur?

The new machinery of the twentieth century had a revolutionary effect on perception. Airplanes allowed vast overviews. Radio separated hearing from seeing. Photography froze realistic sight and separated it from the rest of the

senses. Silent film could then cut up that sight and remount it in a variety of fragmented pieces, counterposing a totally different musical script.

The new creativity was a lot like new war technologies. Grenades shredded
people at a distance from their murderers; airplane bombing removed death's
authors even further. Sophisticated noxious gases aimed at people's senses rather
than their bodies. The living death of the "trench" engraved a new black hole
in the European imagination.[1] And the "whole" of destruction was recorded on
film.

By the time film learned to talk in the 1930s, dadaism, futurism, and surrealism had linked the aesthetic of fragmentation and destruction to an institutionalized artistic avant-garde.[2] As we look back at that art today, alongside the new
warfare and the new entertainment technologies with which its birth coincided,
it begins to seem as highly "realistic" as was, say, naturalism, in its time. Talking
film itself represented a rather different aesthetic advance on an essentially fragmented front: here, finally, was a technology that could restore some of the perceptual unity its own constitutive parts had taken away. For some, the impression of a "restored totality" in the talkies was overwhelmingly positive, while
others complained – quite understandably in view of newly established surrealist
norms – of the "lost art" of the silents and of a regressive return via talkies to
staid representations more appropriate for theater than for film.

But even talking film could not erase from modern perception the ability to
fragment image or to concentrate magically on one sense at a time: sound and
sight had already become too radically divided by the separate industries of radio
and photography for this. And lest we forget, political reality was benefiting
from representation by means of the same new technologies that were dominat-
ing art: the combined possibilities of political photos, newsreels, radio broadcasts, and talking films offered intense possibilities for oral and visual slogans.

In political representations, as in artistic ones, fragmentation of perception
encouraged technologically determined relationships to the subject matter,
whether of fictional characters, objects, or political leaders: the relationships
were "partial." A theory of something called a "partial object relationship" was
developed by psychoanalytic theorist Melanie Klein during the 1930s, when she
herself was forced to flee Nazi Germany for England. "Partial object" refers to
the infant's relationship to the relevant "parts" of the mother's body in the first
few months of life: the breast that feeds, the voice that lulls to sleep, the hands
that wash and caress.[3] Klein's term is not the only one that comes to mind in
this context: we might also think of Winnicott's transitional objects, of the
playthings used by children to soothe the passage toward their independence
from a mother.[4] The oddly charged yet alien status of machinery, or, indeed,
of any manufactured object in modern art, shares certain characteristics with the
toys that constitute a child's first attempts to form object relationships. With the
difference that the "relationship" in question is now that of the writing, painting,

filming, subject to a postindustrial society. New communications media soothe the passage out of nationalist isolation and into the kind of international awareness that the media has made possible in the first place. With the break into a "media-ized" world (both larger and more accessible than the old national one) comes worship of media objects: the cult of the machine, of the recorded, amplified voice, the fascination with the kind of fragmentation and repetition that film has taught spectators to locate.

We can easily imagine Freud's analytic narrators at ease in the company and decor of a novel by Marcel Proust. The object-relations theorists of the "second generation"—Klein, Mahler, Winnicott—might feel better in a movie house or a studio than in a drawing room or salon. Their descriptions abound with the blurred boundaries, the pieces of things, the analytic play techniques that rhyme with modernism. The playfully fragmented modernist language of futurism and surrealism is echoed there. As is physical and sexual violence, shared by the avant-garde images and texts with the more conventional realist work of a Sartre and a Malraux. Subjects, objects, torn apart from one another and from themselves.

A note of caution: the psychoanalytic narratives of Klein and Mahler and Winicott are developmental. Each attempts to account for the changes the infant experiences from the time it leaves the womb to the time it enters the symbolic oedipal stage, and thus to fill a chronological void felt in the work of Freud. I can't simply pick and choose isolated "moments" of this narrative and plop them onto fascist writing. The problem is even further complicated by the fact that I am trying to account for reactions to technology, since there are already metaphors of technology in key psychoanalytic vocabulary, and the connection between the metaphors and the technology is no more random for the psychoanalytic theorists than it was for me: I came to study psychoanalytic terms like *projection* and *screen memory* because the words *projection* and *screen* occurred so consistently in my corpus of fascist texts.

What about the fact that the terms were actually invented when the technologies were becoming culturally pervasive? In writing about projection in the beginning of the century, Freud must surely have been aware of screens—if at first only of magic lantern screens. What is the connection of the analytically powerful screen memory to people's memories of their favorite films? Is film-watching tantamount to building a personal history, an alternative to "lived experience" with a fresh set of images offered to the individual by the culture? And what about the theoretically influential "mirror phase": the moment when the child recognizes itself in the looking glass and recognizes, at the same time, the fundamental "otherness" of its consciousness from its own body? Do people who see themselves represented on film experience the elation of the mirror phase? Do they imagine they have mastered the object world? Or do they fear alienation from their own images? And if, as I argue in chapter 6, fascists experience that elation without fear – if movie-watching somehow constitutes their delusions of immortality and their imagined imperviousness to destruction – does the estrangement in front of the mirror merely get displaced, transferred onto violence against others?[5] I can only *keep* asking these questions of my individual texts, both theoretical and fascist.

First, the theoretical text of Klein. What she terms "projective identification" may be directed toward an ideal object, to avoid separation or keep the ideal "safe" from "bad objects," and toward a "bad object," to gain control of the source of danger or to attack and destroy. In moments of great anxiety, according to Klein, the ego will often fragment itself into many parts, and the projections will be multiple. The socioeconomic anxieties of the prewar years offer many tempting parallels to Klein's children's stories. Unacceptable dilemmas are associated with the Jews, who are projected as bad objects (rootless, ruthless, and persecuting), and the characteristics that seem to offer projection from those dilemmas come to belong to a single ideal man (rooted, omniscient, and beneficent): this man is the fascist leader and the total state that he incarnates.

But Klein's theoretical stories are modern; they always break down their own categories. To remain in their spirit, we would have to emphasize that in this "ideal" projection of the fascist leader by the fascist subject, the imaginary relationship between the two is undifferentiated. The fascist subject incorporates the state, experiences the state within himself: he swallows what he wants and spits out the rest in angry talk. The fascist ideal is being swallowed by the subject at the same time as it is being projected onto the leader. Projection and introjection are not always even that distinguishable. I will return to this problem via the bizarre combination of populism and elitism in fascism: a man rejoices as he disappears into a crowd, deems himself uniquely privileged for so doing. He is taking the crowd within him, absorbing its powers, just as he is rejecting, violently, the societal outcasts that allow him to define a privileged crowd in the first place. As complicated and overlapping as the Kleinian categories may get (Theweleit simply rejects them as abstract "dilutions" of unconscious drives), they indicate one consistent factor: a confusion about boundaries between self and other.[6]

That this problem is *essential* to understanding fascism was firmly believed by Delio Cantimori. Cantimori, a historian of the Enlightenment, had experienced Italian fascism firsthand, and didn't do much work on it until the very end of his career. Then he wrote, still only in fragments, about the problems others had had when undertaking such work. He thought then that when people tried to speak generally about fascism, that is, neither historically nor critically, they always ended up by writing "as if fascism were a species of whale who swallowed everything indiscriminately, or who carried everyman satanically to perdition, like Moby Dick." One must, he countered, "discern the variety of its currents, movements . . . illusions, fantasies, etc. etc."[7] How appropriate, that by means of a seditious after-effect, fascism should do the same kind of work on its theorists that it once did on its subjects: carrying them along or swallowing them! Even from within my struggle to historicize, fascism makes me feel "way in over my head." When I am not nauseated by descriptions of fascist oppression, I am dizzy from the effort of organizing a definition of fascism. The movement that appeals to all people, to all classes, to pacifists in France, to militants in Germany, to neither right nor left, to both revolutionary and conservative, feels like an ocean. I might finally succeed in isolating the fascist phenomenon to cities, or to the petty bourgeoisie; but as the movement grows, the phenomenon shifts along with its supporters. As for the petty bourgeoisie, the "masses" to whom we attribute fascist desires, they turn out to be a class that always responds to the most seductive voice: a class that defines itself by desire.[8] And I can never tell when fascism is inside or out. The projection of hatred onto the Jews surely has to do with fears of a loss of national identity that were aggravated as the "flood" of immigrants came into France in the 1920s and 1930s, from the outside (from the east). Whether that fear can be isolated from the whole complicated historic process and deemed "originally" outside, perceived through certain films or in certain propaganda, or inside, in equally "expressive" private psychoses, is undecidable. I come to similarly dizzying conclusions as I study psychoanalytic theory, the theory of the inside-out. The consolidation of German fascism forms the nurturing background of Klein's theories, but the anxiety caused by fascism is also "inside them": history only made visible to her something that already existed in our infantile pre-selves.

We can also look at the force of the partial object in a fascist text. The prose of media critic Robert Brasillach is tremendously helpful. Fascist leaders in his texts are either seen or heard, rarely both at once, and the separation of the senses itself becomes part of the magic aura of the fascist state: "loud speakers repeat the end of Hitler's phrases in echo" (p. 237); a projector spotlights a red mass of flags, "flowing like a flow of purple lava" (p. 232); Brasillach describes "listening to the sound of (fascist) Léon Degrelle's voice even more than what he said to me" (p. 208). In the context of this last phrase, there was no separation *by* technology; the desire to separate has become automatic. Riding in an auto with Degrelle (already a futurist activity of some prestige), Brasillach continues to operate the separation, this time with assistance from daylight rather than from radio or film: "I don't see his face. I only hear his voice in the shadow" (p. 212). And when Brasillach actually approaches Hitler's headquarters at Nuremberg, he doesn't open a door but "penetrates into the magic fortress [*enceinte*]."[9] We might think here of Margaret Mahler's description of a child somewhere between what she calls the "echo phase" and the "practicing period" of individuation. The child toddles about with great elation from a "sense of sharing in his mother's magic powers."[10] This is not the despairing Echo of Greek myth, the Echo condemned to repeat the sentence endings of the beloved Narcissus.

This is a successful Echo, jubilant in sharing Narcissus's voice, strong in following, in imagining itself repeated, rather than repeating.

Lack of boundaries, the projection of negative and positive energy, the new language of the state, the triumph of Echo: we are in the strange territory of voice. It is hard for anyone studying French literature today to write about voice without measuring the powerful theoretical contributions of Jacques Derrida. Derrida has performed brilliantly close analyses of individual philosophic and literary works, investigating the way that they grant metaphysical privilege to speaking over writing, to presence over absence, to centers over margins. Because of his work, we are closer to being as sensitive to the processes of domination and repression in language as we would wish to be to the same processes in actual physical and political acts. Voice, for Derrida, is always the key to mystification. When we think poetically, we posit voice as a false origin of writing; one to which we think we could return, were we to write the truth. But to write is disappointing. We either kill voice—we write it "down"—or we erect it as a false origin—write it "up." This is easier to understand by considering some of voice's correlates: where there is reverence for voice, reverence for presence, nature, and immediate communication will often follow. "Dictating" (the work of the dictator, the one who speaks) also plays on the desire to recover voice. There is, then, a whole family of terms that denote dangerous desires for the acultural, the antiintellectual, the seductive, the *fascist*. Voice is considered their sponsor, the unspeakable, never-to-be-inscribed "thing" in the name of which all sorts of theoretical errors are made.[11]

To theorize about voice is to tread this dangerous ground. Studying voice is not necessarily like studying music, for even improvised music can be as highly coded as a sonnet. Phoneticians measure intonation and sound patterns and classify the psychic possibilities of voice. Poeticians study the transmission of oral texts "written" only through the processes of memory and performance.[12] Psychoanalysts work daily with an intuitive "third ear" to hear their patients' voices. What about an ideological approach?

A good theoretical starting point for such an approach is already suggested, quite succinctly, in Althusser's definition of ideological "interpellation."[13] His interpellation is not a formal questioning (as in the standard English use), or an interruption by speaking (as in the Latin *interpellare*), but a kind of general "ringing up" of ideology among us. "Hey you!" says the cop on the beat. I look up: I'm the one he wants. I am being called.

The emblem of interpellation in Althusser's text is oral or visual; a call, a whistle, a wave of the hand will suffice to get my attention. Althusser will develop only the visual component, describing ideology in terms of Lacan's "mirror structure". Ideological moments are for him times when people have the illusion of recognizing themselves, each other, reality itself. "That's the way it is"

(Walter Cronkite); "Amen—So be it" (Churchgoers, as quoted by Althusser): such phrases signify that "ideology has been here," has done its work. "Here" can be a TV screen or a church pulpit.

Psycho-phonetician Micheline Veaux has speculated about the vocal equivalent of the mirror phase.[14] Veaux refers to empirical studies that show infants recognizing the specific voice of their biological mothers, well before they "know" any language. The crucial factor in their recognition, it turns out, is not the quality or tonal register of the voice but its intonation. Vocal recognition (interpellation) of the child by the mother is governed by rhythm and repetition. We might put this somewhat differently in order to add our voice to Althusser's theory. Rhythm and repetition, as preoedipal relationships to language, are already "author-itative." This developmentally "first" authority is a musical and maternal one rather than a visual one (assuming we associate visual authority, as does Althusser, with Lacan's definition of the phallus and the "name of the father"). Veaux contrasts the figures of Echo and Narcissus to explain the difference between what she calls the vocal and visual "mirror stages." Echo represents the female parent (the name of the mother); Narcissus, the male. "Echolalia," the stage of development after the child learns it has a voice of its own but before it knows enough language to do other than merely repeat what the parent says, is a kind of sonar mirror phase. Echolalia ends (except in its pathological form) when the child first says no. By saying no, the child discovers it has a voice that is "not" the other's. This is the oral discovery of self.[15]

How might a primitive moment like Echolalia reappear in nonpathological adulthood? Examples abound from academic life alone. Students who, by virtue of a particularly strong attachment to their teacher, are capable of an uncanny repetition or echo of that teacher's "style"; a repetition of the actual rhythms of the teacher's phrases. This can happen long before the accompanying ideas of the teacher have been assimilated on any meaningful level. I imagine that there are, among my readers, teachers who have had just this disquieting experience of seeing the very intonations of their sentence structures so effectively mimicked on a paper devoid of a single one of their ideas. It is for this reason that teachers are motherly. They like good students and prefer students who have "found their own critical voices," but they want the students to find a voice *without saying no*. (One could undoubtedly analyze this triple bind further through textual analyses of the Letter of Recommendation.)

For a similar reason, teachers of composition in a foreign language find that long after their students have mastered the various grammatical paradigms, learned the basic rules for syntax, there can still be problems—subtle, but immediately obvious—that distinguish that student's writing from a native speaker's writing. Punctuation, connected to the natural breathing patterns of the native language, will be all wrong. What the French call the "tournure" of a sentence—

its twists and turns, its flow — will be confused. Sometimes the only way to learn these sublinguistic rhythms is to immerse one's self totally and uncritically in the oral language, like a child acquiring a grammatical unconscious.

The authority I am describing is the authority of the mother tongue, and it is a rhythmic one. Kristeva translates its functions into the vocabulary of linguistics and calls it a *semiotic* register of language. She opposes to the semiotic a *symbolic* paternal register. From this theoretical polarity, she has analyzed the ravings of Céline with a sensitivity to both his poetry and his racism.[16] Kristeva is the first critic, to my knowledge, who has been able to read both Céline's innovative "form" and his reactionary "content" without resorting to moral condemnation or biographic determinism. I differ with Kristeva mainly in the way she extends her theory, my own sense being that this semiotic level is not "inscribed" in any privileged sense in an avant-garde canon, but is felt by even a traditional stylist such as Brasillach. The maternal can be expressed in description or by means of style. My other departure from Kristeva is political. She grants the semiotic a special prestige by characterizing it as a "liberating moment" in literary texts, as one that can negate authoritarian abstractions. I want to study it rather more historically than intellectually. This means focusing on its own authority and its failure to liberate. In the twentieth century, maternal longings get mixed up with technological amplification, with experiments in perception on both the private and the public level. But to see this (and to hear it), I need to take those longings out of semiology and put them back in the world of production.

Brasillach talks about Hitler's New Germany as an apprenticeship in a new maternal tongue. At a work camp, he witnesses a song lesson. "There, this word [presumably "song lesson"] certainly evokes nothing cute [*aucune mignardise*] but the gravity, the virility, the hard and powerful love of the *patrie*, the total devotion, all this expressed in that language of the sounds and the choir which is the true maternal language of Germany."[17] The fascist voices are echoing here in the proliferation of commas and the stringing out of clauses, as well as in the descriptive content.

We have only to look at the curious marriage in Brasillach's prose to realize that there is no choosing between mother- and father-bound fascist desires. Fascist subjects are virile, phallic, their devotion to the language they learn is total, boundary-less, and the language itself is a maternal one. In order for the state to generate a whole new type of man (*homo fasciens*, Brasillach will call him), it has to be female. Its subjects are men; fascism itself is a woman, a new mother. The maternal language obviously makes them phallic, but authority is still feminine, its subjects masculine. There are many potential substitutions going on here: if fascist authority is feminine, then the leader is a woman of sorts. Singing the song to follow the leader is a womanly pursuit made acceptably virile by the leader. Something very powerful is happening, precisely because the categories feminized language, masculine language users, virile love, maternal sounds are so unstable. Many ordinarily unacceptable activities (singing, loving, being together – and other activities from the realm of "cuteness") are being done in the name of acceptable masculine ones: a lot of mother-bound pleasure is being "snuck in" to the fascist state in the name of virility.

If the idea that fascists were somehow mother-bound appears antifeminist, my argument has been misunderstood. For it is rather my contention here that theory informed by feminism can show how the maternal is always being *substituted* for other things in later life, how even the repressed semiotic register of language shows up in the most seemingly phallocentric places. Though I do not agree with Kristeva that the female register is necessarily privileged in stylistically revolutionary texts, I do think that what we call "literary texts," in their relative rhetorical "associativeness," are generally easier places to look for constantly shifting gender markers than what passes for rigorous theoretical discourse, whose self-imposed rigidity often successfully masks the female element. I am sure there are many, many exceptions. One might be Drieu la Rochelle's essay *Mesure de la France*, which tells us even more about the ideology of procreation than his self-consciously poetic *Gilles*.[18]

I should clarify along the way that I do not mean to condemn biological mothers instead of fathers as the disseminators of authoritarianism, but rather to show how extraordinarily flexible and varied is the reappearance of emotions about both parents (parental functions) in adult emotional life. These two functions operate in culture by traveling in couples. As Brasillach shows us, the fascist man can't be virile without a female fascist state to teach him the right songs: sexism is highly interactive. As Marinetti's Mafarka will learn, a fascist avant-garde can come to life only by replacing the mother it kills. We need to realize how dependent the phallic fascist is on mother-nation, mother-machine, mother-war. I concentrate on mother-bound rather than father-bound feelings in fascism not because the father-bound doesn't exist, but because mother-bound feelings do not, as I write, have an established place in political theory.[19]

But before exploring the mother-bound theories further, I want to turn briefly to Freud. Freud teaches us exactly what must be passed over in order to make a metaphor of authority-as-father the backbone for a theory of culture. Freud believed that cultural evolution might best be studied in terms of manifestations of the superego. Though the superego is, upon a very close reading, the internalization of the authority of "one or both parents,"[20] a more persistent definition of the superego associates it with an abstract notion of "cultural father" passed down from generation to generation through tradition. We can measure that persistence by examining the treatment of Oedipus in Freudian interpretation. The myth of Oedipus, which involves a structural triangle among child, mother, and father, is read by Freud as the story of a child who dared to usurp his father's power for the love of his mother. On the level of the individual, the desire for the mother plays a crucial role. But as Freud translates the family drama into a cultural context, "mother" is so abstracted as to virtually drop out of the picture: one has the feeling that Freud simply can't keep track of the place of both parents at once. The result is uncannily faithful to Freud's real world: father-child relationship goes to work in the analogies between man and society, mother-child is left at home.

Much has been made, by feminist critics, of Freud's attachment to the formation of the superego and his subsequent lack of desire (his fear, say some) to interest himself in psychic life previous to it—that is, to interest himself in the analysis of preoedipal children, and in the relationship of mother and child. The passage that post-Freudian feminists light upon in their critique of Freud is one where Freud admits his bafflement at the idea of "oceanic feeling": the limitless, *unbounded* sensation that characterizes the religious experience. With this oceanic feeling, the ego feels inseparable from the outer world. After some musing about his own imperviousness to this feeling, Freud decides that it must be tied to the infant's feeling of helplessness and longing for a protective father.[21]

One telegraphic way to describe psychoanalytic theory and feminist theory since—a whole range of work from Klein and Balint to Theweleit, Chodorow, Flax—is as an effort to work through this one simple Freudian phrase: "I cannot think of any need in childhood as strong as a need for a father's protection" (p. 19). If we think of psychoanalytically oriented feminism as both a critical and a reconstructive art, that working-through is at least twofold. Its first task is to explain why the mother is absent from Freud's conclusions about the oceanic, why Freud *cannot* think about any need in childhood except the need for a father. This amounts not merely to explaining why Freud, as a nineteenth-century Victorian intellectual, was a sexist, but to giving a broader account of why "mothering" has been absent from theoretical work in general and, hence, to historicizing (and demoralizing) our own reading of Freud. A second part of the project is the rewriting of oceanic feeling, or what Margaret Mahler renamed "symbiosis," now with specific reference to the mother as the culturally determined first "caretaker." If I were writing in French, I could pun here about rewriting the oceanic [*la mer*] to echo the maternal [*la mère*].

Given the importance of mother-bound theory in thinking about culture "beyond" Freud, it is not surprising that the mother-daughter couple has received much of the theoretical attention once reserved for the father-son duet. This includes theoretical controversy. In a recent anthology of feminist thought, for example, one essayist argued that no daughter can separate from a mother unless the mother herself has successfully separated, but that the strength of that relationship is the key to the development of a strong successful female individual. Another essayist emphasized the oppression of all mothers at the hands of the father (as a kind of home agent of the state) and argued that *separation* from the mother is the key to freedom.[22] The potential of the maternal element is perhaps nowhere as elliptic as in Kristeva, for whom the maternal has a superior aesthetic value. Between a semiotic language—consisting in the rhythms and babbling nonsense of a child still one with its mother—and symbolic language—the Cartesian language of the Law, of theory, and of Order—Kristeva chooses the semiotic one. She shows it surfacing quite beautifully in much avant-garde art with a liberating, even revolutionary effect. She also shows it "returning," as in the case of certain psychotic or fascist writers, along with symptoms tied to the weight of the Law: here she suggests a definition of fascism as an "institutionalized unconscious" (the unconscious being a semiotic force).[23]

It seems to me crucial to insist on the difference between something conceived aesthetically, but used politically. Symbiosis and oceanic feeling are produced in fascism's "gathering" stages—produced in its rhythms, the intonations of its mass rallies, and in other sorts of its ideological broadcasts. Now it is a leader, not a mother (or a poet) speaking, and there is no question of a successful "regression" to the preoedipal stage, any more than to a pure textuality. What was liberating, in aesthetic terms, can look dangerous the minute it is socially conceived. There is no real choice to be made between the semiotic and symbolic: only, as Kristeva herself seems finally to agree, accounts of their shifts.

However oceanic the theoretical problems presented by this "shift to the maternal" might be, I believe the shift can allow us to understand certain unexplored aspects of fascism, just as the new metaphor of mother as a cultural authority allows the exploration of certain heretofore baffling religious attachments and oceanic feelings. We miss the oceanic aspect of fascism when we look at it as the result of manipulations by evil-fathers Hitler and Mussolini. And since, in that view, the leader is a pied piper and prime mover of all, the role of people (bewitched followers) in fascism is analytically nonexistent. A more sophisticated understanding of fascism that equates it with images of the established Nazi state, that is, with black shirts and swastikas and with political sadism, still explains only one aspect of fascism's appeal. Even theories of fascism as a totalitarianism (isn't one bound to think oceanic thoughts along with the totalizing state?) insist on the paternal qualities of bureaucracies, not on the desires that put the bureaucracies in power in the first place.

## Mal de Mer(e)

To test some of these feminist hypotheses on ground closer to my specific subject, I want to look at the way a thinker writing specifically about French fascism has trouble explaining its utopian, oceanic element. No one could be a more obvious choice for me than Sartre, dean of antifascism and father of postwar letters, whose existentialism might be read as a departure from the practice of "collaboration" in its specifically historical as well as broadest metaphysical senses.

In an essay entitled "Qu'est-ce qu'un collaborateur?" [what is a collaborator?], Sartre aimed his existential question specifically at the fascist intellectuals.[24]

The essay is quite remarkable to read now, forty years after it appeared. It was written with the passion and anger of a man who has found his true nemesis, and yet, at the same time, it quite coolly surveys every major problem and contradiction that theories of fascism in France have faced since. First, the problem given in the title. In analyzing the occupation years, historians have identified a huge split between two groups: a conservative elite at Vichy, and the Parisian hard-line fascists who rejected them as "softies."[25] They both collaborate. Because he is interested in collaboration as pathology, rather than compromise, Sartre concentrates on the Paris extremists. And it is to the intellectuals among them—to Montherlant, Drieu la Rochelle, and Brasillach—rather than to the politicos—Doriot, Déat, and so on—that he devotes the greater part of his argument. Though he states that "it would be an error to confuse collaborator and fascist," Sartre does just that: he (or his editors) even inadvertently(?) nazify Brasillach's name by spelling it *Brazillach*!

The gist of Sartre's argument is that the fascists are outsiders. In an uncharacteristic accumulation of the patriotic first person plural, he insists that these men have "no real ties with contemporary France, with our great political traditions, with a century and a half of our history and of our culture" (p. 48). It is, according to Sartre, because they don't belong to anything recognizably French that you can't do a class analysis on them: they can no more belong to a class than to anything else in France. And because they don't belong to a class, these "intellectuals . . . have neither the courage nor the simple possibility of integrating into the proletariat" (p. 46). Case in point, Drieu la Rochelle, "who was obsessed his whole life by Italian fascism and Russian communism at the same time" (pp. 46–47). As an outsider, the fascist is prey to "the attractive force of a foreign community" (p. 48). His deviation originates with a "fixation on collective foreign forms, badly assimilated by an indigenous community" (p. 46).

In just a few sentences, Sartre has seized on the three major stumbling blocks that fascism presents to the theorist: the coexistence of left and right wing in fascism, the "heresy" that fascism constitutes in terms of class analysis, and the erotic dimension of fascism (people's "fixation" and "attraction" to it).

Sartre is extremely sensitive to fascism at the same time that he makes his analytic error about it. The fascism of "Qu'est-ce qu'un collaborateur?" invades France strictly from the outside and affects only the people in France who are already fundamental outsiders. The fascist is empty (of Frenchness) and (hence?) weak: prey to foreign forces, without the courage to integrate. The emphasis on weakness persists in the essay and becomes gradually more and more "feminized." Collaboration (and now the model seems to switch momentarily back to Vichy) is "historicism" or interpretive *passivity*: "since France fell, let's make the best of it." The resister is the political version of Spitz's individuating

Robert Brasillach. Photo Harlingue-Viollet.

child: he's strong enough to say "no" to reality. The fascist is womanly: "One can pick out all over articles by Chateaubriant, Drieu, Brazillach [*sic*], curious metaphors which present the relations of France and Germany under the aspect of a *sexual union where France plays the role of the Woman*" (p.58, my emphasis). The collaborator, he will conclude, sees in himself the "seductive charm" of French (feminized) culture.

The writer foremost in Sartre's mind when he wrote this essay was undoubtedly Brasillach, for Brasillach was tried and condemned to death in January 1945. Simone de Beauvoir, a spectator in the courtroom, would use the trial as a vehicle to analyze the responsibilities of the Purge in *Les Temps Modernes*. Newspaper reports of the event were brief, but vivid. They gave birth to a life-long interest in fascism on the part of one American who happened to read them in Le Havre on the day of the execution: this is, at any rate, how Robert Tucker explains his personal reasons for undertaking a political biography of Brasillach in 1975.[26]

Let us imagine, then, that Sartre knew the following quotations from an article published by Brasillach on February 19, 1943, since they were repeated with great outrage by the judge at his trial:

> If one wants to know my entire opinion, I will say that I was not a Germanophile before the war, nor even at the beginning of the politics of collaboration; I was only looking out for the interests of reason. But now, things have changed; I've contracted a liaison with the German genius [*génie*], I will never forget it . . . Like it or not, we have lived together; French(men) of some reflection during these few years will have more or less slept with Germany, and the memory of it will remain sweet to them.[27]

I am tempted to argue after reading the trial transcript in its entirety that these single lines did more than any other text or action to condemn Brasillach as a traitor. What the prosecutor finds despicable is Brasillach's avowal of having given in to irrational sexual political feelings about Germany. What interests me, when I juxtapose the Sartre description of the fascist-collaborator to the actual words of Brasillach, is the fragility of Sartre's idea that *France plays the role of the woman* in those feelings, or, as in another Sartrian statement, that the collaborator sees in himself the "seductive charm" of French (feminized) culture. Sartre's statement seems to presuppose that the French fascist and French collaborator, both of them imaginary girls, enjoy the same thing: a (sexual) occupation by a phallic (Nazi) authority. Brasillach himself, though suspected of homosexual leanings by some critics, does not, at least not in this particular passage, "play the role of the woman." He is writing about liaisons, sleeping together, and sweet memories: whether France plays the woman or the man is left to the imagination of the reader.

The myth of Germany and France as a male-female couple is probably as old as the difference between *Geist* and *Esprit*.[28] One finds its prewar variant in the German philologist Curtius's 1930 *Essai sur la France*: Curtius argues that Germany has a technologically-oriented "civilization," and France an arts-oriented "culture."[29]

But Brasillach reverses that cliché, since his most typical intellectual gesture is, as I have already shown repeatedly, to *maternalize* technology. Coming back from "100 hours with [*chez*] Hitler" in a period in which, as Brasillach told his judge, he was not yet Germanophile, Brasillach writes:

> Faced with German National Socialism one remains full of doubt and worry. I'm not thinking only of the struggle against the Church, which is just one aspect of the question. But looking at this construction of a new man, one asks oneself: is it permitted? Isn't there an effort here which bypasses [*outrepasser*] the boundaries of the nation? Tomorrow,

will Hitlerism be anything more than a gigantesque historic curiosity? Isn't it all too much?

. . . When one tries to remember these days, so full, when one evokes the nocturnal ceremonies, lit obliquely by torchlight and spotlight, German children playing like wolves around their recollections of civil war and sacrifice, the Leader rousing this subjugated crowd with plaintive cries into large swells [*houles*], one says to oneself, in effect, about this country—so near a neighbor—that it is, first of all, in the full sense of the word, and prodigiously, and profoundly, a foreign country [*un pays étrange*].[30]

And if this same Germany is described elsewhere in the essay as surprisingly "oriental," it is because Brasillach is struggling with the fascinating "otherness" of Germany: he does so with an ambivalence reserved in the classical literature he knew so well for the strange female monster-goddesses of the Odyssey, for Virgil's Dido. As he says in the passage quoted at his trial, he is not a Germanophile before the Occupation: he is a man of reason, a Maurrassien, tempted with the exotic femininity of national socialism. His ambivalence is an ambivalence toward the feminine.

And what if we take seriously the repetition in the text of words like *shocked*, *surprised*, *disturbed*, *stunned*, along with *sacred*, *magic*, *terrible* (in the French sense of awesome); the bizarre proliferation of commas; and the awkwardly manifold qualification ("in effect," "that it is," "first of all," "in the full sense of the word," "prodigiously", "profoundly") of the word *étrange* in his last line? We will then, I think, have to do as he suggests and consider the word *étrange* in its full sense, that is, à la Rimbaud, literally and in all its senses, most especially in its German one: *unheimlich*—uncanny, disquieting, strange—and its antagonistic mate *heimlich*—homey, canny, but also disquieting.

It is my own memory of Freud's curiosity about the uncanny as an aesthetic property that lead me to pause at these lines. Freud admitted to being as baffled by "das Unheimliche" as he had been by the oceanic: both reminded him of his incomprehension of the maternal element in culture. "The 'uncanny' is that class of the terrifying which leads back to something known long to us, once very familiar. . . . This *unheimlich* place, however, is the entrance to the former heim [home] of all human beings, to the place where everyone dwelt once upon a time and in the beginning."[31]

Brasillach's Germany, complete with an oceanic crowd and wolf-children sucking at the mother state, is a veritable convention of the maternal elements that baffled Freud. "Cent heures chez Hitler" is an important essay in the literature about French fascism, though not for the reason I've just given. It is quoted by French historians to demonstrate that even the most canonical of French fascists found nazism "foreign" and "weird." The essay is, hence, evidence for a ground-breaking idea in French historiography: the idea that French fascism was *not* the foreign import that analysts in the tradition of Sartre would have it be.[32]

But if foreign and weird mean "unheimlich" rather than "unattractive"—if Brasillach is both attracted to and repelled by Germany—the French situation becomes somewhat more complicated, both rooted in France and moved by nazism.

Following French fascism in its Frenchness, as well as its unheimlichness, leads me to an entirely different Sartrian approach to the fascist matrix. This work may be closer to understanding Brasillach than the postwar essay in which, as we saw, Sartre mentioned Brasillach but misspelled his name.

I am thinking of Sartre's novella of ten years earlier, "L'Enfance d'un chef."[33] The fiction goes unmentioned in "Qu'est-ce qu'un collaborateur?,'" perhaps because it describes an attraction to fascism in which there is no overt mention of foreign forces. "L'Enfance d'un chef" begins with a remarkable series of gender substitutions on the part of the adorable young "chef," whose mother's friends treat him like a "true little girl." The boy, Lucien, is fascinated by his mother. "What would happen if they took away Mama's dress, and if she put on Papa's pants?" he wonders. "Perhaps it would make her grow a black mustache—just like that" (p. 156). Lucien converts when an acquaintance in the "Camelots du Roi" (the Action Française youth corps) has him read Barrès's *Les Déracinés*, a novel about discovering one's identity with French provincial soil. Here, then, the fascist becomes a fascist when he recognizes his own roots. Sartre's narrative makes clear that only by the pleasure of excluding imagined "non-French" Jews does Lucien feel he is making the world safe for more Barresian narratives, and that he himself is existing. Before becoming an anti-Semite, Lucien has passed through a fascination with psychoanalysis and even an abortive homosexual episode with a surrealist mentor. Only anti-Semitism succeeds in giving him the gift of masculinity he has sought since the first scene of the novel, when, not yet separate, *he sought it for his mother*. The story ends with a repetition of those first scenes. Lucien looks in the mirror as he had once looked at his mother, finds himself still not awesome enough, and decides to grow his own mustache.

The mustache, a clear cultural signifier, by 1939, of Hitler and, hence, of a foreign fascism, is a complex ideological sign in this novel because it is marked, from the beginning, as an imaginary attribute projected by Lucien onto his powerful mother's face, onto the geography of the motherland. Had Sartre read, as early as 1937, Brasillach's analogous literary gesture: "Every Frenchman returns from Germany persuaded that his country, his youth, could do at least as well as our neighbors—and better, if we first restored certain universal virtues and felled democracy. As for the rest, what a shock, and what strangeness [*quel étonnement et quelle étrangeté*]."[34]

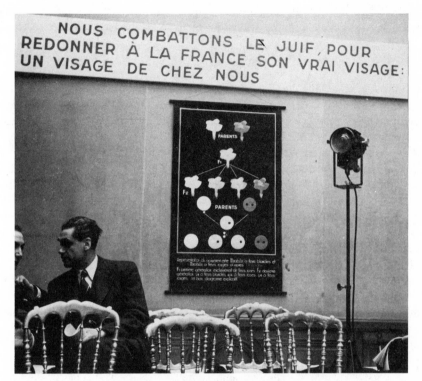

NOUS COMBATTONS LE JUIF, POUR REDONNER À LA FRANCE SON VRAI VISAGE: UN VISAGE DE CHEZ NOUS

Genetics at the Institut d'Etudes des Questions Juives, 1941. Photo Roger-Viollet.

Even Lucien's homosexuality, which would seem to portend the portrayal of the French fascists in *Situations* as weak pederasts, is in "L'Enfance d'un chef" the result of having mistaken the seductive voice of a surrealist elder for a true mentor, an error on the way to mother-bound fascism.

One has the feeling reading "Qu'est-ce qu'un collaborateur?" that Sartre himself, preoccupied by the traumas of the war, has forgotten his own story of the "childhood" of French fascism, a story in which a Frenchman merely borrows Hitler's mustache as a power emblem (a *fasces*) to help him redesign his mother-country's true French face. We might put this somewhat differently by acknowledging that Sartre's thinking, "like France," was "invaded" by the Germans. It was impossible in 1946 to think about fascism apart from occupation. Obviously, too, it would have been dangerous for Sartre to write about the fundamentally French *desires* of French fascists at the very moment when he was trying to rebuild an intellectual climate that would effectively undo the deleterious effects of the fascist traditions. When we remember Sartre's forgetfulness, it is important to keep in mind how many interpretive "errors" about fascism are grounded in pragmatic political reality.[35]

## Voices on the Left

But the aversion to the question of desire wasn't limited to the occupied French: it characterized theories of fascism from 1919 on. Of the many theorists reluctant to consider the problem of desire in fascism, perhaps the most influential were the members of the Third International.[36] The Third International first understood fascism as a new tool of the ruling class, and even as a logical continuation of social democracy (as in Stalin's infamous "social fascism" theory). According to Poulantzas's critique, the Third International is to blame not only for not organizing workers in opposition to fascism but for thinking in "nationalistic terms" about the Soviet Union instead of continuing the struggle for an communist movement. In this way, Poulantzas believes, the Third International let certain fascist values subtly penetrate its own ranks. Why was it so blind? Laclau blames its basic understanding of ideology as economic class interest. This, he says, made the Third International refuse to see that any working-class person could desire a movement so elitist and so obviously opposed to marxist-leninist principles. Since a fascist worker's movement was held to be inconceivable, no antifascist popular-front strategy was proposed by the Third International until after fascism had gained parliamentary power in German and Italy—by then it was too late.

The extent of this interpretive failure should explain why some of the best literature on fascism in the marxist tradition has as its foundation a lengthy explanation of the various erroneous positions taken by the Third International, followed by analyses of the ways those positions contributed to the success of fascism.[37]

Critiques of fascism that dwell on an analysis of the Third International may seem tedious to the American reader removed from marxist polemics. But these critiques have had an effect of great general importance on marxist theory. By studying its errors with respect to fascism, western marxism has seen fit to abandon a purely economic model and to take seriously Marx's caveat: economics analyzed "first," before an analysis of other kinds of production, won't be good economics. Laclau proposes, in response to Third International economism and to Poulantzas's rather depressing analysis of a "floating petty bourgeoisie" (Moby Dick?), to give much more importance to ideology: ideology understood as a reproduction of desires and *discourse*, that is, in terms of the persuasive language used by fascists. A study like Jean-Pierre Faye's *Langages totalitaires*, concerned with the way fascist language spread from text to text and became more and more acceptable, is cited negatively by Poulantzas and enthusiastically by Laclau. Something has happened in between: Althusser's notion of ideological interpellation in language has made a bridge between linguistics and politics, between politics and psychoanalysis. What we find in Laclau's work is not so much the synthesis of a Freudian and a marxist analysis of fascism as an attempt to work through the newer theories of Lacan and Althusser; here the effect of fascism is understood as perversely indirect, traveling through language, through rhetoric, through what Althusser has called "the imaginary relationship of individuals to their real conditions of existence."

Indeed, Laclau will conclude, the experience of fascism blasts any easy notions we might have of class identity and the role of class alliances in political struggle. Class identity is a flexible notion, subject to all kinds of mutations in culture. In fascism, an old Jacobin notion of "the [classless] people" is called up and rearranged to be buoyed up by racism, so that "people" are appealed to as a "race."[38] Fantasy, creativity, dreaming are not inappropriate political terms.

But a "father," or perhaps I should say "mother," of desire-oriented political theories predates the Althusserians. It is in Wilhelm Reich's 1933 *The Mass Psychology of Fascism* that all my theoretical concerns—political, psychoanalytic, and vocal—find their first articulation.[39]

Reich was an outcast of the Third International and of the analytic community. He conceived of fascism as inherent in the circumstance of the individual living in the authoritarian family. The father is the dictator of the family, just as the dictator is the ruler of the state. If we see no way out of such structures, it is because of our own ways of thinking. Putting our "head first," we try to make it rule over a body that we like to think of as some imperfect version of the machines we create. In racism, we cast "others" as the animals we hate to be. In mysticism, we express the sensual side that rationality has left behind. Reich also notices the gaps between economics and ideology in fascism. The modern economic structure developed so much more quickly than the human one, that twentieth-century ideology remains primitive in its response to twentieth-century life. Fascism is entirely understandable in such a situation because it satisfies so many desires ignored by the "head first" approach to living. It reconciles ancient longings with the new machines.

In discussing the emotional ties that ground susceptibility to fascism, Reich takes on both parents. "The tie to the mother is the basis of all family ties"(pp. 56–57). "National feeling is derived from the maternal tie (home feeling)" (p. 136). But when it comes to the family, it is the father who rules, and the father who "perceives *himself* in the führer, and in the authoritarian state [Reich's emphasis]" (p. 136). The conclusion exactly echoes Freud's clause on the oceanic: "the childish need for protection is disguised in the form of a feeling at one with the führer"(p. 63). The final equation is this: "On the basis of this identification he feels himself to be a defender . . . of the nation" (p. 63). The pattern is familiar: recognizing oneself as manly and safeguarding mother-nation go together.

Directly below (that is, on the layout of the page) such evocations of the father is an odd little footnote, addressed to Reich's readers:"He who has not freed himself from his own tie to his family and to his mother, should not seek to investigate the formation of ideology" (p. 59). Yet since Reich decides that it is the father who constitutes authority, information on the fundamental tie to the mother is sparse in Reich's analysis of the authoritarian family. One could almost say that the mother-bound is but a "force" in his writing, without thorough articulation.[40] What information he gives us, however, points to a connection between maternal authority and national or home (*heimlich*) feeling. In a developmental aside, Reich remarks that infantile maternal longings should give way in adolescence to sexual relationships, but that when sexuality is repressed, the maternal longings are frozen in place and eternalized as extreme nationalism (pp. 56–57). Adolescent sexuality is displaced onto those very "unheimlich" politics we saw in Brasillach's essay on Nuremberg.

Reich's analogy, however slight, is invaluable for what it can contribute to our understanding of fascism's appeal to youth. We usually think of young men in fascist youth corps "in search of cultural fathers." But wasn't adolescence also that time of life when, attempting to "leap" toward adulthood, we were open to great boundary crises—to massive crushes, to daydreaming, to all kinds of intoxications? Friendships and group rituals of adolescence translate preoedipal feelings into revolt and communal experience. The teen-age is a symbiotic halfway house to differentiated adult life.[41]

Reich insisted that the workers' movement had to address the desires of the youth, or the reactionary movements would do it instead. His simile for political allegiance among youths is "marching to the music": "It is our contention that children and adolescents will march just as happily to fascist music tomorrow as they march to liberal music today" (p. 196). Marching to music is presumably not just finding a pied piper; it is *euphoric*. When he insists that youth can't distinguish between revolutionary and reactionary propaganda, Reich is perhaps forgetting his earlier claim that workers' movements couldn't address young people's desires. Youth, not so much out of naïveté as out of need, supports the movement most attuned to the oceanic. And, not to mistake youth as a literal category, we might add that so do those whom oceanic feelings make feel young.

I hope it is clear by now that when I refer to mother- or father-bound feelings, they don't have much to do with male or female people in the biological sense. If they did, people wouldn't experience mother-bound love for their male analysts, or symbolic fear of their female bosses. Hitler, even and especially Hitler, can be mother in a utopian moment, father in an authoritarian one. As Reich suggests, people can identify with a leader-as-father, in that they imagine the leader's power over the state as being their own over their smaller world. But we could just as easily characterize the same moment as one in which a leader-as-mother "gives birth" to people's feelings of power and euphoria.

Herein, I think, lie the shortcomings of purely biographic studies of fascist desires.[42] A given author can just as easily have "fled from his mother" into a phallic military atmosphere (like Theweleit's Freikorps officers), as have eternalized the mother-bound with a hyperromantic nationalism, as Brasillach did. There is a correspondence between biography and political feelings, but it is not direct or overt.

As a connected caveat against literalism, I should repeat that all this mother-bound feeling in fascism must not make us forget that fascist theories of sexuality confine the woman to the kitchen and nursery; that fascist terrorism used so-called Aryan women on baby farms; and that fascist administrators had women tortured in concentration camp fertility experiments. Reducing women to reproductive machines allowed fascists to feel eternal, just as reducing "others" to inferior races allowed them to feel like a superior race.

The elusive mother-bound can't be biographic. It ends up doing the very opposite of giving real power to actual women. How, then, can an analysis of the mother-bound contribute anything to real political analysis? What can it explain that wasn't explicable before? People have a lot of trouble figuring out why everyone thought Hitler was going to solve the unemployment problem. But the fascist mother nourishes. She nourishes through speech, so that real nourishment seems less important. With the advent of radio and the transformation of all the political figures into disembodied "speakers," wooing the public on microphone, the 1930s became a veritable festival of oral gratification. Fascist regimes weren't the only ones that "used" voice: Roosevelt did too. My point is not that all disembodied political voices were fascist but that the machinery of the media gave birth to a new kind of ideological vulnerability. It was mother bound, and fascism "knew" it. The side effects are numerous. Crowds in the nineteenth-century had been metaphorically female, but in the twentieth-century, they could play male to the maternal voices guiding them. And so on.

What ideology could make it clearer than fascism does that people have a sexual, as well as material, interest in their political life? The anger and excitement with which political issues are debated is not merely because of abstract commitments to liberty or social justice: when people discuss politics, they are discussing their ability to manipulate the world that houses them, to make intimate a gigantic "outside." We could describe such feelings in terms of connection, of possession, of power: all eminently erotic ones, as "old" as our infantile grasping and sucking at life.[43]

A standard metaphor of American politics exhibits a good understanding of this. Long before the women's movement made literal gender an issue, political organizers referred to certain issues as being "sexy issues." These "sexy issues" are sometimes referred to in the vernacular as issues that "hit home." Certain tax laws are "sexy" because they affect daily life—everyone can feel their effect and get angry about them. Sexy issues aren't abstract.

Nor are any of the desires appealed to by fascist rhetoric, foremost among which is the desire to have government "hit home." "Presence," "immediacy," "real leadership," "restored unity": back to the ubiquitous maternal other. After this imaginary unity has put fascism in power, the rhetoric can change. The fascist bureaucracy consolidates the control of big business; artificially raised wages go down; labor unions are destroyed; and, orally, the utopian element is shunted in favor of a more pragmatic militaristic authoritarianism.[44] Then the fascist state starts looking grotesquely paternal.

It is precisely at this stage that there are massive defections among those intellectuals to whom mother-bound fascism looked creative. They detect a new style, and they're uncomfortable with it. A funny thing happens after Ernst Jünger, a fascist of the "first phase," has rejected Hitlerism. He finds himself stationed in occupied France, surrounded by French fascists still in the grip of fascist enthusiasm. He is disgusted by them. It's not merely that Jünger has been "cured" of fascist longings; it's that by traveling to France, he crosses over to a fascist phase no longer appropriate to his own experiences.[45]

One can't "decide" between the mother-bound and father-bound elements in fascism. They get bundled up in fascism's totalizing machinery and offered up in fascist language to appeal at different emotional registers at different moments of fascism's history. Their coexistence might serve as a reminder that fascism works by binding doubles, a process that leads to persistent blindness to the fascist machinery in theories that insist on deciding between two parts of fascism. Is fascism modern or antimodern? Is it revolutionary or conservative, left or right? When I originally discovered the mother-bound element of fascism in my reading, I had just such a desire to split fascism into two parts and "pick" one. This was my own inadvertent attempt to reduce fascism's power by intellectually stopping its binding mechanism. But splitting, after all, is really much the same activity as binding done in reverse. It haunted me that the fascist anti-Semite was also a "splitter," separating what he feared from what he desired by projecting all he didn't understand in modern life onto the Jews, and all that he wished to recuperate in modern life onto the fascist state.

Splitting and binding in fascism empty its language of the kind of content or consistency that usually helps explain political doctrines. Reich and Poulantzas both write that fascism will take on whatever language its listeners want to hear. Faye and Laclau attempt to analyze such mutations structurally, but to do so they must abandon straightforward categories and concentrate on processes like cross-pollination and displacement, mechanisms so all-encompassing and dangerous, they lead us back to Cantimori's wonderful metaphor of fascism-as-Moby-Dick.

What follows is a longer description of some of these startling "bundlings" performed in fascism. I will write now at a level of abstraction I want ultimately to reject. But by describing an ideology in formal terms, I can show how theorists are lead by fascism to decide that fascism is "either/or," or that it has "no content." My own verbal acrobatics will gauge the effects of the slippery beast as they mime it: what I lose in textual detail, I will try to recapture in speculation.

### The Polarity Machine

*Modern and Antimodern*

Critics of such fascist writers as Drieu la Rochelle, Céline, and Brasillach pose the question of fascist ideology in terms of a contradiction between these writers' modernist and anti-modernist sympathies with remarkable consistency.[46] It is assumed by them that a modernist is an iconoclast, a writer who experiments with traditional forms, who incorporates into his text images of the industrialized city and its alienated citizens, who participates in the questioning of traditional moral values often associated with the political left. An antimodernist, according to this view, is nostalgic — both for an era in which moral values and social hierarchies seem to have been defined clearly, and for the landscapes (feudal, pastoral, or agrarian) that accompany his particular retrospective utopia. In France, for example, the antimodernist would use and idealize archaic literary forms, as Brasillach adapted Corneille, or as Céline interspersed in his *Mort à crédit* a medieval story called the Tales of King Krogold. Or the antimodernist would portray and laud the survival of an archaic life-style, as Drieu la Rochelle does with his Norman hero, Carentin, in *Gilles*. Carentin, an avuncular Action Française country philosopher, is the *porte-parole* of antimodern anti-Semitism: "Well! As for me, I can't tolerate the Jews, because they are *par excellence* the modern world that I abhor."[47]

Then we get to the complications. Anti-Semitism, for example, can be modern — you only have to look at Céline's condemnations of the Jews in *Bagatelles pour un massacre* to see how they are linked both to a modern urbanism and to an archaic plot by the Elders of Zion. The imagined Jewish enemy can be as new as machinery or as old as the desert. Racism is flexible, and it would be dangerous to reify it too quickly. Céline's modern epic, or even Brasillach's admiration for the feudal overtones of a modernist phenomenon like cinema, confuses the categories of modernist and antimodernist. Are these categories useful in approaching a fascist text?

Part of the problem lies in the fuzziness of the words used to talk about what is *modern*, divided lexically between the aesthetic, political, and economic realms. Variants on the word are slanted toward one particular realm of social production: *modernization* usually connotes some technological advancement;

*modern* is frequently historical; *modernism* has a stylistic bent. Obviously, the words can only continue to be meaningful as long as those realms remain isolated.

And this is the case with much late nineteenth- and early twentieth-century popular French and German fiction. Antimodern aesthetics appear to be a standard feature of work whose social function was quite simply to defend against the horrors of technological modernization. The canonical French novel that best demonstrates this strategy is Barrès's *Les Déracinés*, in which the narration is fueled by an ethnocentric philosophy linking various forms of modern unhappiness to corrupt Jewish industrialists, to centralization, and to the city itself.

But since fascism can be characterized formally as an entry of aesthetic criteria into the political and economic realms—the effective smashing of barriers between the three realms mentioned above—it makes way for the possibility that a social defense against modernization can itself be (aesthetically) modern.

Certainly, fascist literature shares with traditional antimodernism a reverence for nature, a desire for community and for revolt against modern life. In Brasillach, for example, camping and hitchhiking are lauded from an antimodernist perspective. Yet that same literature appears to join the modernizers in its glorification of technology, its sophisticated understanding of propaganda, its reverence for mechanized war. Witness Marinetti's "Electric War," Brasillach's love of the sound track, Rebatet's belief in radio.

In more straightforwardly political fascist rhetoric, when revolt against bourgeois society takes the form of nostalgia for a feudal community, or when an ostensibly revolutionary consciousness of "the people" works in the service of an archaic racial or tribal consciousness, a modernist value is paradoxically in the service of an antimodernist one.[48] Neither category, exclusive of the other, can be useful in the analysis of either political or literary fascism, precisely because of the way that fascist ideology, as interpellation, has been able to collapse such polarities and attract modernists, antimodernists, and those inbetween.

Here is an example of the dilemma of choice: Henry Turner, an American historian, puzzles over what he calls the desire of the Nazis to "have the products of industry—automobiles, airplanes, tanks, etc. . . . but without an industrial society."[49] His question (modern or antimodern fascism?) contains its own response: that is, that the posited coexistence of modern industry and the life-style of "organic" preindustrial society was a basis of fascism's totalizing appeal. The isolation of desired products from a social whole is emblematic of other mechanisms at work in fascist ideology: its disregard for the utility of technology, its separation of technology from economic production, its aestheticization of the political ground of technological modernity.

Other theorists cut the situation into different conceptual portions. In Jacques Ellul's view, nazism cultivates the revolt of the masses against decadence in order to align antimodern political impulses and modern techniques into a rigorous social order.[50] Turner's remark has divided what Ellul calls "technique" into two further components: an industrial consciousness (rejected) and the industrial products (fetishized). Ellul describes the rejection of industrial consciousness within the category of the political. It is not surprising that the literary critic Walter Benjamin was the first to recognize the separation of objects from their use value in fascist ideology, because that kind of separation is part of the standard distancing that makes people recognize things as works of art.

In the case of fascist art, however, the autonomy of industrial products is granted as protection against the real—against street violence, economic depression, faltering parliamentary governments, against the success of bolshevism, and therefore against an increasingly visible working class. It is granted with, if you like, "the refusal of the real." As though the "automobiles, airplanes, tanks" were so many aesthetic showpieces, decorating a primitive mentality. Thus, the elitist, aesthetic tradition that culminated with the decadents at the turn of the century can, and often does, turn fascist when applied to the new consumer society of the 1930s—as a cure. "We will solve the social problem artistically," claim the Italian futurists. The writers negatively affected by the actual social basis of modernity, that is, by the working relations resulting from large scale industry, can still remain decidedly modern by lauding the products of that industry while depoliticizing, or ignoring, its process. Here I quote an early example from Marinetti:

> One can say of the great French railway strike that the organizers
> were unable to persuade a single mechanic to sabotage his locomotive.
> To me this seems entirely natural. How could one of these men have
> been able to wound or kill . . . his beautiful steel machine that had
> so often glowed with pleasure beneath his ardent caress?[51]

Marinetti makes people laugh because he is so wonderfully obvious. The bribe by which the means of production is repressed is not aesthetic (the aesthetic bribe referred to by Freud in his essay on daydreaming) so much as it is sexual. Marinetti offers the reader an industrial pornography, where substitutive gratification is immediate. The notion of gratification is, of course, highly relevant to an aesthetic that posits concrete modern and antimodern elements in a fight against the fantasized abstractions—read: fascism's Others—Jews, Immigrants, or Workers. It is against the negative background of the "other" that fascist totality takes place. The totality can be either backward- or forward-looking, but it must go *far*. Other ideologies do this, but fascism does so in hypertrophic style—way, way back and way, way forward, running the gamut from medievalism to the most radical futurism. References in fascist texts to a feudal community or to a primitive nature—the epic setting of Marinetti's *Mafarka le futuriste*, or Brasillach's reference to cinema as a modern "chanson de geste"—are not incompatible with reverence for the machine as long as both are understood as part of an aesthetic—or, in the case of Marinetti, a libidinal— shielding of the human condition beyond and before the actual contradictions of industrialized life. We might also think of this approach to technology as an anticipation of the consumer's approach. It allows the artist to celebrate modernity without delving into its social consequences. It allows the artist to disregard a painful social context with the shield of an avant-garde sensibility. The stance is not necessarily fascist; we have seen it since. Its consequences depend on a context.

I hope it is clear by now that the important question for me is not whether, or even how, fascism is modernist, but how one of the avant-garde approaches to art served the fascist movement. The major theoretical stumbling block for all critics of the period seems to be in distinguishing aesthetic and sociological modernism: sometimes antimodernist rhetoric appears as a reaction to industrialization; sometimes industry itself is simply rendered aesthetic. References in fascist texts to a feudal community or to a primitive nature accompanied by reverence for the machine are not necessarily antagonistic, since both can result in a comfortable distancing of the human condition from the actual contradictions of industrialized life. Marinetti's gleeful prose, so eminently amusing and quotable, is a particularly successful example of compatible archaism and modernism; with its tremendous linguistic verve, it more than compensates for any context it may erase.

*Construction and Destruction*

Walter Benjamin has analyzed Marinetti's aestheticization of war as an extreme moment in this distancing process. War, writes Benjamin, has a crucial imaginary, that is, ideological, function in the binding of two more polarities, *Construction* and *Destruction*. Benjamin's writing on war and fascism is dazzling, even by his usual standards, since fascism requires that he constantly leap from the aesthetic cynicism that nourishes fascism to the authoritarianism that characterizes its praxis, and back. In one piece, after citing avant-garde artists to whom fascist ideology "owes" (Benn and Bronnen in Germany, Marinetti in Italy, and Oscar Wilde in England) Benjamin concludes dramatically: "Never has decadent art been interested in the construction of monuments. It has been left to fascism to unite the decadent theory of art to a monumental praxis. Nothing is more instructive than this meeting of elements which are, in themselves, contradictory."[52]

A disguise of the actual uses of technology unites aestheticism to fascist art. Aesthetes can describe objects that are used to kill as though they were purely creative. Fascism makes use of such description. An aesthetic of "art for art" applied to the concept of war gives us both art for war (promilitaristic art) and, more crucially, "outside" the established art form as such, war for the sake of art, war *as* art.

War, in Benjamin's view, is that *imaginative* place where the modern aesthete acts out a desire to destroy the foundation of technology in production. The war machine is a means of restoring to modern life qualities of visibility and effectiveness, of restoring the sensory presence that has always been assumed in the relationship of the thinking subject to its biological body. But with a twist: the aproductive products of war are justified fetishistically. By festishistically I mean independently of their actual function and at a distance from the admiring subject, the all-important *viewer*.

Benjamin is probably the first "comparatist" of fascism, as well as its first cultural critic. He passes easily from reference to reference in the French, Italian, English, and German tradition.[53] On how many more texts might his point have been made? He could have used as his example Brasillach and Bardèche's statement, in the 1943 edition of *Histoire du cinéma*, that the Second World War was a spectacle, founded in the collective imagination of moviegoers between the wars.[54] Here again, destruction in the real is justified beforehand by an aesthetic device—in this case the newsreel—that distances and controls war, rendering it a safe fantasy, and ultimately, a real possibility. The Second World War, they wrote, was staged in our collective imagination, in our moviegoing imagination, before the war actually began.

What Benjamin has named the "aura"—the authenticity and uniqueness of the work of art before technology rendered it radically reproducible—is replaced in fascist art by the "total" appeal of something on the verge of aura-lessness. Fascist aesthetics has a debt to masterful moderns like Céline and Marinetti, on the one hand, and an embryonic allegiance to new, authorless form production in radio and cinema, on the other. The private language of literary modernity is one brilliant signal of aura's death throes. Cinema is another. By drawing the spectator into an illusory, complete other world, it looks toward a new system in which art appeals as totality. Here was a medium that would engineer a break with individually authored art forms and that could, at the same time, forge together the most appealing elements of the modernist and antimodernist aesthetic. Alongside cinema, we can list the microphone, the poster, and the rally as other fascist forms by which the primitive appeal of ritual and tradition can obfuscate the alienating, mediating aspects of modern art production and still remain decidedly modern.

In an article whose title—"Drieu la Rochelle and Modernist Anti-Modernism in French Fascism"—is emblematic of this whole theoretical problem, Robert Soucy called Drieu's work "a modernism shot through with anti-modernist longings."[55] Rather, in the work that concerns us, expectations and values that precede industrialization (the desire for faith, meaning, goals) are applied to the most alienated aspects of modern life. War no longer instills the victor with prestige because of the land or booty gained but because the fight itself, the weapons and bombs, creates a spectacle that is then recorded on film and broadcast throughout the world. It is now the reproduction of war, instead of war itself, that is "shot through" with ritualistic value. Fascism recuperates modern man's lost rituals with the help of the very factor that has threatened them in the first place: technology. And this is precisely how fascist art can appear both nostalgic and avant-garde, how it can construct by representing destruction.

## Selfishness and Selflessness

The contradiction Benjamin describes between decadent art and monumental art undergoes a developmental shift (much as mother-bound desires cede to father-bound ones) as fascism and bureaucracy become more intertwined. As fascism takes power, Benjamin remarks, it will have less and less need for refined intellectuals; it will be able to employ "less exalted spirits" to administer largely mechanized propaganda. Its avant-garde practitioners will give way to dull realists who construct mammoth phallic statuary and buildings. Fascism loses its own imagination: it decides simply to return to Rome.

But when this happens (and in France, we remember, it never quite does), that earlier fascist art has already been there, giving the masses a sense of direct participation in the state. This directness, or sense of unmediated participation, is created with sophisticated art technologies that foster a psychological link between citizen and state by representing the citizen to the citizen. "When we see the sturdy bloom of the young nationalists opening out on the silver screens, we must take part," wrote Brasillach of his own commitment to fascism.[56] The link between film and political power is equally clear in a futurist manifesto on cinema: "this is how we decompose and recompose the universe according to our marvelous whims, to centuple the powers of the Italian creative genius and its absolute pre-eminence in the world."[57]

## The Other and the Self

In order to convey the illusion of a total state and of a resuscitated preindustrial community, fascist ideology must somehow put under its control everything about modern life that would seem to render that community impossible. The increasing importance of colonialism as a source of nationalist strength and the improved methods of communication between distant peoples are two such threatening factors. The arrival of masses of immigrants in Germany and in France, coupled with the international economic depression of the 1930s, are two more. All these "internationalizing" events interfere with the possibility of a mythic uniracial existence such as that proffered by fascist utopias. Fascism reduces such threatening international factors to concrete groups of people. They come to stand, in the case of the Jews, for all that fascism wants to hide (its sympathy with imperialism and acquisitiveness) and for all that fascism fears (rootlessness, lack of national identity, "free-floating identity"). In fascist Italy, where anti-Semitism plays a minor role, we see bourgeois parliamentarianism linked to female "inactivity." Fascism must define "outsiders" to safeguard its own illusions. The Jew represents the aspects of modernity unacceptable to fascist communalism, and the woman represents the "token waste product" of the nineteenth century – that which fascism must leave behind. But to claim that anti-Semitism is simply antimodern and that misogyny is modern is unsatisfactory: the terms are far too flexible. They mutate according to the political tensions of the moment, and we will see them working differently in different texts.

In a fascinating study that explores such mutations, Moishe Postone sets out to show how anti-Semitism allowed the German fascists to appear as anticapitalists by tying the Jews to everything about modern capital that was confusing.[58] By linking the Jews to what Postone calls "abstract finance capital," the Jews could be blamed for inflation. Industrial production, so necessary to the fascist state, could then remain "innocent" or even become glorified in fascism as the descendant of artisan labor. For this to happen, finance capital and abstract reason are linked to Jews; direct industrial labor is deemed "concrete" and is made safe for the support of the fascist state. This is not so much a theory of the Jew as scapegoat as it is a description of political splitting.

We might think about fascist racism in these terms: the imaginary state itself becomes a nourishing mother who only produces one kind of child. Thus, the illusory unity of modern and antimodern mentalities, of revolutionary and conservative thought – in short, the illusion of the total, maternal state in fascism, depends for coherence on siphoning off or projecting contradictory material onto the Jews. They are the "strangers to the mother."

## Abstract and Literal

Just as the regime art practiced by the established fascist state is cloyingly unimaginative, consolidated fascist ideology relies more and more on literal characterization and representations of its chosen negativity. Nazism partakes in the actual extermination of its projected negative fantasy in the concentration camps. Postone (again, a methodological model in terms of his treatment of symbolic "identities" in nazism) argues that the work of the camps was to render the Jewish people – the threatening and the abstract – into a nonpeople, into abstracted shadows (skeletons) of humanity. Camp administration "proved" that Jews were "reducible" by ritually wresting from the masses of exterminated bodies all that remained on them of use-value, such as clothes, gold fillings, hair, and so on.

The purported desire in many fascist texts to get "down to earth" – the valorization of the organic, the literal, the everyday – depends for its validity on the transference of polar opposites—the abstract, the figurative—to actually specified groups of human beings. The spiritual notion of "the people" becomes a specific, pseudoscientific group of people, the Aryans. The threat of national dispersal is reduced to a Jewish threat, because of historic Jewish mobility.

This basic structure has many variants. In France, where linguistic unity has long been endowed with qualities akin to the sacred, I find literalizations at the level of voice. Internationalism is a Jewish mélange of languages; fascist nationalism can then safeguard an organic spoken language. The Italian futurist version of the "down to earth" is less recognizable: it is an "up in the air," at the expense of the dullards below. The fascist desire to control lived experience works in both directions.

## Revolutionary and Conservative

The contradiction between modernism and antimodernism in fascism is, in a sense, a false one. It covers up the manner in which old and new human reflexes are being recycled to serve a politics of destruction. Fascism puts ideology over economics. In Germany and Italy, the economic structures of the fascist state are basically unchanged from those of the capitalist one, with the difference that the failing market economy is buoyed by preparations for a war economy and that weary parliamentary in-fighting is infused with the unity of purpose that comes with one-party rule. These fascisms, as perceived by their supporters in neighboring France, offer the appeal of a revolt without threatening property relations.[59] This situation is especially appealing to the intellectual, who dreams of gaining "community"—a metaphor for support—without losing "self"—a metaphor for creation. Fascist intellectuals hate communism because it threatens to strip them of their identity as artists, and they hate capitalism because it appreciates money over art. Fascism seems to be about making life into art—a transformation that promises to give artists an enormous role.

The lip service of the fascist intelligentsia to rebellion and destruction, as well as to safeguarding and restoring, confuses the opposition between revolutionary and conservative politics that we rely on for making political judgments. In the absence of altered property relations, what kind of order does fascism set out to destroy; what values does it consider worth safeguarding?

The appeal of fascism had to do with its presentation as a total state—one that could reconcile the nationalism of the right and the syndicalist revolt on the left. This is the state of things that most interests Jean-Pierre Faye when he describes the total state as both completely revolutionary and completely conservative. Faye remarks that the revolutionary aspects of the polarity contribute ironically to the most reactionary aspects of fascism. Faye describes a process of cross-pollination in fascism. Popular revolutionary consciousness (left) is influenced by nationalism (right) and translated into people's racial consciousness (fascistic); neither left nor right are noxious until "set off" in combination.[60] Ellul's technosociety depends upon a similar exploitation of primitive impulse. Before them, Wilhelm Reich described the fascist mentality as one that applies reactionary concepts to revolutionary emotions. The fascist reaction to the riots of February 6, 1934, furnishes us with a specifically French example of this cross pollination: Jacobin popular sentiments are mixed with royalist (Action Française) ones.

Sternhell's study of the class origins of French fascists confronts this confusion on an empirical level.[61] French fascism appeared to be on the rise whenever the traditional right took a beating, but conservative electoral and social victories (from Poincaré to Pétain) always managed to stave off fascist success. Sternhell's research uncovered one fact that the new philosopher Bernard-Henri Lévy would repeat in his own flamboyant post-marxist style: collaborationists and fascists of the 1940s tended to be exsocialists and communists more often than they were "cross over" members of the Action Française.[62] Sternhell concludes from his findings that French fascism could only come to power on a right-wing grave. French fascism didn't succeed because a stable conservative right, allergic to political action, was there to stop it.

There is an interesting symmetry between Sternhell's view and that of the marxist critics who argue that a successful workers' movement could have prevented both Italian and German fascist rule. Left and right, in other words, must *both* be weakened for fascism to "be" both. All standard systems of political representation must be on the blink.

*Populism and Elitism*

As I have suggested, fascism works with binding and with splits. Faithful to our temporarily formalist approach, we can also say that its history corresponds to a topological shift.

After an initial, rallying period, during which a left-sounding movement appeals to a populist petty bourgeoisie, the movement's power is consolidated in formal bureaucracy; populist ties are severed or dissolved into party ties; and economic power passes back into the hands of the traditional capitalist channels. Visible political power remains in the hands of the fascist party, increasingly militaristic and authoritarian in its rhetoric. From maternal nourisher, source of national identity, and poet of a classless society, the fascist leader becomes an employer, a protector, a warrior king. The populist ideal mutates toward an elitist one.

Even this shift, however, involves a certain amount of overlap. There is thus a bizarre compatibility of elitism and populism in fascism, whereby every man, in imaginary proximity to the body and soul of a leader, can feel like *the* Man. Marinetti, for example, in promoting "artecrazia," evokes a Dionysian cycle of the subject-as-artist, scattered and destroyed in creative orgy in order to re-emerge with greater powers. Marinetti replaces the traditionally "whole" subject with a scattered ubiquitous one, just as in a modern understanding of art, the aura of the individual work is replaced by the total presence of art. (We have posited that art is received as modern when it is able to be continually reproduced and represented in a number of places at once, to attract a number of senses, a number of subjects, either simultaneously or separately.) In Céline's texts, the same modern loss of subjectivity is obviously out of hand—the destruction of the subject occurs in such a way as to efface all boundaries between self and other, life and death. The constant re-creation of death and destruction of boundaries in his imaginary tableaux, coupled with his extraordinary racism and fear of others, create a new totality: a total chaos, but also a self without limits; a pseudoindividual who is everywhere and nowhere at all. Certain aspects of institutionalized fascist art that still bear some relation to avant-garde precursors continue to function "beyond the populist shift," giving the masses a sense of *direct* participation in the state.

We can now posit some very general observations: what fascism transforms is not the means of production or distribution of wealth in the state, but the technical means by which the state reproduces its own legitimacy before individuals. When fascism took power, it took charge of the imaginary, using the most advanced sophisticated agents of representation available—cinema, radio, architecture, staged rallies—new elements in the "design" of everyday life that few knew to take seriously as political forces. It would be an error to describe fascist state media as an endlessly fascinating emotional coup. It was highly clichéd and boring, even to its devotees. But it was ubiquitous, and it had been prepared in several generations of higher brow art and literature. Today our received ideas about "media manipulation" strike me as a long-term intellectual side effect of fascism. When we think of media as mechanically controlling a homogenous "mass," we are still giving Goebbels too much historic credit. We can no more reduce fascist media to maniacal manipulation than we can reduce the rest of fascism to pied piperism: too many peoples' desires and too many hard working imaginations stand in the way.[63]

The title of Robert Brasillach's fascist newspaper tells us this about the elitist-populist subject in fascist art: *Je Suis Partout*, "I am everywhere," and its double entendre, "I follow everywhere." In fascism, the reproducibility (rather than the content) of the media offered a new sense of mastery. The traditional mastery promised by nineteenth-century liberalism was one in which the individual subject owned and controlled a small universe (the nineteenth-century subject-as-small businessman). This mastery collapsed, for many, and was succeeded in fascism by a sense of being able to *follow* and *belong to* a limitlessly large world. To be everywhere is to see or hear images of one's own progenitor everywhere: on the screen and on the radio, echoing at rallies and staring from every poster.

The crowd at a fascist rally, beneath *Je Suis Partout* posters. Paris, 1942. Photo Lapi Viollet.

Pied piperism actually has its origins in the illusion of "being followed" by fascist art. Participation in fascism was not as selflessly masochistic as its most outraged, disbelieving critics would have it appear, for it gave the masses the impression of intimacy, not just with the leader, but with the myriad representations of themselves supplied by the state. This seductive fascism is not, as Fromm would have it, a "flight from freedom" but an imagined "flight to freedom" in the collective will to breach all limits.[64] Fascism allowed people to say that they were (following) everywhere: their fascism was utopian in the very real sense of being "not in one place."

## Notes

1. Paul Fussell, *The Great War and Modern Memory*.
2. Benjamin describes the way Dada seemed to anticipate the destruction of war in his "The Work of Art in the Age of Mechanical Reproduction," p. 238: "By means of its technical structure, the film has taken the physical shock effect out of the wrappers in which Dadaism had, as it were, kept it inside the moral shock effect." See also note 20 of the same article: "As for Dadaism, insights important for Cubism and Futurism are to be gained from the movie. Both appear as deficient attempts of art to accommodate the pervasion of reality by the apparatus."
3. Melanie Klein's "Mourning and Its Relation to Manic-Depressive States (1940)" is a good example of her inadvertent "reading" of modernism.
4. See D. W. Winnicott, *Playing and Reality*. His seminal essay "Transitional Objects and

Transitional Phenomena" first appeared in 1951. Victor Tausk, "On the Origin of the 'Influencing Machine' in Schizophrenia (1919)," pp. 31–64, is also useful reading in this context.

5. This important question was first posed to me by Nathaniel Wing.

6. Theweleit, *Männerphantasien*. Laplanche and Pontalis's essay on projection in *The Language of Psycho-Analysis*, pp. 349–55, implies that projection is something of a failure as a psychoanalytic tool. The authors begin by stating that projection is "badly demarcated" in theory—like the function it would describe, it rejects boundaries. We might think of the many different definitions of projection as pasteups in a collage. It is the whole badly demarcated collage, not the individual pasteup meanings, that is useful in understanding fascist desires. To show what I mean I will outline the four kinds of projection suggested by Laplanche and Pontalis: (1) creative projection: a child creates a drawing, and the drawing is used as a tool to interpret the child's personality. She has "projected" her personality onto the drawing. This normal sense of projection can be extended to (2) mythological and artistic projection: all cultural production presumably projects aspects of human existence; (3) positive and negative projection: in racism and idealization, people can transfer good and bad feelings onto other people or objects (we're nearing Kleinian territory here); and (4) double projection: an unacceptable feeling is erased by being turned into its opposite. Later, the very thing that has been repressed returns to haunt us. Laplanche and Pontalis translate this last form of projection into two examples: either we rediscover in the world something we once struggled to get rid of in ourselves, or, like moviegoers, we send out into the world an image that exists in us in an unconscious way. This second definition interests me because it is both cinematographic (technological) and profoundly reactionary in the ideological sense: we don't recognize the connection between ourselves and the rest of the world (we refuse it), yet, like the fascists I am studying, we refuse *aesthetically*, by representing the world to ourselves.

7. Delio Cantimori, *Conversandi di storia*, p. 134, my trans. Cantimori was mentor to Renzo De Felice, biographer of Mussolini and the major contemporary Italian theorist of fascism. Felice describes with great affection his working relationship with Cantimori and recounts the history of each man's interest in the study of fascism in Renzo De Felice, *Fascism*, pp. 22–28.

8. Poulantzas, *Fascism and Dictatorship*, defines the petty bourgeoisie as a class caught between the master-slave dialectic, a kind of Hegelian failure. Sharing the interests of neither the bourgeoisie nor the proletariat, the petty bourgeoisie can only exist by aspiring in one direction or the other. Susceptible to myth, and especially to the myth of education and culture, the ultimate petty bourgeois is the intellectual. This fact, in Poulantzas' terms, would make the intellectual more susceptible than others to fascism.

Laclau, *Politics and Ideology in Marxist Theory*, takes a somewhat more encouraging position in stating that class identity is nowhere near as rigid as Poulantzas describes it. Class, for Laclau, is not a "representational" notion (a "*signifié*" in harmony with its "*signifiant*"). Workers are not going to identify with working-class ideology any more automatically than the children of the very rich are going to identify with industrialists instead of terrorists. People can imagine for themselves any class alliance they want (that's what ideology is all about). Laclau's view makes room for all kinds of shifting alliances, for bourgeois populism as well as for working-class fascism of the Déat-Doriot variety.

9. Brasillach, *Notre Avant-Guerre*. Page numbers are noted in parentheses in the body of the text. Theweleit (vol. 1, ms.) quotes a newspaper description of the procession of the banners at Nuremberg in which the images are so close to Brasillach's that Brasillach might have copied them. Here it is: "Dr. Ley announced the 'Entry March of the Banners.' For a moment, one could see nothing. But then they emerged from the blackness of the night, over on the south side. In seven columns, they poured into the spaces between the formations. You couldn't see the people, couldn't recognize the standard-bearers. All you saw was a broad, red, surging stream, its surface sparkling gold and silver, advancing slowly like fiery lava. Feeling the dynamism of that slow advance, you got some small impression of what those sacred symbols meant." Brasillach would write, "It's because these

ceremonies and songs signify something that we should pay attention to them" (p. 233), and in his original 1937 article, "Cent heures chez Hitler," he added: "and, without a doubt, keep ourselves on guard." Theweleit insists on the way that the fascist ceremony "converts the flowing 'feminine' into a rigid 'masculine.' " From Brasillach's romantic distance, fascism is always flowing; rigidity exists only in the afterthought, the defense against fascism (*"et, sans doute, nous tenir sur nos gardes"*).

10. Margaret S. Mahler, "On Human Symbiosis and the Vicissitudes of Individuation," p. 20.

11. See Jacques Derrida, *Grammatology*.

12. See Ivan Fónagy, *La Vive voix: essais de psychophonétique*, and Paul Zumthor, *Introduction à la poésie orale*.

13. Louis Althusser, "Ideology and Ideological State Apparatuses."

14. Micheline Veaux, "Réflexions Vocales dans un miroir et Voix mythiques," pp. 435–47.

15. Here she draws heavily on René Spitz, *No and Yes in the Genesis of Human Communication*.

16. Kristeva's work on Céline is represented in *Polylogue* and *Pouvoirs de l'horreur*. Essays from *Polylogue* have been translated along with earlier work with a helpful theoretical introduction and glossary of terms in a volume entitled *Desire in Language*. *Pouvoirs de l'horreur* has been translated in its entirety. See also Irving Howe, "Céline: The Sod Beneath the Skin," pp. 54–66. It was interesting to discover that Irving Howe's early essay on Céline, though almost entirely thematic, anticipates Kristeva's formal attention to the "abject." Howe, offended by Céline, takes a much greater theoretical (and pragmatic) distance from the texts than does Kristeva: but then he is also closer to them historically.

17. Brasillach, *Notre Avant-Guerre*, p. 234.

18. *Gilles* is generally considered the ideal type of the fascist novel. See my reading of these two texts in chapter 6, "Bodies and Landscapes: Drieu la Rochelle." I thank Denis Hollier for recommending *Mesure de la France*.

19. American feminists are undertaking just such a theoretical project. See Hester Eisenstein and Alice Jardine, eds., *The Future of Difference* (see reference entry under Chodorow, Nancy) and an important single article, Elizabeth Berg, "The Third Woman," pp. 11–20. Jardine's "Ideology and Writing Couples" was also helpful to me in formulating my argument.

20. See *Civilization and Its Discontents*, p. 125, on the genesis of guilt: "the place of the father or the two parents is taken by the larger human community."

21. *Civilization and Its Discontents*, p. 72. Theweleit's exegesis of this passage in the context of a theoretical dialogue between Freud and Reich is of great importance. Jane Flax discusses the same passage in "Mother-Daughter Relationships: Psychodynamics, Politics, and Philosophy," p. 26. Flax departs from Freud via Monique Wittig, who, she notes, reads *Civilization and Its Discontents* as "a struggle among men after women are dominated."

22. I am referring to Nancy Chodorow, "Gender, Relation, and Difference in Psychoanalytic Perspective," and to Jane Flax, "Mother-Daughter Relationships," in *The Future of Difference*. Flax analyzes an identity bind: in order to differentiate from her mother, a woman must identify with her father, and thus with his oppression of the mother. Chodorow, describing a somewhat more perfect world, believes that the female child who perceives the mother as a successfully "separated self" can value herself.

23. Kristeva, *Polylogue*, p. 17.

24. "Qu'est-ce qu'un collaborateur?" pp. 43–62. Translations are my own. Page numbers are noted in parentheses in the body of the text.

25. The distinction is made by Stanley Hoffmann in "The Fall," part 1 of *Decline or Renewal?*, pp. 1–62. Paxton's *Vichy France* also contains a detailed analysis of Vichy and the intelligentsia. Lucien Rebatet, who returned to Paris after a brief stint at Vichy, is the most vocal in his disdain for the followers of Pétain (see *Les Décombres*).

26. Simone de Beauvoir, "Oeil pour oeil," pp. 813–30; Robert Tucker, *The Fascist Ego*, Preface.

27. Brasillach's 1943 article "Lettre à quelques jeunes gens" is reprinted in its entirety in Brasillach, *Oeuvres complètes*, vol. 12, pp. 610–14 (the famous phrase can be found on p. 612 of that edition). The phrase is quoted by government prosecutor Reboul in defense attorney Jacques Isorni's edition of the Brasillach trial, *Le Procès de Robert Brasillach*, p. 138.

28. See Andrea Gisela Snell, " 'Die Franzosen' and 'Les Allemands': Cultural Clichés in the Making (1650–1850)," for a broad historic view of these stereotypes. Only in the late eighteenth century, Snell argues, did German Francomania find its echo in France. With Madame de Stael's *De L'Allemagne*, the French began to see the German spirit as something "essential" and "profound."

29. See the Benoist-Méchin translation of Curtius's *Essai sur la France*, pp. 60–61. Curtius's is only one of what seems to have been a whole series of books written between the wars—and across the political spectrum—on the murky subject of "national character." A laudatory typology of the genre is developed by Georges Hardy, in *La Géographie psychologique* Hardy mentions such titles as Regis Michaud's *Ce qu'il faut connaître de l'âme américaine* (1929), and Paul Gaultier's *L'Ame française* (1936).

It is also worth noting in this context that translator Benoist-Méchin was to be a cultural ambassador of French-German relations as a Vichy delegate to the German government in Paris. His literary emblem for the fall of France would appropriately echo Curtius: the fall was a harvest (*La Moisson de quarante* [Paris, 1941]).

The male German and female French stereotypes before the war may have had as much to do with traditions of export between the two countries as with social mores within them. As for stereotypes during the war, Richard Cobb points out that the collaborationist topos of a marriage between Ceres and Vulcan (evident everywhere from Benoist-Méchin to the daily news) had "an increasing ring of truth as the occupying authorities set about pillaging France of her resources in food and drink" (*French and Germans/ Germans and French*, p. 161).

30. Robert Brasillach, "Cent heures chez Hitler," p. 74. Brasillach's revision of this text for inclusion in his 1941 memoirs, *Notre Avant-Guerre*, is marked by the abolition of much of his antithetical feelings: gone, for example, is the entire first paragraph of the above quote. Was this for the benefit of the censors, or was it a result of Brasillach's growing Germanophilia?

31. Freud, "The 'Uncanny'," pp. 123–24, 152–53.

32. See Robert Paxton, *Vichy France*, p. 230: "even fascist ideologues like Robert Brasillach found Nazi party rallies foreign and slightly ludicrous," and Gérard Miller, *Les Pousse-au-Jouir du Maréchal Pétain*, p. 205: "The French right remembers the accounts of notorious fascists returning sympathetic, but skeptic, from Germany." (Miller substantiates this remark by quoting Brasillach's *"unheimlich"* passage.) I should insist that it is only because these writers have so carefully distinguished French fascism both from Pétainism and from nazism that I now enjoy the intellectual luxury of examining ambivalence *within* that ideology. As Roland Barthes wrote in his introduction to Miller's text, "to believe that there is never but one fascism would be politically dangerous."

33. Jean-Paul Sartre, "L'Enfance d'un chef," pp. 151–245. Page references noted in the body of the text are to the French edition; translations are my own.

34. Robert Brasillach, "Cent heures chez Hitler," p. 73. Absent from the 1941 version of this essay is the qualifier "and better" and the rejoinder about "beating down democracy." The sentence beginning "As for the rest" is replaced by "And this is a valuable lesson for all" (*Notre Avant-Guerre*, p. 239).

35. Michael Riffaterre pointed this out to me in a slightly different context on the occasion of the 1981 Columbia University Poetics Colloquium, "The Poetics of Ideology," by stating simply that a "poetics" of ideology must never disregard the political necessities of the moment.

36. The Bolshevik victory in the October Revolution of 1917 was the motivating force behind the founding of the Third International, Communist International, or Comintern, in 1919. The Comintern Congress of 1935, representing more than three million communists in sixty-five different parties, finally called for a united front between communists and socialists against fascism and

helped inspire the Popular Front governments in France and Spain. The same Comintern endorsed Stalin's 1930s purges. The organization was officially dissolved in 1943 on the grounds that the war made international communist organizing impossible. See Tom Bottomore, ed., *A Dictionary of Marxist Thought*, pp. 236–38.

37. See Nicos Poulantzas, *Fascism and Dictatorship*; Martin Kitchen, *Fascism*; Ernesto Laclau, *Ideology in Marxist Theory*.

38. Laclau's work has obvious implications for a "mise en question" of class determinism in marxist theories of the French Revolution.

39. Wilhelm Reich, *The Mass Psychology of Fascism*. Subsequent page references are in parentheses in the body of the text.

40. Theweleit treats this problem with extensive reference to Reich's complete works and to Deleuze and Guattari's *Anti-Oedipus* (a book that may prove to be to Reich's discoveries what Lacan's work is to Freud's). Reich, by Theweleit's account, sensed the complications of family power, but his straight-on attachment to Freudian conceptual topography presumably prevented him from developing more than the father-side of his theory.

41. Peter Blos, "The Second Individuation Process of Adolescence," pp. 162–86, confirmed some of my own ideas on the subject from a clinical perspective. Blos chooses interesting cultural examples for his descriptions of adolescence: the alienated stance of the protagonist in Camus's *The Stranger*, and the rebellious dressers among young German men in the late eighteenth century.

42. See, for example, a thorough psychoanalytic study of Brasillach's literary works by Josette Wilburn, "Le Travail de l'inconscient dans la création romanesque chez Robert Brasillach." Wilburn is especially attentive to Brasillach's father's early death and to Brasillach's attachment to his powerful mother. Richard Cobb quips in *French and Germans/ Germans and French* that both Brasillach and Montherlant were egoists spoiled by their mothers.

43. Klein, Theweleit, Dinnerstein, and others have insisted that mother is "the first outside."

44. See Poulantzas, *Fascism and Dictatorship*, for an analysis of the consolidation of fascism.

45. See Ernst Jünger, *Premier Journal parisien*.

46. See, for example, Robert Soucy, "Drieu la Rochelle and Modernist Anti-Modernism in French Fascism," pp. 922–37; Henry Turner, "Fascism and Modernization," pp. 547–64. Tarmo Kunnas's *Drieu la Rochelle, Céline, Brasillach et la tentation fasciste* presents fascism as primarily antiprogressive and irrational; hence, antimodern.

47. Pierre Drieu la Rochelle, *Gilles*, p. 159.

48. Jean-Pierre Faye, *Théorie du récit*, and Ernesto Laclau, *Politics and Ideology in Marxist Theory*.

49. Turner, "Fascism and Modernization," p. 557.

50. Ellul believes that traditional marxist explanations of fascism abdicate responsibility when they insist that fascism was the fault of the economy, of big capital, or of a petty bourgeoisie afraid of becoming a proletariat. See *De la révolution aux révoltes*.

51. Marinetti, "Multiplied Man and the Reign of the Machine," p. 90.

52. Benjamin, "André Gide et ses nouveaux adversaires," p. 217.

53. Benjamin's essays on fascism available in English include: "Theories of German Fascism: On the Collection of Essays *War and Warrior*, edited by Ernst Jünger," pp. 120–28, and "The Work of Art in the Age of Mechanical Reproduction," pp. 217–52.

54. See chapter 8.

55. Soucy, "Drieu la Rochelle," p. 937.

56. Robert Brasillach, *Les Sept Couleurs*, p. 160–61. The quotation is discussed at greater length in chapter 8.

57. Marinetti, "The Futurist Cinema," p. 134.

58. Moishe Postone, "Anti-Semitism and National Socialism: Notes on the German Reaction to 'Holocaust,' " pp. 97–117.

59. Fredric Jameson's narrative study of Wyndham Lewis, entitled *Fables of Aggression*, shows the satirist reacting to this fear.

60. Faye, *Théorie du récit*, p. 77.

61. Sternhell, "Strands of French Fascism," pp. 479–501.

62. Bernard-Henri Lévy, *L'Idéologie française*.

63. For a discussion of our myths about media, see Jean Cazeneuve, *La Société de l'ubiquité*.

64. For a thorough discussion of Eric Fromm's *Escape from Freedom*, see Kitchen, *Fascism*, pp. 14–19.

# Chapter 2
# Fascism and Banality

Everyone who writes fears being misread: let me say that while writing a book on fascism, that fear has been great. The subject, I am told by friends and colleagues alike, is dangerous. So it seems even more important than usual to write about how I "intend" my textual analyses. I don't intend them as a pristine scholarly defense of "minor" authors, and surely not as an argument for making those authors "major" (the major-minor distinction being more relevant to baseball than to the study of culture). I don't intend them as a condemnation of the political errors of the same "minor" writers, as though their politics were the barrier to their literature, rather than part of it. I am not even interested in these writers as authors, so much as in their writing as symptomatic of a *major problem* — fascist desire — and some of its manifestations in France.

And, if I succeed in saying anything at all about fascist desire, one of my hopes is that I will have added a question mark to the unquestioned dominance of literary studies centered on the canon or "great thinker" approach to culture. This is not solely out of some personally felt antielitism; although, as someone who learned to read and write in a decade that saw the renewal of a radical women's movement as well as vigorous protest against imperialism in opposition to the American invasion of Vietnam, my skepticism when faced with elites might be said to be historically "overdetermined." My early education may well have led me to question the canon, but my cultural research has led me to insist on those questions.

Limiting one's reading to the canon of great thinkers no more guarantees a privileged understanding of ideology than does a study of "junk culture." The two kinds of study must be considered together. The canon also has an important relationship to what a society deems "appropriate" to remember. Some books survive because they belonged to the victors, and they survive at the expense of the defeated people's books. The books written by the French fascists, embarrassing and long ignored, have "needed," in some recuperative social sense, to be repressed, but along with their repression has come a repression of information about the climate that produced them in the first place.

Much archival information on the period 1940–1945 is restricted; the daily lives of many would be compromised were it not. Some of the best historical and biographical research on French fascists has been written by people living outside France—the subject may still be too sensitive for an "in-house" treatment. Emblematic of that sensitivity is the fact that "Holocaust," an American serial dramatizing nazism and the German-run camps, was aired on the French television channel 2 in 1979; but in the same year, the French television stations refused (for the second time in eight years) to purchase *Le Chagrin et la pitié*, a documentary that treated the same war years in France.

The fact that there was never an established fascist state in France and that the presence of fascist enthusiasts in the country could be blamed—post hoc—on the Nazi occupants can account for the ease with which French fascism is often simply denied. Yet the memory of fascism within their ranks haunts French intellectuals, and the question of a specifically French version of fascist ideology has hovered over that country's collective intellectual conscience since the execution of Brasillach and Sartre's 1945 essay on collaborators, returning to the polemical forefront with nearly every major political and cultural crisis since. The events that elicit a debate about fascism involve "themes" echoing from the Popular Front and Vichy years—most frequent among them are French racism and the politics of immigration. From the time I began research on this book, new occasions for debate have been numerous: the violence by French workers against immigrant workers; the emergence, in the late 1970s, of a culturally defined New Right, promoter of American sociobiology and European elitism; the New Philosophers who insist on the presence of fascist elements on the French left as well as the French right; the interview in the weekly magazine *L'Express* with Darquier de Pellepoix, former racial administrator of Vichy France; the wave of terrorist attacks in the early 1980s on Jewish synagogues and monuments, and the massacre at Goldenberg's restaurant; the declaration by an obscure archivist-lecturer at the University of Lyon that there were never any gas chambers, and the educational campaign organized against him by leading historians; the capture and pretrial controversy over Klaus Barbie, murderer of Resistance hero Jean Moulin; the attempt by his defense to discredit the French Resistance. And, most recently, the notoriety of long-time right-winger Le Pen, whose Front National takes as its emblem the familiar slogan "La France aux Français!"

The intellectual vocabulary with which the French discuss fascism is still a highly ethical one, a vocabulary of "memory," of "responsibility," of "prediction," of sensitivity to fascist symptomatology. What seems to be at stake is the persistent role of intellectuals as cultural watchdogs, and the persistent role of fascism—over and above the most recently coined term totalitarianism, as *the* social danger (and temptation) par excellence.

And at the same time, since I began writing, academic work on a few fascist writers and intellectuals has flourished in and out of France: Céline has been lauded for his writing and has furnished the ground for an important debate on the politics of style; Drieu's political writings have given rise to a body of work on political ambivalence. The French reaction to such work is invariably heated; fascist writers are still "argued" rather than "read."

But in spite of a renewal of literary interest in a few authors, it is certainly not the case that the sum of work by French fascists—much of it catalogs of bigotry and crude denunciations—might by now be rereadable, out of context, as stories that overcome the ideology which informs them by some great human drama accessible to all. Nor is it as truly educational to read a fascist novel as to experience positively a great masterpiece of Western literature. Though the texts I read were often highly disturbing to me, they were just as often banal, unworthy of an intellectual's interest. *Banal*, however, has as one of its meanings the sense "open to the use of the entire community"—"*a common* (shared) place," as well as "trivial." It is an ambivalent word by definition and has a complicated history of its own within the study of fascist ideology. Since the term is crucial to the ideas about ideology that I bring to my study of French fascism, I want to interrogate that history at some length.

Why do I feel the need to study other-than-masterpieces? The answer may be self-evident to a political scientist or historian, but not to a literary critic. One of my reasons is time bound. Electronic media are blurring the distinction between mass and elite experience of culture. There is more culture now than there used to be; it takes more forms than it ever has; and it is experienced by greater numbers of people from a greater variety of social classes than ever before. This cultural explosion begins with the advent of film and radio before the First World War. The writers in this book are deeply affected by it—some of them vehemently hopped on the bandwagon of the new media. This gives them interest as cultural pioneers of a sort.

Analysts of the period have shown little interest in this aspect of fascist writing, though they paved the way for my own work in many other ways. Among Zeev Sternhell (who tends to see the French fascist intellectuals of the 1930s as "mere" journalists, circulating degraded versions of the more serious political thinkers of the previous generation), Jeffrey Mehlman (who has chosen to analyze a fascist by-product, anti-Semitism, in its most veiled "respectable" forms), and Klaus Theweleit (who, confronting German culture, sets out deliberately to enter the revoltingly misogynist world of the fascist Freikorps officers), it's the last whose approach comes closest to mine.[1] I, too, intend to enter the world of the authors I describe.

Each of the critics mentioned above has made my own work easier by combating one of the many well-congealed myths that have sprung up as "defenses" against the study of fascism. Sternhell, for example, in a recent book in which he continues his research on the intellectual origins of fascism into the 1930s, favors the unacknowledged, apolitical (in the card-carrying sense of the phrase), and philosophical expressions of fascist ideas as the most efficacious "carriers" of fascist ideology. So, for example, while Sartre long ago dismissed the bourgeois conservatism of prewar intellectuals like Thierry Maulnier as being merely temporarily aligned with fascist interests, Sternhell sees Maulnier rather as a "pure" philosophic producer of fascist texts, a thinker more faithful to the essential French fascism than even Brasillach or Drieu (p. 264). He writes, for example, that the refusal to enter into active politics renders the work of Maulnier still more significant than theirs. Maulnier's journal *Combat*, though it had only one thousand subscribers, "counts" ideologically because "the ideas elaborated in the little reviews with limited circulation, penetrate very quickly the major part of the big press and become so many received ideas" (p. 247). *Combat* can penetrate precisely because it is "less virulent," "less vulgar" than *Je Suis Partout*: "The review develops a political ideology more subtle that that of the fascists who say their name (who call themselves fascists), without one being able to discern any true basic difference between them" (pp. 247–48).

In Sternhell's work, a prewar New Right and New Left take more of a beating than the prewar fascists themselves. By finding strains of French fascist ideology in nonfascist work, he is able to give fascist ideas a frightening normalcy and consistency in French intellectual history. Using the respectable academic critic Maulnier as his fall guy, Sternhell gives a final blow to the traditional identification of French fascists with pro-German collaborators: "[the agents of prewar fascism] are not only the men and the movements stigmatized by the post-war purge, but some of the most eminent intellectuals of the early 20th century in France"—this despite the only relative importance of the fascist phenomenon in France (p. 268).[2]

Mehlman's project is similar to Sternhell's. Rather than taking on fascism in French political theory, he takes on anti-Semitism in French literature. The connections he makes between the literary canon and anti-Semitism are even less intended or conscious in the texts he cites than fascism is in the texts cited by Sternhell. This gives to his analysis a certain gloomy mysticism, or what Ann Smock has called an "occulted" sense of an anti-Semitic tradition in French letters, one whose time boundaries and extent are uncertain.[3]

Theweleit's basic stance in his analysis of the fascist Freikorps officers is a rejection of moralism in the analysis of fascism. Part of his strategy involves leading his readers to a real acknowledgment, in themselves, of the same repulsive misogyny he cites in his militant male corpus. This he does, in part, by showing that the misogyny so obvious in the writing of the Freikorps officers is to be found as well in certain marginal works of "correct" thinkers such as Brecht, Freud, and Marx. By making the link between fascism and misogyny "speak for itself," Theweleit finds judicial *guilt* and *innocence* analytically useless terms for working on fascism.[4]

My authors are not as literally brutal or militant as Theweleit's; they are not as philosophically coherent as Sternhell's; and they are not as successfully aesthetic as Mehlman's. One might say that, unlike Mehlman, I'm dealing with literary producers rather than authors, with textual "material" rather than [*belles*] "letters." Many of the texts I've studied are unreadable and ridiculous by most standards. Marinetti's *Mafarka* landed him in jail; Céline's *Bagatelles* was censored by the Popular Front government; Brasillach was shot for his writing; Rebatet was ruined for his. As I noted above, Drieu's political reputation has fared best, probably because his political *ambivalence*—seen as more interesting than a straight-on fascism—makes him a sympathetically "tempted," instead of simply "fascist," writer. Drieu had a large number of "great thinker" friends and is easier to locate in the canon than the others.

The waxing and waning of these writers' respectability is a cultural phenomenon worthy of a separate study. Céline has reentered the canon through the vestibule of a critical avant-garde that has placed him in a respectably revolutionary poetic tradition, one that borders precariously on psychosis in one direction and on fascism and totalitarianism in the other.[5] Marinetti survives as a designer more than a writer. Brasillach's film history continues to sell, and there was enough controversy about his execution to fuel a hot polemic in *Le Monde* on its thirtieth anniversary.[6]

But, although the question of fascism in retrospect is important, it is one I want to save for the end of my study, where I will describe my visit with Maurice Bardèche. And although fascism takes hold in each writer in a highly individual psychological manner (Marinetti's fervor, Brasillach's innocence, Céline's rage, Rebatet's cynicism, Drieu's defeatism), I am not interested primarily in a study of ideologically susceptible personalities.[7]

As an example of what interests me more, I offer the fact that all these writers were tremendously sensitive to their writings as commodities. The new breed of free-lance intellectual was a marketer rather than a scholar, as aware of selling politics as of creating prose. Brasillach, who is often extremely difficult to take seriously as a novelist, is interesting as a manic recycler of prose: passages from articles in *Je Suis Partout* show up in his memoirs, bits of the memoirs reappear as descriptive interludes in the novels. In so much repetition, there are inevitable changes in detail—and the changes are rich in "obvious" ideological content. Rebatet, with even fewer resources and intellectual prestige than Brasillach, was a veritable ideological disc jockey. Marinetti, intellectual entrepreneur and master of ceremonies of modernism, might be described as a role model for them all.

What interests me is French fascist aesthetics at its most obvious and most banal. Because I am convinced that, like Poe's purloined letter, so visible it can't be found, the "obvious" is quite often the last place we look to study ideology.

Perhaps I should say more about what I mean by the *obvious*, what I call in my title the *banal*, in ideological criticism. Somewhere along the way of my research on fascism I became interested in theories of everyday life. The theories confirmed something I had always sensed in my work on fascism but hadn't yet grounded in my own methodological perspective: namely, that the expressions of fascism in my authors did not lie *solely* in their relationships to political events (though these certainly were a good starting point for my investigations), but that they could be found in odd but obvious places like the authors' attitudes to their perceptions of time and space, in their relationship to lived experience.

One way to understand this obviousness may be by analogy to a certain kind of description that arises in psychoanalysis, and which Freud named a "screen memory."[8] Screen memories, he thought, were so useful that a thorough interpretation ought to be able to extract from them the *essential* of the analysand's childhood experience. In his own description of the screen memory, Freud insisted upon the following paradox: The screen memory is noteworthy for its clarity, its persistence, and its apparent *triviality*. The patient who produces a screen memory is, in fact, surprised that such a banal memory survived so well intact.

So, I think, is the case for the topoi around which I have organized my chapters—not events in the lives of writers, not major empirical connections to politics as such, but banal obvious "things" they share with everyone in Europe: their bodies, their landscapes, the movies they go to, the radio they listen to, the appliances in their houses, and their machines at work. I've read precursory texts they proclaim in their most diligent scholarly voices, but I've also tried to examine through their writings their daily preoccupations as lazy readers and skimmers of texts, as Frenchmen gazing at the ads on the evening metro or squinting at the newsreels.

This, then, is how my approach differs from that of the many intellectual historians who have worked on the same writers, also with an eye to situating French fascism.[9] Like them, I am interested in fascist pronouncements and "engagements," but since fascism seems to me to have been an attitude that was lived from day to day, I've tried to look as well at the most everyday, unofficial versions of it.[10] Marinetti's relationship to flying, Céline's diagnoses, Drieu's teeth, Brasillach's and Bardèche's love of the movies, Rebatet's radio, a certain use of language as "slogan" or "broadcast" by all of them—these banal elements interact ideologically with the more accepted "events" of French fascism: the Stavisky affair, the riots of February 6, 1934, the horrors of the Occupation, the more self-consciously ideological moments in fascist prose. The official and daily events are cemented by the ideological properties of fascism: anti-Semitism; the cult of youth, of the body, and of the leader; the ideal community. If screen memories, those most trivial yet persistent and lucid recollections, are indeed a gift to the analyst, presenting desires and traumas in condensed and displaced form, so might these banal but persistent topoi condense the traces of a fascist sensibility.

## On Banality

I approach fascism in its *banality*. Since the term has a complex history with respect to the study of fascism, let me outline it in order to separate the received idea of fascist banality from my own.

The most prominent notion of fascist banality is an American one that comes from a series of articles published in *The New Yorker* in the early 1960s. Their subject was the trial of Nazi war criminal Adolph Eichmann in Jerusalem in 1961. Their author was the renowned critic of totalitarianism Hannah Arendt.[11] Eichmann, writes Arendt, astonished the judges simply because he had *no conception* of what he had done; *no imagination*. Even as he was about to be hung, he uttered a cliché of "grotesque silliness" from the funeral oratory: "After a short while, gentlemen, *we shall all meet again*. Such is the fate of all men. Long live Germany, long live Argentina, long live Austria. *I shall not forget them*" (p. 252, Arendt's emphasis). The "lesson" taught by Eichmann, concludes Arendt, is the "fearsome, word-and-thought defying *banality of evil*" (p. 252, Arendt's emphasis). As controversial as it was originally, *banality* has become a widely accepted descriptive term for totalitarian sadism.[12]

The "banality of evil" thesis is founded on a judgment of the intellect of fascists: this, I think, is its greatest appeal and its greatest weakness. Eichmann, the model fascist, shocks people because he is neither "Macbeth nor Iago"; nonetheless, he is capable of heinous crimes against humanity. I am certain Arendt was accurate in calling Eichmann an idiot. But can we assume, as many accounts of fascism have done since, that fascism itself is an exercise in mediocrity? There is common ground between Arendt's analysis and statements like the following one, by Zeev Sternhell: "Though philosophers and scientists cannot be held responsible for the uses made of their teachings, for the way they are interpreted and the meaning read into their thoughts, it was nevertheless their teachings which, when put into the hands of a thousand minor intellectuals who frequently had little aptitude for careful philosophical reasoning, shaped a new intellectual climate. . . . that intellectual climate allowed fascism to burgeon and grow.[13] Many fascist intellectuals were indeed minor, but would "careful philosophic reasoning" have prevented fascism? Sternhell's words give us reason to hope.

We have seen that Arendt's definition is applied to a Nazi bureaucrat, someone who may not have read much at all. Arendt had earlier experience with "degraded" racism: in 1933, she went to the Prussian State Library to copy excerpts from official anti-Semitic tracts. The tracts were to be used as "horror propaganda" at the eighteenth Zionist Congress scheduled for August 1933.[14] She was caught doing the research and arrested, but a kindly policeman released her in a few hours. It was after this incident that Arendt decided to flee Germany.

But what did she have to say about the "thousand minor intellectuals" who contributed to the burgeoning of fascism, particularly in France? When Arendt moved to Paris in 1933, she did more extensive work on both degraded and "respectable" anti-Semitic literature there: she even kept a notebook of quotes and statistics and spoke to the Women's International Zionist Organization on antisemitism in France since the Dreyfus affair.[15] She quoted everyone from the Marquis de Morès to Charles Maurras.

And if we advance in time to part 3 of her *Origins of Totalitarianism*, it becomes even clearer that her view of Eichmann as an idiot did not grow uniquely out of her experience covering the trials. Her avowal of Eichmann's banality actually *echoes* her analysis of French intellectuals of the 1930s.[16]

In *Eichmann in Jerusalem* she describes Eichmann's "remoteness from reality" (p. 288); whereas in *Totalitarianism*, noting the "attraction which the totalitarian movements had for avant-garde artists," she condemns it as "the elite's lack of a sense of reality" (p. 335). Her prime example is André Gide's admiring review of Céline's anti-Semitic pamphlet, *Bagatelles pour un massacre*, "not because he [Gide] wanted to kill the Jews of France, but because he rejoiced in [Céline's] blunt admission of such a desire" (p. 335). Surprisingly, for an intellectual, her attitude toward the petty bourgeois bureaucrat and the man of letters is strikingly similar. Arendt was no snob: she used Gide as a model for understanding Eichmann.

This last hypothesis turns out, upon rereading Gide's review of Céline, to be more true than one might imagine. For it is in the review that Gide himself first coined this use of the term *banal*. Although he reads *Bagatelles* primarily as a parody of racism, he speculates about the book's "real" effect in one small passage: "If we had to see in *Bagatelles pour un massacre* something other than a game, Céline, despite all his genius, would be without excuse for stirring up the banal passions with his cynicism and offhanded frivolity.[17] Arendt most likely discussed the review with fellow Parisian exile Walter Benjamin and may even have seen a letter written by Benjamin to Max Horkheimer about it.[18] The letter zeroes in on the phrase about banality:

You've probably seen Gide's critical discussion of Céline in the April NRF: "If we had to see in *Bagatelles pour un massacre* something other than a game, Céline, despite all his genius, would be without excuse for stirring up the banal passions with his cynicism and offhanded frivolity." The word *banal* says it all [le mot *banal* en dit long] [Benjamin's emphasis]. Céline's lack of seriousness, you'll remember, struck me as well. Besides, Gide's moral side sees only the intention of the work, not its consequences. Unless, that is, Gide's satanic side has nothing against those consequences.[19]

For Walter Benjamin, then, banality is an important truth about fascist discourse: a truth grasped momentarily by Gide but obscured, ironically, by Gide's propensity for moralizing. (We might say, in more contemporary terms, that Gide believed in the ideological intentionality of the writing subject, but that Benjamin is a "reception" theorist, a critic of ideological effects.)

Benjamin, as his "you will remember" reminds us, had long been planning his own work on literary fascism, but the times and his own material limitations were getting in the way. In a July 2, 1937, letter to Gerhard Scholem he apologizes that the economic climate in Paris is bad, and that he is so pressed with work that he hasn't even had time to go to the 1937 Exposition Internationale. (Since Benjamin's work on the nineteenth century exposition was an important part of his analysis of Paris as capital of the nineteenth century, his absence from this big exposition of the twentieth century indicates real hardship.)[20] He was thinking about an article on medical nihilism, linking Jungian notions of archetypes and the collective unconscious to the poetry of Benn and Céline and what he called the whole "fascist framework" or "fascist anatomy." The project was never completed, but this brief mention of it, juxtaposed with the quotation from Gide, gives us some clue about what Benjamin thought *banality* had to offer in an analysis of fascism.

*Banality*, for Benjamin, was an amoral category. There was no intellectual indictment attached to the word, as there would be for Arendt. On the contrary, if a study of fascism meant reading medical nihilism in the work of Céline, Jung, and Benn, then it was an intellectually challenging and, presumably, highly *imaginative* construct.

How radically different, then, is Arendt's banality: for her, the fascist lacks a sense of reality but is at the same time *devoid of imagination*. Eichmann, the prototype, can speak only in clichés.

The problem with her definition is that it makes the writers attracted to fascism "unsuccessful" artists (since devoid of imagination), on the one hand, and "unsuccessful" realists (since devoid of a sense of reality), on the other. One gets the idea that if only the intellectuals had been more realistic and less avant-garde and the bureaucrats had been a little smarter, neither group would have succumbed. How interesting it would be to know more about what Arendt made of her early mentor and lover Heidegger's initial attraction to national socialism. According to her biographer, she found it a comic lapse.[21] An interview late in her life shows the importance she gave at one time to fascism among respectable intellectuals: "The problem, the personal problem, was not what our enemies might be doing, but what our friends were doing." She was determined, upon leaving Germany, to leave the purely intellectual life: hence her interest in "practical" work with Zionist groups. But here again, her biographer concludes, her intense friendships with antifascist exiles in Paris made her forget the profascist colleagues she had left behind. Would remembering what *those* friends were doing (in the sense that Benjamin was remembering Benn and Jung) have dealt a blow to some of her assumptions?[22]

As it is, any analysis of fascist aesthetics that took Arendt's theory as its starting point would be finished before it began, condemned merely to denounce the eminently denounceable neoclassical artworks of fascism's late bureaucratic phase, and to pass over the more complex works of the populist phase.[23]

As work on fascism continues, and grapples with the dilemma of its growing distance—and freedom—from the horror of fascist events, the list of "respectable" and "brilliant" people who were drawn to fascism or who were fascist fellow travelers for one time or another gets longer and longer. As we look back, the "common sense" revulsion that grounds a theory like Arendt's gets harder and harder to take for granted as the pervasive reaction of "sane-thinking people" or "intelligent people" to fascist prose.[24] As we grow historically further from the experience of fascism, it has become possible to reject the view of fascism as an "accident" or "temporary illness" in order to get analytically closer to fascist ideology in all its banality. In order to recognize it. It should be clear by now that I think Benjamin's understanding of banality does this better than Arendt's.

By *banal*, I have also tried to mean one other thing, now tied to the actual process of my research and to my own daily life. Whenever my archival resources allowed it, I have attempted to link the everyday elements in my readings to their existence in the culture at large. Radio, cinema, fear of depopulation, immigration are shown by reference to the daily news, the almanacs, and the geography manuals of the 1930s and 1940s to exist at other levels of society and in other kinds of text production than strictly "poetic" or even "political." I interviewed a surviving fascist intellectual, not for any "true" account of the events, but for a sense of the man's world. And once, as I was skimming the *Marie Claire* women's magazine of the war years, I found a color fantasy drawing of the ideal modern apartment for newlyweds: three tiny rooms and bath, daybed, a buffet for storing dishes that folds out to dine, and a deco lamp. It looks very much like the 1930s apartment behind the Ecole Normale where Brasillach spent those years with his sister, and where she and her family still live. What seemed remarkable for me about the magazine apartment (what I can see in the magazine but couldn't notice in the Brasillach apartment as it's laid

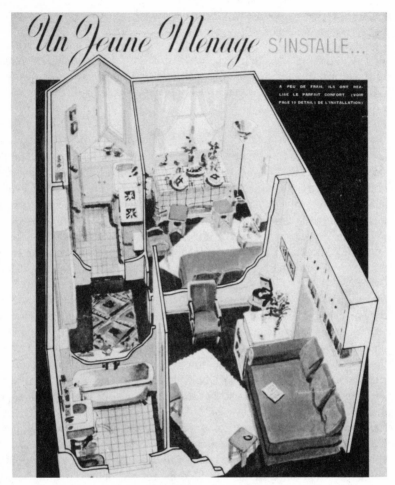

Newlyweds' apartment, 1942. Pierre Pagès/*Marie-Claire*.

out today) is that the seating drawn in each room is organized around two machines: a phonograph in the salon, a radio in the dining room.[25] The discovery of the drawing was thrilling because it quite literally mapped out for me something about which I had already read many times in theories of modernism.

And, of course, without having read the theory, I may not have recognized the interest of the ad in the first place. So on the important theoretical level, I need to make clear that my interest in the everyday comes from my commitment to a marxist criticism using as much material as possible from the "base" in its analysis of culture. My inspiration, then, comes not only from *Marie-Claire*, but from "superstructural products": from books by Henri Lefebvre, T. J. Clark, and Fredric Jameson, and from work by Kristin Ross and Molly Nesbit in an ongoing project on everyday life.[26]

By arguing for a theory of everydayness *with* fascist texts, I hope in some small way to celebrate the following paradox: that discourse so unquestioningly imbued with the führer principle, that is, with the most grotesque form of great-man ideology, be made to work critically in the service of its own demise.

## The Case of France

But, I've been asked, why write a book about fascism in France, since fascism was never an established political power there? And what could be obvious about that? One reason, as I've implied above, is the fact that France continues to be haunted by its unresolved, partially acknowledged flirtations with fascism at various junctures in the past. Anyone who follows today's polemics in the French press is bound to become curious about what a French fascist might have been — or might be. Another — and more roundabout "theorist's" reason — is the important role that France has come to play in theoretical work about fascism in general.

France, a place where politics and style are never strangers to one another, is a "promising" place for the study of fascist forms. (It is a place where, to make a small joke at the expense of Jacques Lacan, even the unconscious has a rhetoric!) This study has traditionally taken two directions.

First of all, it's quite remarkable how often episodes from French political history show up as models for analyzing Italian and German fascism — not to mean, then, that France is fascist, but that France is a pedagogical place with respect to theories of fascism.

Marx's analysis of the rise of Louis Napoléon in postrevolutionary France is used by Thalheimer and Gramsci as an analogy for the rise of Mussolini and Hitler.[27] In this model, the dominant classes temporarily sacrifice their political control to the fascists in order to safeguard their real economic dominance from the workers, just as the ruling class used Louis Napoléon and his lumpen to temporarily protect them from another workers' revolution. The analogous symptom in nascent fascism is the fact that traditional parliamentary parties give way to paramilitary oppositional groups. The marginal power groups that form are culturally attractive to the dominant bourgeois intellectuals as well as to the "marginals" themselves. Even the bourgeois parties become radicalized, and political rhetoric of all kinds becomes explosive. According to Bonapartist theory, this is what gives the initial stages of fascism their mass oppositional flavor.

French critics Poulantzas and Laclau and Italian critic Felice see in this situation something quite different than the lumpen military base of a Bonapartist farce.[28] Fascism, for them too, is a crisis of representation, but the crisis corresponds to a prerevolutionary Jacobin moment rather than to a Bonapartist one.

Fascism takes power when political life seems less mediated by laws, when the possibilities for action seem ripe. Laclau calls this Jacobinism a populist one. Classes don't represent what they used to: communists, royalists, petty bourgeois from the city and countryside are drawn by a popular "interpellation" or calling (see my discussion of this Althusserian concept above, p. 8); they stop thinking of themselves as members of a socio-economic class and feel united as a people. In fascist rhetoric, the popular feelings are translated into nationalist and racial ones. The best way to measure the salient ideological formations in fascism is in the changing political language of the period, and especially in oppositional language.

A new generation of theorists in Germany (the group of writers known in this country through the journal *New German Critique*) takes a somewhat different pedagogical approach by emphasizing what nonfascist intellectuals in France have to offer to theories of German fascism; Theweleit's intellectual debts are to Bataille and Leiris — contemporaries of the fascists — and to Deleuze and Guattari, radical French psychoanalysts whose work dates from the 1960s.[29]

There is another trend in studies of fascism toward a direct consideration of a fascist ideology as it evolved in France. Emphasis is placed on France's precursory role in the movement. Stanley Payne, a political scientist who has compared the varieties of fascism, sees it as an outgrowth of the more Promethean aspects of the Enlightenment, the headquarters of which was in France.[30] George Mosse, the eminent intellectual historian, traces the intellectual origins of the Third Reich to as many French as German racial thinkers.[31] Barrès and Sorel are studied by Soucy and Sternhell as protofascists.[32]

My book, however, is not about sources; rather, it is concerned with their "bloom." I do treat two writers whose work preceded fascism. I discuss Sorel for the extent to which his own writing becomes "sloganized" in the writing of others. I discuss Marinetti, who, though widely published in France, is Italian. And, like Sorel, he writes a full generation before Brasillach, Céline, Drieu, and Rebatet. That Marinetti, an "outsider," is included in my work is not an indication that I think fascism infiltrated France from somewhere else. Rather, I find his style and themes particularly instructive (as well as inspirational to the others) in casting fascism in the aesthetic, rather than purely intellectual or social, role. The fascism of Céline, Drieu, Brasillach, and Rebatet is neither purely French nor an echo of the Italian and German movements: I will try to indicate their national and international moments in individual studies.

I am most interested in yet another kind of relationship between France and its fascist neighbors in Germany and Italy. Recent metacritics of fascism point out that the most neglected and needed studies are those of the period before fascism gains actual state power. This is sometimes referred to as its "gathering" stage. They explain that when the fascist states did take power, many of the dimensions that had characterized their success in rallying simply disappeared because of the needs of bureaucracies: among them, what is called fascism's communal, utopian dimension—the very thing that appealed most to artists and intellectuals, and that also might be said to have attracted what some call "the people" and what others call "the petty bourgeoisie" to the movement.[33] This is surprising, and counter, in some sense, to people's expectations about what the initial period of fascism was like. In differentiating between communist and fascist ideology, for example, it is generally acknowledged that communist utopian thought advances revolutionary practice; not the bureaucratic authoritarianism that has resulted in the soviet experience. Fascist utopias, however, include the idea of dictatorship—one would think, then, that the fascist state, the fascist praxis, would not be at odds with the forces that brought fascism to power.[34] Yet it is. One of the first things to happen in established Nazidom is the suppression of the left-wing communal component, which is at odds with the fascist program of national supremacy and war-waging at all costs. Thus, in the established fascist state, some of the elements of the initial binding energy disappear: fascism becomes less popular and more elitist.

And this is where France becomes important for an understanding of fascism, albeit somewhat paradoxically, because state fascism was never successfully established there. Let me take a brief detour to outline some of the reasons why it wasn't.

The French democratic bourgeoisie was too strong to be pushed aside, even by severe economic crisis. Another way to look at this strength is as a better established form of the liberal–competitive capitalist duo than had had time to develop in the uneven economies of Germany and Italy. In Germany and Italy, modernism was both industrially and culturally precocious: modernity tottered precariously on feudal agrarian structures. Nowhere, perhaps, is there a better description of that precociousness than in Marinetti's "Founding and Manifesto of Futurism." The manifesto begins with the evocation of a Victorian study that might have been Freud's consulting room, and it moves quickly from locomotives and steam engines—nineteenth century machines—to trams, and to the auto that the narrators themselves will use to escape into the future through the streets of Milan. The narrator describes hearing two noises: the "muttering devotions of the old canal" and the "roar of famished motor cars." Marinetti's house on the Via del Senato, we are told by critic Reyner Banham, really did face one century on each side: the decaying renaissance canal was out back, trams and autos were, as in the text, "beneath the [front] windows." The futurist narrator is shut up at home, literally "between two worlds": even if he wanted to close his window to progress, the new machinery would still reach him through his ears.[35]

So, unlike Italy, where the passage from the back door to the front was a shock, France was "prepared" for modernism. A century of bourgeois revolution had helped transform the country from liberal bourgeois democracy to international monopoly capitalism, with some help from its colonies.[36]

Whether one believes that it was an overwhelmingly democratic tradition or a smooth economic adjustment from a national to an international market economy that prevented the coalescence of fascism in prewar France, it is generally agreed that the "national revolution" at Vichy, provisional and founded upon defeat, was only a watered down, conservative echo of a fascist state. Yet racial politics thrived in Vichy's conservative bureaucracy without German intervention.[37] And in occupied Paris, the dream of a specifically French fascism remained "in the air." The hard-core fascist writers were not satisfied by the national revolution. They refused Pétainism, set up shop in Paris, and used the fascism in neighboring countries to various degrees as "grist for their mill." What they had in mind was not allegiance to Germany; it was fascism by and for France. Sometimes they seemed to adapt to, and sometimes to react against, the German influence on "their" fascism. With some exceptions among the precursors (some of the early Faisceau members and francistes who had since evolved to the conservative right, and occasionally to communism or to the liberal left), the fascists didn't resist: they did, however, worry about maintaining their nationalism in defeat.

Thus, in France, the analysis of the puzzling utopian, communal element in fascism is possible both before and during the war. That the utopian appeal of fascism was for many of them an aesthetic one only confirms what Western marxist critics, convinced of "economic determinism only in the *last* instance" (and after a lot of interpretive work), have concluded: that fascist ideology must first be measured in discourse. What better place to study the discourse than in France, where it existed longest without a state, as criticism, narrative, artform? And, at the same time, it may be precisely the embryonic aesthetic-utopian quality of the movement that makes it so painful for French scholars to examine today.

In other words, French fascism in the 1930s and 1940s is not a degraded expression of a "real" theoretical fascism that may have preceded it. This period is, in the *banal* sense of the word and, I think, essentially, French fascism's most real moment: the years when an odd assortment of writers struggle, against the evidence of heavy-handed Nazis and the purge of a fascist left wing in Germany and Italy, to make the utopian communal dimension of fascism survive beyond its time.

## Notes

1. Zeev Sternhell, *Ni droite ni gauche*; Mehlman, *Legacies*; Theweleit, *Männerphantasien*.

2. Sternhell's attack on Maulnier is anticipated, though Sternhell himself does not seem aware of it, in an article by Walter Benjamin on Maulnier and Gide published as a "Letter from Paris," in *Das Wort* I, 1936. It appears in a French translation as "André Gide et ses nouveaux adversaires," pp. 211–24.

3. In a letter to the author, February 15, 1984.

4. The idea of letting fascism "speak for itself" is also at work in an interesting analysis of Vichy radio broadcasts by Gérard Miller, *Les Pousse-au-Jouir du Maréchal Pétain*.

5. See Kristeva: "I might have spoken about Maiakovski or about Artaud: I will speak about Céline" (*Polylogue*, p. 150). I discuss Kristeva's analyses of fascist language in detail in the chapters "Theoretical Voices" and "Bodies and Landscapes: Céline."

6. Pascal Ory, "Apologie pour un meurtre."

7. In the tradition of the Frankfurt school work on the authoritarian personality (see entry under Adorno in the references) or in terms of Reich's "armored" personality. Although Theweleit couldn't disagree more with the "rationalist" outlook of the Frankfurt school, his study is also concerned with susceptibility to fascist feelings at the personal (bodily) level. The Frankfurt study errs by assuming that the political liberal is impervious to violent, authoritarian feelings. If there is error in Theweleit's study, it is of the opposite kind: his fascist may look to some readers like an "everymale."

8. See "Screen Memories," pp. 303–22; "Childhood and Screen Memories," pp. 43–52; "Remembering, Repeating and Working Through" (1914g).

9. I hesitate even to attempt listing them, since I know I will most certainly omit one or two. Limiting myself to English and French work (and primarily to book-length studies), I first note the following intellectual biographies of fascist writers:

Pierre Andreu and Frédéric Grover, *Drieu la Rochelle*.

Dominique Desanti, *Le Séducteur mystifié* [on Drieu].

Frank Field, "Drieu la Rochelle and Fascism," in *Three French Writers and the Great War*, pp. 81–138.

Frédéric J. Grover, *Drieu la Rochelle and the Fiction of Testimony*.

James Joll, "F.T. Marinetti: Futurism and Fascism," in *Three Intellectuals in Politics*, pp. 133–84.

Tarmo Kunnas, *Drieu la Rochelle, Céline, Brasillach et la tentation fasciste* [largely apologetic].

David Schalk, "Fascist Engagement" [on Brasillach], in *The Spectrum of Political Engagement: Mounier, Benda, Nizan, Brasillach, Sartre*, pp. 76–109 [some interesting analogies with Vietnam era American intellectual politics].

Robert Soucy, *Fascist Intellectual: Drieu la Rochelle*.

——. *Fascism in France: The Case of Maurice Barrès*.

William R. Tucker, *The Fascist Ego: A Political Biography of Robert Brasillach*.

Pol Vandromme's studies of Rebatet, Céline, and Drieu (full citations given in the references) are apologies.

The following volumes might better be described as intellectual histories:

P.-M. Dioudonnat. *Je Suis Partout: les maurrassiens devant la tentation fasciste*.

R. Girardet, "Notes sur l'esprit d'un fascisme français, 1934–1948," pp. 529–46.

A. Hamilton, *The Appeal of Fascism: A Study of Intellectuals and Fascism, 1919–1945*.

Pascal Ory, *Les Collaborateurs, 1940–1945*.

J. Plumyène and R. Lasierra, *Les Fascismes français*.

P. Sérant, *Le Romantisme fasciste*.

M. Winock, *Edouard Drumont et Cie: Antisémitisme et fascisme en France* (especially "Une parabole fasciste: *Gilles* de Drieu la Rochelle"). Winock's essays represent a mélange of history of ideas and cultural history.

Robert Wohl, *The Generation of 1914* (especially the discussion of Drieu in chapter 1, "France: The Young Men of Today").

Eugen Weber's *Action Française* and Sterhell's two volumes on fascism in France offer essential cultural and political background.

10. Richard Cobb has a marvelous sense of lived experience, of what he calls the rare intersections of private and public life. But his connections of private and public are so straightforward that he often equates political nastiness and personal nastiness; that is, he doesn't acknowledge the odd alienated relationship between individual and social psychology. Brasillach and Montherlant were nasty egotists spoiled by their mothers; other successful fascists were "utter asses and woolly bores"

("The Anatomy of a Fascist," in *A Second Identity*, p. 301). What I find remarkable about Cobb's work, however, is that he can sneer in this way at his subjects while continuing to breathe life into his descriptions of their lives. See *A Second Identity* and *French and Germans/Germans and French*.

11. Republished as Hannah Arendt, *Eichmann in Jerusalem: A Report on the Banality of Evil*. Subsequent page references are noted in parentheses in the body of the text.

12. It even showed up in *The National Lampoon* in 1976 in a piece entitled "The Banality of Evil, the Evil of Banality" (I rely on my memory for this date in the absence of any index for that magazine). That it leant itself to parody was no indication that the phrase had simply been adopted: it had been debated and discussed endlessly in both the popular and the scholarly press. Arendt was criticized especially by Zionists, who thought she had implied a lack of resistance to fascism, even on the part of the Jews. See a description of the controversy in Elisabeth Young-Bruehl, *Hannah Arendt*, pp. 338-94.

13. Sternhell, "Fascist Ideology," p. 322. This is consistent with the attitude Sternhell takes to the journalists of the 1930s in *Ni droite ni gauche*.

14. Elisabeth Young-Bruehl, "From the Pariah's Point of View," p. 7.

15. Some of this research on France was published in the United States in "From the Dreyfus Affair to France Today" (pp. 173-217) and formed the basis for part 1 of *The Origins of Totalitarianism* ("Antisemitism," pp. 3-122).

16. Hannah Arendt, *Totalitarianism* (especially pp. 326-40). Subsequent page references from this section are noted in parentheses in the body of the text.

17. André Gide, "Les Juifs, Céline et Maritain," pp. 630-36. The translation is mine.

18. They met in a study group, usually in Benjamin's apartment, 10 rue Dombasle. Young-Bruehl, *Hannah Arendt*, p. 122.

19. Walter Benjamin, letter to Max Horkheimer, April 16, 1938, p. 753, my translation. The sentence "The word *banal* says it all" is written in French in the original German text.

20. Walter Benjamin, letter to Gerhard Scholem, July 2, 1937, pp. 730-31.

21. Young-Bruehl, *Hannah Arendt*, p. 69.

22. From Reif, *Gespräche mit Hannah Arendt*, p. 20, quoted in Young-Bruehl, "From the Pariah's Point of View," p. 8.

23. Yet another theorist of fascism takes "banality" seriously. Although Wilhelm Reich shares some of Arendt's intellectual disdain for "banalities," those "seemingly irrelevant everyday habits" (his initial examples are "the lower middle-class bedroom suite," "the decent suit of clothes for Sunday," and "proper dance steps"), he nonetheless acknowledges that the appeal of these "details of everyday life" is understood and used by the fascists much more successfully than are the "thousands of revolutionary rallies and leaflets" by the workers' movements. See his *The Mass Psychology of Fascism*, p. 58. The renewed interest in Reich's approach to fascism, combined with the contributions of feminist psychoanalysis to theory, resulted in an interesting conference at Ohio State in 1983 entitled "Women, Fascism, and Everyday Life in Germany."

24. Suleiman's reading of Drieu's *Gilles* ("Ideological Dissent," pp. 162-77) is excellent for the way in which it theorizes how such a commonsense approach, if it worked, would work (unfortunately, it doesn't).

25. Pierre Pagès, "Un Jeune Ménage s'installe" (1942), back cover, *Marie Claire*.

26. See, for example, Fredric Jameson, *The Political Unconscious*; Timothy Clark, *Image of the People*; Henri Lefebvre, *Critique de la vie quotidienne*; Molly Nesbit, "Atget's Seven Albums"; Kristin Ross, "Rimbaud and the Transformation of Everyday Life"; Kaplan and Ross, eds., *Yale French Studies*, special issue on everyday life, forthcoming.

27. See, for example, Gramsci, "Caesarism," pp. 219-23, and Thalheimer, "Über den Faschismus," pp. 19-38. Or see the discussion of Bonapartism in Kitchen, *Fascism*, pp. 71-82.

28. Poulantzas, *Fascism and Dictatorship*; Laclau, *Politics and Ideology*; De Felice, *Fascism*.

29. See the reference section for selected publications by these theorists.

30. Stanley Payne's summary of theories of fascism, as well as his section on fascism in France and Belgium in *Fascism: Comparison and Definition*, is a model of concision and lucidity.

31. George L. Mosse, *Toward the Final Solution*.

32. Sternhell, *La Droite révoloutionnaire* and *Ni droite ni gauche*; Soucy, *Fascism in France*.

33. See also my discussion of Poulantzas and Laclau above, pp. 20–21.

34. For a broad theoretical discussion of the divergence between ideological goals and ideological practice, see Seliger, *Ideology and Politics* (especially pp. 200–205).

35. Marinetti, "The Founding and Manifesto of Futurism" (1909), pp. 39–44; Reyner Banham, *Theory and Design in the First Machine Age*.

36. That bomb wouldn't explode until the revolt of the generals in the Algerian crisis (May 13, 1958), which is commonly referred to as a protofascist putsch.

37. Marrus and Paxton, *Vichy France and the Jews*, have emphasized how many of the political actions that we recognize in France as being fascist actually developed independently from German pressure.

# Chapter 3
# Slogan Text: Sorel

Sartre goes straight to the heart of Georges Sorel's relationship to fascism when he urges us, however offhandedly, to dismiss Sorel's *Reflections on Violence* as a lot of "fascist prattle."[1] What does it mean to say that Sorel's writing prattles or talks too much? Did the writing itself talk too much, or did people talk too much about it? And what, beyond inviting insult, do fascist writing and prattling have in common? It is certain that this work on violence lent itself to being used in fascist ideology. But to figure out why and how, I need to study both the language of the text and the ways it entered the language of fascist enthusiasts of the generation that followed it. I will begin, however, closer to home, by studying the problems critics still have in evaluating Sorel. From their problems — and mine — I can glean a surviving "Sorel effect" on the reader. I can then use the effect to work backward toward the original Sorel text and its historic situation.

Sorel's influence on European fascism was as immediately obvious and superficial as the infamous Mussolini quip "Everything I am, I owe to Sorel." The result is that his work is often automatically considered fascist. What is true for later fascist writers is also true for their alleged precursor: rather than encouraging investigation, Sorel's connection to fascism has threatened serious consideration of his thought.

The Sorel scholar is thus always faced with a critical imperative: to decide if Sorel was a true fascist or merely misunderstood. A few examples will illustrate the dynamics of the dilemma. When American political scientist John Stanley introduces Sorel's work in 1981, he must carefully separate Sorel the "fascist bad boy" from Sorel the theorist: "It is a grave mistake to demand necessary causal relationships between a man's theoretical system and his practical politics: they are all too often at odds with each other even in the most brilliant men."[2]

Stanley's warning is surprising because Sorel was never much of a political practitioner outside his writing. Sorel's brief vacation from syndicalism as an Action Française monarchist, for example, was a strictly textual affair: a favorable article on Péguy's catholic nationalism, a signature at the bottom of an obscure declaration announcing a syndicalist nationalist alliance, a few contributions to a nationalist journal, *L'Indépendance*, and what Talmon has called a "reluctant" patronage of the Cercle Proudhon, in which the nationalist socialist synthesis was being worked out mainly by a younger group of disciples of Sorel and Maurras.[3] Because any link between Sorel and fascism is much clearer in Sorel's disciples than it is in Sorel's own writing, it has become standard in "proving" Sorel's fascism to quote Georges Valois, the founder of the Faisceau and active member of the Cercle Proudhon. Sorel's own politics are deranged by his style—unstable, piecemeal, metaphoric. As Michael Curtis quips, Sorel's writing always looks like "rough drafts for a book he never wrote." Curtis accounts for the frustration of the critic faced with the Sorelian corpus with the following attempt at political catalog:

> He was in turn a traditionalist in 1889, a Marxist in 1894, a Bergsonian in the same year, a Vician in 1896, a Socialist critical of Marxism in that year, a reformist syndicalist in 1898, a Dreyfusard in 1899, a revolutionary syndicalist in 1904 to 1905, a disillusioned ex-Dreyfusard in 1909, an ally of the nationalists and monarchists in 1910, and at the time of World War I a philosopher of morals.[4]

Implicit in all these evaluations is an obvious defense for Sorel against the charge of a premeditated fascism: how could such a jumbled thinker have been a premeditated anything? Stanley suggests as much: "It might even be asked whether the seemingly quixotic changes in Sorel's political allegiances are the cause for suspicion that we are dealing with a *less than serious* writer."[5]

Rather than being a fascist prattler, might not Sorel be merely an innocent chatterer? Being less than serious is certainly better than being a fascist. Yet the phrase "less than serious," coming as it does in my own text after Benjamin's remarks on Céline and Marinetti, Arendt's on Gide and Eichmann, Gide's on Céline, ought to send off some critical alarms in my readers.[6] "Less than serious," I have argued, has the sense of *banal*—easy for the critic to ignore or repress—and the sense of *pleasurable*—repeatable "blabberings" or idle talk. Both kinds of "less than seriousness" made fascist talk travel better than serious talk and made it more impervious to serious criticism, hence easier to accept.

Zeev Sternhell, who has probably worked more on the intellectual history of Sorel's generation than anyone writing today, describes the same situation in terms of an intellectual hierarchy: "The men who put together the ingredients of fascist ideology on the eve of the great war [Sorel, Maurras, Barrès] brought within reach of the general reader a system of ideas which was not easily understood and which they themselves from time to time deformed or oversimplified."[7] According to Sternhell, the eve of the Great War is a moment of general prattling: both Sorelian reader and Sorelian text are guilty of misinterpretations.

Jack Roth echoes Sternhell and Curtis when he describes Sorel's method as irresponsible political free association:

The work of Sorel gave little evidence of systematic or thorough scholarship, or, for that matter, of consistent intellectual orientation and growth. The studies he published were little more than confused collections of annotations on a variety of matters, divided by no apparent system into paragraphs and chapters. The book review was generally the first form in which an argument was presented, followed by an article, and, if it proved to be worth elaborating, by a book. Moreover, he was invariably content to use second-hand sources.[8]

Emphasizing Sorelian (or Maurrasian or Barresian) thought as error, oversimplification, and sloppiness is very much in the interpretive tradition of Arendt: as though these thinkers "ought to have known better." But what if Sorel wanted to think this way; what if he *chose* to prattle? And what if, as Sartre inadvertently suggests, it was precisely in his prattling that he was most fascist? I ask this in part because the work most beloved to the French fascists, *Reflections on Violence*, is probably the most piecemeal of them all: in its present French edition we note a 1909 letter by Sorel to Daniel Halévy explaining why a 1906 series of articles from *Mouvement Socialiste* was to be collected in one volume, followed by a preface to the original 1906 publication in *Mouvement Socialiste*, followed by the body of the text, a note for the third edition of 1912, and three appendixes.[9] Stanley considers *Reflections on Violence* a stumbling block to an understanding of the "real Sorel"; a book that, in the context of the complete works, is merely a sweeping of theoretical dust under the carpet category of myth. He bemoans the fact that *Reflections on Violence* is continually singled out—as I am doing here—as *the* contribution of Sorel, since he sees it as the part of Sorel's opus least worth reading. The fact remains, however, that the book least worth reading was the book most often cited and probably the only book the fascists knew much about.

Sorel wrote *Reflections on Violence* in reaction to two failures: the failure of a sustained proletarian revolution to take place in France and, in a larger sense, the failure of workers to know what they want, and to know themselves as workers rather than as the "subjects" of a parliamentary system.[10] The book contains a certain amount of socialist history; Sorel outlines the lack of progress of the working-class movement under democratic socialism and criticizes the parliamentary system for oppressing the workers with compromises. In what we might judge to be an ironic defense against parliamentary rhetoric, the book noisily argues that there is too much talk in socialism, and not enough action. Sorel then arrives at his central, obsessional idea, around which the rest of the book is articulated: the general strike. With a general strike, the workers will be able to manage their own political life and their own working space. They will get politics out of the senate and back to the factory. The general strike will furthermore unite a working class badly fragmented among marxist, syndicalist, and democratic socialist groups. It will give them visibility and identity as workers: it will make of the workplace the place of an event.

One oddity of Sorel's book must be examined. The general strike itself, however much Sorel claims it as the great materialist basis of his revolutionary project, remains unarticulated. The strike event is never planned in detail. Indeed, it turns out that Sorel isn't really interested in the strike as much as in the image it creates: "The myth itself must be judged as a means of acting on the present; any attempt to discuss how far it can be taken literally as future history is devoid of sense. *It is the myth in its entirety which is alone important*" (Sorel's emphasis, p. 126).

Furthermore, there is very little suggestion of violence in *Reflections on Violence*, but rather a suggestion that the images be imposed violently on workers' consciousness. When Sorel outlines the success of early Christianity as a model for the proletarian revolution, he insists on the actual comfort of the early believers, the paucity of "blood spilling" necessary to create an image of bloody heroism for future generations: "there was no necessity for the martyrdoms to be numerous . . . " (p. 184). What is important, then, is not violence itself, but reflections on violence.

We are, in *Reflections on Violence* always one step away from the problem of direct political action and firmly immersed in the problem of recognizing and mythologizing politically influential actions or events. This small observation is crucial, for it takes us very far from the received idea of Sorel as a proponent of direct action and spontaneous bloodflow, and closer to a Sorel we might call a slogan man or publicist.

The Christian experience, for example, is discussed from the point of view of revolutionary publicity. Sorel tells us that the early Christians received no attention whatsoever from the Romans, who treated them like any other dissidents. But he insists here that attention from the enemy is unimportant. Myth is not a defense against others but is an inside track: it works best when it is truly "ours," and when "they" couldn't even recognize it if they saw it. This is precisely the principle that advertisers use when they design an ad campaign to appeal to a specific group of the population. It makes no difference if the revolution doesn't make sense outside the targeted market.

Workers, then, can learn from early Christianity the following lessons in conversion and mass rallying techniques: (1) not much actual violence is necessary—a few well disseminated myths of martrydom will suffice; and (2) the key to success is in recognizing what events to mythologize and figuring out how to do it.

As a reflection, perhaps, of the anxiety surrounding this burden of recognition upon the worker, *Reflections on Violence* is invested with an extraordinary amount of visual metaphor, painterly vocabulary, and linguistic *vouloir mettre en scène*. The general strike itself is called a *tableau*:

. . . a body of images capable of invoking instinctively all the sentiments which correspond to the different manifestations of the war undertaken by Socialism against modern society. (p. 127)

The general strike groups [sentiments] in a coordinated picture, and by bringing them together, gives to each one of them its maximum of intensity. (p. 127)

It colors with an intense life all the details of the composition presented to the consciousness. (p. 127)

We do nothing great without the help of warmly-coloured and clearly-defined images, which absorb the whole of our attention; now, is it possible to find anything more satisfying from their point of view than the general strike? (p. 148)

If we were to seek out actual tableaux to illustrate these quotes, we would require pictures that structure a heroic consciousness in the very heart of a vibrant object world. What does this better than the futurist paintings of the period around 1910? Any number of canvases by Severini or Boccioni would have made brilliant illustrations for an Italian edition of Sorel's book. But the quotes that sound so much like descriptions of futurist painting are attributed by Sorel in the footnotes of *Reflections on Violence* to the influence of Henri Bergson's *Introduction to Metaphysics*.[11]

To understand the notes, we need to consider Sorel's writing situation. When he retired from his job as a bridge and road engineer at age fifty to pursue his writing, Sorel moved to Boulogne-sur-Seine, near Paris and engaged in the traditional activity of the aspiring French intellectual: he went to the Collège de France and began attending the seminar of Henri Bergson, reigning star at the time. Sorel acknowledges the Bergson influence in his preface to *Reflections on Violence*, the "Lettre à Daniel Halévy." He mentions specifically how useful it was to have *heard* Bergson, and he describes the sympathy that spoken words establish between people. Questioning his own inability to rewrite or even complete his own work, Sorel asks if he isn't marking, in this way, his own loyalty to Bergson. Bergson, after all, saved his own harshest words for thinkers who rewrote too much and thus became their own disciples. By keeping his work in draft, Sorel could hope to safeguard in his writing the quality of the Bergsonian lectures he so admired, and he could also hope to avoid the great Bergsonian sin—intellectual abstraction or reification of thought. The connection between Sorel's own intellectual habits and his intellectual apprenticeship, listening to Bergson, ought not to be forgotten when we examine what is called the "incoherence" or "laziness" of Sorel's work. Couldn't the "sloppy," "unpredictable" writer be understood as someone attempting to take seriously what Bergson calls the "essentially active, I might almost say violent, character of metaphysical intuition" (p.56)?

It is clear in reading *An Introduction to Metaphysics* how seductive Bergson's entire critique of representation must have been to the engineer-philosopher. The philosopher, says Bergson, must start with the real, rather than with the abstract. At the heart of reality is what Bergson calls "duration," a lively physical principle. Representing duration is another problem, and faced with a choice between concepts and images in writing, Bergson chooses images:

> Mental life cannot be represented by images, but it is even less possible to represent it by concepts. The image has at least this advantage, that it keeps us in the concrete. No image can replace the intuition of duration, but many diverse images, borrowed from many very different orders of things, may, by the convergence of their action, direct consciousness to the precise point where there is a certain intuition to be seized. By choosing images as dissimilar as possible, we shall prevent any one of them from usurping the place of the intuition it is intended to call up, since it would then be driven away by its rivals. (pp. 99–100)

Bergson searches for analogies adequate to good metaphysical thought: he tries out a color spectrum, a small elastic body, an unrolling or rolling coil. None are quite right separately, but together they make something of a contribution to philosophy. Indeed, Bergson's idea of good metaphysics, like Sorel's of the good revolution, sounds a lot like futurist paintings—"supple, mobile, and almost fluid representations, always ready to mould themselves onto the fleeting forms of intuition" (p. 21). It isn't hard to imagine that the road builder in Sorel felt personally "interpellated" by analogies like this one: "Great discoveries, then, serve only to illuminate, point by point, the already drawn line of this logic, just as on the night of a fête we light up one by one the rows of gas-jets which already outline the shape of some building" (p. 86).

We must also keep in mind that Sorel listens to Bergson as part of a process of initiation into a new life of writing. *An Introduction to Metaphysics*, with its reassuring "recipes" for realistic thinking, must have appealled very strongly to Sorel as a place where his old applied world met his new intellectual one. Bergson even has some specific advice to offer to writers:

Something more is needed [beyond simple note taking] in order to set about the work of composition itself, and that is an often very painful effort to place ourselves directly at the heart of the subject, and to seek as deeply as possibly an impulse, after which we need only *let ourselves go.* (My emphasis, p. 90)

Sorel's "less than serious" style can now be understood quite differently: as a painful effort, a rite of initiation, an homage to a mentor. Bergson's ideal writer is a lot like the unrolling coil of his metaphysical-physical analogy. Sorel is a great student of the Bergsonian "unrolling coil" school of style, letting himself go with his intellectual impulses, intuiting his way through the history of Western philosophy. The distance between writing and writing about politics is not great: Sorel wants to solve the problem of political representation with an intuited image. By thinking about a strike, by belonging to a group because of a shared image of a strike, workers represent themselves – they suddenly stand for something, or "sit in" for something.

One can see other areas in which Sorel has taken Bergson's advice about thinking in general, and applied it to his thinking about politics. The working class under the yoke of parliamentary socialism, like the intellectual thinking under the burden of Kant, can only arrive at an abstracted shadowy understanding of true representation.[12] In parliamentary government, a bourgeois ideologue is supposed to stand for the worker, but in fact stands only for the law that is always, in the final analysis, pro-capital. The law mediates; no one stands for the worker, the worker disappears – even to him/her self.

Since intuition depends so much on consciousness, Sorel is also concerned with individual motivation. The revolution must compete with capitalism by moving each member of the working class to act with the same fervor with which profit moves the bourgeois individual to pursue acquisition.

Here Sorel turns to a life or death analogy in war. In the Republican Army of the Wars of Liberty, "the soldier was convinced that the slightest failure of the most insignificant private might compromise the success of the whole and the life of all his comrades, and [that] the soldier acted accordingly" (p. 240). The implicit contrast here is to a situation of mere individual obedience, typified in parliamentary democracy. In Sorel's critique of democracy, the legislation of a leader is arbitrarily connected to the lives of the people represented, and the leaders end up identifying with the law, and not with the people. Democracy, we might say, is "badly metonymic." In the Wars of Liberty, Sorel offers a curative description of perfect (populist) synecdoche: the behavior of each part radically affects the success or failure, indeed the very life, of the whole. Each individual literally stands (or falls) for the group. And he follows through the analogy:

The same spirit is found in the working class groups who are eager for the general strike; these groups, in fact, *picture* the Revolution as an immense uprising which may yet be called *individualistic*; each working with the greatest possible zeal, each acting on his own account, not troubling himself much to subordinate his conduct to a great and scientifically combined plan. (p. 241)

Epic belonging without loss of identity; aesthetic pleasure; freedom and revolt: these were the very founding ideals, first of Italian futurism, then of fascist aestheticism as read in Drieu, Brasillach, and Rebatet one generation later. All want fascism to restore to daily life a sense of epic belonging to the state and individual glory in the state, values seen as being threatened by rapidly developing technology, the proliferation of factories, assembly-line work—the very same factors because of which Sorel's myth of the general strike comes into being.

By conceiving of victory over the technological world in aesthetic terms, Sorel is responding not to the identity crisis of the working class but to a similar crisis in the bourgeois intelligentsia, the members of which are both drawn to and appalled by what Sorel calls "so many novelties introduced in an unexpected manner" (p. 134). Indeed, it is the appeal of Sorel's basic model of revolt to the middle class, as well as to the working class, that makes Georges Valois, founder of the Faisceau and architect of the Maurras-Sorel intellectual merger, see Sorel as the "intellectual father of fascism."[13] For fascism to work, all kinds of representation had to fail; the bourgeoisie had to be as convinced as the workers that parliamentary democracy was no good. Sorel's intuitive writing, with its wild historic examples and insistence on energy and intensity above and beyond analysis, begins to unravel the representational cords.

Here we've come to the limits of Sorel's loyalty to Bergson as an engineer of concrete thinking. The limit is ironic: precisely because Bergson influences Sorel to "go with the flow" of his intuitions, the result is a view of revolution that is anything but concrete: "the general strike must be taken as a whole and undivided, and the passage from capitalism to Socialism conceived as a catastrophe, the development of which *baffles description*" (my emphasis, p. 148). Here, I think, is where Sorel's "coil" finally unwinds. If, as critics have accused him, he counters every intellectual doubt with a belief in the final veracity of the strike event, it is not so much that he is intellectually lazy as that he is seduced by the category he has invented. He puts it best when he states that "the idea of the general strike has such power behind it that it drags into the revolutionary track everything it touches" (p. 133). Sorel is operating in a state of fascination where the general strike is concerned. It emerges in his energetic, euphoric sense of revolution, his polemical verve, his bafflement. I imagine that this is the Sorel-effect Stanley refers to when he writes of the "peculiarly disturbing" quality in Sorel, the aspect that makes it difficult for contemporary social theorists, trained in political models, to deal with him. Yet it's this explosion of models in Sorel that needs to be understood to make the link between his text and its fascist reception. For where he "explodes," he opens up his work to multiple variants and to sloganization by others.

If we put aside temporarily the question of Sorel's authorial intentions and focus on the appearance of the author's name or on more or less veiled references to *Reflections on Violence* in French fascist polemics of the 1920s and 1930s, we find that Sorel's legacy to the fascist movement was exactly what Sorel thought the revolution needed: a few suggestive words that could connote an entire image of revolt.

First of all, Sorel was a slogan, an intellectual flag around which a certain ideological discourse could rally. How odd, in view of the confusion he creates in political theorists today, that all of his euphoric prattle should have been so easily reduced to encapsulated form. What remains to be asked about slogan is a question I've asked of ideological condensation in general. Is it visual—a banner to be waved, a recognizable rallying point, a vision of revolt? Or is it oral—a battle cry, a song? Highly operative slogans are both. They are also, in Sorel's nascent modernist era, multigeneric, filling a space between poetry and advertising created at the crossroads of avant-garde art and poster politics. *Reflections on Violence* is in this sense a great unread political text of the fascist movement, comparable to other circulating slogans of modernity, to Proudhon's "Property is theft," and to Rimbaud's "Il faut être absolument moderne." There must be a whole category of texts—call them "open books"—whose revved up rhetoric encourages their being claimed by everyone and their being so greatly reduced and bandied about. All of them would be fascist texts to the extent to which they lend themselves to a binding of ordinarily inimical ideologies. Is this the quality that leads both to their being quoted, rather than read, and to the zeal with which they are appropriated?

In the case of Sorel, the proper name alone is often enough to carry to weight of an entire slogan. For Mussolini ("Everything I am, I owe to Sorel"), the name was a kind of gate key to the passage from socialism to fascism, and from respectably intellectual France to Italy. For Drieu la Rochelle in 1940, Sorel was the first name on a list of strong thinkers, the ones the French *should* have read in order not to fall: "the France that had read Sorel, Barrès, Maurras, Péguy, Bernanos, Céline, Giono, Malraux, Petitjean was not strong enough to impose itself on the France that was reading A. France, Duhamel, Giraudoux, Mauriac, Maurois."[14]

Brasillach flew the Sorel banner in 1942 to remind the French how much credit Mussolini had given them in his founding of fascism: "And we oughtn't to forget, we French, that the initiator of the Italian movement declared that 'in the great river of fascism one can locate currents that go back to Sorel, Péguy, Lagardelle of the Socialist movement,' that is to say, to Frenchmen."[15] Sorel's name flows from text to text, like a refrain, picking up more proper names along the way. Didn't Sorel himself think that every nation needed songs to be sublime, and needed to be sublime to nourish revolution? Again, something ideologically interesting is happening here, in that the sublime, an ordinarily visual category, takes on oral meanings through Sorel's suggestion.

In some cases, the Sorel text doesn't need to be read but merely spoken or displayed. In other instances, Sorel's energy flows through every metaphor, without his name ever being mentioned. This use of Sorel as the fertilizer of revolutionary myth is even closer to that spark of an ongoing narrative flame that Sorel thought revolutions needed. If slogan in this second sense is a kind of lifeline between writing and politics; if, in Barbara Spackman's terms, slogan is "language which threatens to move beyond language",[16] we might be able to see it working in political rhetoric as a kind of self-fulfilling prophecy. A slogan might, for example, offer a particular metaphoric suggestion in its accounting for history, and if that suggestion is sufficiently powerful in the *social* sense of the term, it will be, as it were, "present" for the interpretation of the next histori-cal event even *as it happens*. In this way interpretive form actually carries its effect into the real: history is telling and making at once.[17]

Several events function as mythological stock in fascist literature: the civil war in Spain; the French riots of February 6, 1934; Hitler's Nuremberg rallies. Though we could probably find in all of them some "translation" of Sorel, the most useful example may be February 6 — closest to an actual strike as Sorel de-fined it, and closest to a peculiarly French fascist moment.

A Jewish immigrant banker by the name of Stavisky is discovered to have used connections with the Radical party to fund a fraudulent banking operation in Bayonne. When the scandal hits the press, it is quickly harnessed in the ser-vice of a total analysis of economic depression, government corruption, and the evils of immigration. Here, from the point of view of many, is a perfect vehicle for explaining the number of bankruptcies and capital failures threatening French economic life.[18] Veterans' leagues and splinter groups from far right and far left rush to the streets and approach the Palais Bourbon; the government will ultimately fire on them. Eighteen people die. The event structures anti-parliamentarian France into a position of martyrdom and revolt — every fascist intellectual hopes desperately for someone to "seize the time."

Drieu writes of the event in *Gilles* as the apocalypse of the French nation.[19] He orchestrates it, with World War I veterans singing the Marseillaise and a group of communists singing the International. The key elements of a Sorelian revolt are right there — song, march, unity between warriors and workers, the proven failure of a parliamentary leadership. Drieu describes the ensuing spectacle — the flames from an overturned bus on the Champs Elysées, the con-fused crowd — as a scene from a new Greek tragedy:

In an instant he [Gilles] was transfigured. Looking to his right and his left, he saw himself surrounded by Fear and Courage—the divine couple who preside over wars had returned. . . . Like an evening in Champagne, like that morning in Verdun, when he arrived with the 20th Army Corps. . . . On his right, at the entry of the Champs Elysées, an overturned bus was burning. Some men were moving around the instant auto-da-fé, warming themselves with its flame. Beyond them, near the rotary, one could perceive a great mass draped with flags, shifting a bit—the veterans. From that moment on, he was in a whirlpool of crowds which were battering and soft in turn, spurting and abating, heaped up and lost. On a beauteous theater of stone and sky, a people and a police separated like two halves of a chorus. (pp. 595–96)

The next morning, Gilles runs to his old friend Clérences, a disgruntled radical, to announce the moment of no return: Gilles has experienced the Sorelian moment of recognition. Entering Clérence's study, he starts shouting in slogans: "This is the first time in 20 years that I've felt alive," and so on. Gilles tries to convince Clérences that this is the day he can go out in the streets and capture the Jeunesses Patriotes, the Croix de Feu, the Action Française, and the communists all in the same net. Attacking Daladier (the reigning parliamentary leader) or defending him suddenly seems irrelevant. The important thing is to abandon the old political routine—parties, manifestos, meetings, articles—that is, writing.

"The barriers between left and right will be broken forever," he announces, "and streams of life will precipitate in every direction. Don't you sense the moment of the great crest? The stream is before us: we can divert it in whatever direction we want, but we have to do it right away, at any cost." (p. 599)

Gilles, primary actor here as well as narrator of his own actions, remarks at this point that everyone in Clérence's study now fidgets belligerently in their armchairs "like movie-goers the moment the machine guns start blasting in a gangster movie." When Clérences responds to Gilles's speech with "You are a fascist, Monsieur Gambier," the narrator attributes his words to "a little Jew" who doesn't speak, but rather "flutes" this "fatal speech." "And how," exclaims Gilles—the triumphant adolescent—as he leaves the room.

Brasillach's description of the same event is really a reading of Drieu's, thus giving to February 6 the additional weight of the already recognized:

A great hope was born in [our] blood, the hope of a National revolution. . . . It was formed throughout that tragic night among the most diverse rumors, of the resignation of the President of the Republic, the announcement of hundreds of deaths . . . anger, worry. The divine couple Courage and Fear, wrote Drieu la Rochelle, who had sensed so well that exalting night, Courage and Fear organized themselves and set out throughout the streets . . . the German papers announced, "The dawn of fascism is rising over France."[20]

Like the name Sorel in the quotes above, we see the Sorelian event flow from one text to the next, joyous as a "stream of life," violent as a "blasting machine gun," taking on new proper names. In Drieu, the sterile left-right dichotomy that has so long divided the nation has been reduced in the magic space of the Place de la Concorde (analogous to the general strike space), to its original arbitrary spacial meaning, which the heroic fascist consciousness can easily "control" by looking to both sides. Gilles, the fascist revolutionary, thus "looks to his right and his left" and sees not the parties of the sterile senate, nor even the royalists and the communists, but a presiding mythic couple, Courage and Fear, who control them all in the moment of catastrophe. In Brasillach's account, all that really remains of Sorel's original left syndicalism is the verb *organized*: now it is Drieu's mythic couple, rather than workers, organizing themselves to preside over the war against the modern world.

Brasillach tried to institutionalize February 6 – he would return to the site of the event each year to commemorate the dead. Echoing Sorel, he wrote: "Only the revolutionaries have understood the meaning of these myths and ceremonies."[21] In a sense he was wrong. February 6 scared a lot of people about the possibility of a French fascist coup and may have been partly responsible for the victory of an antifascist popular front government two years later. Nor was February 6 forgotten by the end of the Second World War. The Liberation government, in what it must have hoped would be its own final gloss on the event, chose February 6, 1945, as the date of Brasillach's execution. But Brasillach fought to the end to hold the Sorelian banner in his own hands. His lawyer, Jacques Isorni, records Brasillach's penultimate words (to his sister) as these: "Today is the 6th of February. You will [henceforth] think of me and you will think as well of the others who died the same day 11 years ago."[22]

Brasillach and Drieu, in moving the Sorel scenario from the factory to the Place de la Concorde, have merely operated a change that Sorel's own work, with its insistence on energy, on aesthetic unity, and on a national sublime, already suggests. What drops out of the equation entirely in the fascist context is the identity of worker as worker. Drieu and Brasillach gloss instead Sorel's politics of aesthetic discrimination and creation; they metamorphose the worker into a spectator of political ceremonies "looking to his right and left," "diverting the great flow," and being "transfigured" into a political mythmaker in so doing. Clérences and his friends can't join the revolution because they are mere spectators: hearing Gilles's speech, they remain in their armchairs instead of rising as political warriors. In this respect, they are all, like Clérences, "little Jews": they can't sing the sublime revolutionary tune; they can only squeak like flutes. It is as strange, squeaky parliamentary speakers that they kill Gilles's revolutionary plan. Brasillach's racial dig is slightly more epic and abstract: hope for national revolution is born "in the blood." By a series of substitutions, the synecdochical joy Sorel proposes for the individual striker in the factory becomes linked in fascist politics to the situation of the individual in the nation, to blood urges and Aryan energy. But behind the Sorelian myth are radically new supports for mass political persuasion. Fascist propaganda had at its disposal collective art forms such as cinema and radio, technical mythmaking machines that gave passive individuals lost in their armchairs a chance to retrieve themselves as fascists, if only in their imaginations.

*Reflections on Violence* rhymes better with these sleek machines than with what Reyner Banham has called "the cast iron, soot and rust of the Victorian age" into which Sorel was born. Why did Sorel's ideology lend itself so well to the next generation? Why, in a sense, are his politics a generation ahead of the factory technology of his times—compatible with the world of heroic, individually operated technology, foreshortened distances, and speed?

I think we tend to forget the basic facts of Sorel's life. The man was an engineer who had spent his working life in the provinces, in an arid Corsica, in the colonial Algerian desert. The year he received a legion of honor and a promotion to chief engineer of roads and bridges, he resigned, refused a pension, and moved to the outskirts of Paris to start an intellectual life at age fifty. He succeeded so grandly as an intellectual that his return to Paris survives on the books as one of the great puzzles of twentieth century intellectual biography. Sorel, in fact, is our "reverse-Rimbaud". (Rimbaud left Paris, and poetry, in his early twenties for an obscure business career in Africa). Nothing must have pleased Bergson more than to observe the intellectual progress of a writer who really had started with the concrete, whose philosophy was built upon years of practical work.

Curtis tells us that Sorel spent a lot of time at the end of his engineering career in the Perpignan library reading architecture and archeology books. In Paris, he seems to have left his profession definitively: his reading is proliferative but strictly philosophic. We can only glimpse his working life through some of his conclusions: while Bergson, the old-style aesthete, is afraid that humans will start acting and thinking like the machines they worked on—that they will become automatons—Sorel, whose own work with machines had been creative, sees a harmony between humans and machines as a goal. What did he know about technology that Bergson didn't?

When Sorel returned to a post-Haussmanian Paris in 1892, he must have been amazed at the changes he saw. He might have felt exhilarated: this was the era of the great international expositions, the Eiffel Tower, the iron-worked metro stop. Paris's engineers had taken over the functions that architects had once held; private elitist creations were passing into the domaine of public works. Technology was becoming art: in a world like this, why couldn't a builder of bridges and roads do philosophy? Sorel doesn't write specifically about building, but his writing clearly conveys all the excitement of his crossover, his belated discoveries, his "coil sprung." The pleasure of engineering emerges as a sense of finding a new way around a problem, "liberating the spirit of invention in my readers" (letter to Halévy, p. 30), "to break through the bonds of what has been previously constructed for common use" (letter to Halévy, p. 28), to "readily skip the transitions between these things because they nearly always come under the heading of commonplaces" (letter to Halévy, p. 28).

As violent in his admiration as in his criticisms and his abrupt changes of heart, Sorel's thinking is the very embodiment of a second adolescence. This is exactly what disturbs critics about his work and exactly what made him appeal to the excited political journalists of the younger generation, to the Brasillach's and Drieu's, the poetic engineers of fascist ideology. His remarks on Bergson, to return to my early example of his adult student life, are not proof of his Bergsonism so much as indications of his capacity for temporary passionate excitement over a new system of thought. He can wax the same way about Marx, Renan, or Nietzsche. Given that enthusiasm tends to come across in his work as advocacy on the verge of publicism, it is not surprising that those who quoted him did so as a kind of banner text for a revolution fascinated by its own publicity.

What Sorel might have intuited in 1909 was that the creative energy he had experienced in his engineering, and which he brought to his writing, was going to be felt by everyone as soon as machines left the factory and entered daily life. The machines would enter daily life in two ways—in individually operated machines like cars and airplanes, which would give people an enormous sense of control over space and time, and in entertainment machines like movies and radio, which would represent the new world to people from great distances and in epic proportions. The great blast furnaces and railways that capital needed to expand itself had already been produced. The new machines had to create a new market, and they did so by creating a new buyer—the consumer. With radios, sewing machines, vacuum cleaners, everyone could be a home capitalist, a domestic engineer. Their machines bore no reminder of the scene of production, they weren't class specific; and though they were in existence as early as the First World War, they weren't truly popular until the period between the wars.[23]

When this popularization takes place, every person becomes an engineer, a Sorel. Daily-life machines also give people in different classes something important in common. It is at this moment—this departure of the machine from the factory—that Sorel's rhetoric of revolution is successfully recyclable minus its specific working-class element. Georges Valois, the first fascist engineer of that move, embraces Sorel for his suitability to an energetic middle-class, as well as to a working-class, revolution. Sorel's own writing helps the process along. Since he offered no specific strategy for the general strike, one could easily substitute people—or, as Brasillach does, *blood*—for *worker*, *nation* for *factory*, *revolutionary genius* for *ingenius revolutionary*. But I don't think the substitutions could have "taken" in any world. The day that the shopkeeper and the factory worker both become consumers, sit next to one another at the movies, or exchange some words about motor oil at their local garage, the day that everyone can map the world from behind the wheel, we can begin to talk about a specific twentieth-century populism, and about fascist rehearsals of Sorel.

## Notes

1. The context is Sartre's introduction to Frantz Fanon's *Wretched of the Earth*: "If you bracket Sorel's fascist prattle [*bavardages*], you will find that Fanon is the first person since Engels to illuminate the midwife of history" (my translation). The standard English translation renders *bavardages* as the neutral *utterances* (p. 14).

2. John L. Stanley, *The Sociology of Virtue*, p. 3.

3. See Eugen Weber, *Action Française*, pp. 73–76, and J. L. Talmon, "The Legacy of Georges Sorel," pp. 57–60, for information on the Sorel-Maurras merger.

4. Michael Curtis, *Three against the Third Republic*, p. 52.

5. John L. Stanley, introduction to *From Georges Sorel*, p. 5.

6. See chapter 2 of this volume ("On Banality"), pp. 47–52 above.

7. Sternhell, "Fascist Ideology," p. 323.

8. Jack J. Roth, *The Cult of Violence*, p. 259.

9. Georges Sorel, *Reflections on Violence*. Page numbers appear in parentheses in the body of the text.

10. The reading that follows grew out of a special session of the MLA the title of which repeated the title of this best-known work. I thank Reed Dasenbrock, Barbara Spackman, and Paolo Valesio for contributing to my thoughts about Sorel on that occasion.

11. Henri Bergson, *An Introduction to Metaphysics*. Subsequent page references to this edition will appear in parentheses in the body of the text. For a political analysis of the English-language translator of both Sorel and Bergson, see Miriam Hansen, "T. E. Hulme, Mercenary of Modernism," pp. 355–85.

12. See Bergson's critique of Kant in *An Introduction to Metaphysics*, pp. 80–88.

13. Georges Valois, *Le Fascisme*, p. 5, quoted and analyzed by Sternhell, *Ni droite ni gauche*, p. 23.

14. Pierre Drieu la Rochelle, "Ecrit en Juin 1940," p. 173.

15. Brasillach, "Pour un fascisme français," pp. 499–500. Brasillach's quotation of Mussolini comes from the widely translated entry on "Fascismo" in the *Enciclopedia Italiana*, ed. Treccani, p. 848. The entry is signed Mussolini but is generally attributed to Giovanni Gentile.

16. From her MLA paper, a version of which was published in *Quaderni D'Italianistica*, under the title "Il verbo (e)sangue: Gabriele D'Annunzio and the Ritualization of Violence."

17. Here I need to acknowledge two theorists whose critical goals have inspired my own work. J. P. Faye has written that "to account for the way language makes oppression possible is a first step

toward 'liberation' " (*Théorie du récit*, p. 136). Edward Said's political criticism is written in a similar spirit (see *The World, the Text, and the Critic*).

18. For interesting quotes on the affaire from the right-wing press, see Jean Plumyène and Raymond Lasierra, "Le 6 fevrier 1934," in *Les Fascismes français*, pp. 64–79.

19. Subsequent references in this chapter to Pierre Drieu la Rochelle's *Gilles* are in parentheses in the body of the text. Translations are mine. For further analyses of Drieu's work, see the section on Drieu la Rochelle in chapter 4 ("Bodies and Landscapes").

20. Brasillach, *Notre Avant-Guerre*, pp. 135–36.

21. Ibid., p. 136.

22. Jacques Isorni, *Le Procès de Robert Brasillach*, p. 26.

23. Sternhell, *Ni droite ni gauche*, pp. 289–93, insists quite rightly on the fact that "machine" civilization is already present in the last decade of the nineteenth century and that the rise of both revolutionary syndicalism and the radical patriotic leagues should be understood in terms of this period of intense industrialization and abundance. I disagree with him, however, when he argues further that the fascism of the 1930s had nothing to add to turn-of-the-century fascist themes. Industrialization, circa 1870–1910, and the popularization of machines for entertainment and sport in the period between the two world wars have different political consequences. Ernest Mandel, *Late Capitalism*, gives an important explanation of the growth of durable consumer goods and its relationship to the production of machines and to the exploitation of raw materials in the European colonies. The relationship between fascism, colonialism, and consumerism will be discussed further in subsequent chapters.

# Chapter 4
# Bodies and Landscapes: Marinetti, Drieu la Rochelle, and Céline

## Marinetti

The first account we have of the metamorphosis of an artistic avant-garde movement into a fascist lobby is written into the novels, plays, and endless manifestos of F. T. Marinetti.

It is now a well-established fact that Marinetti's futurism was a "seminal" moment in European modernism and that it had profound influences on almost every avant-garde movement in twentieth-century Europe: on Russian constructivism, on vorticism, on dadaism and surrealism. It's no wonder, then, that we have so much trouble even thinking about the fascist element in futurism, for to do so is to threaten the reputation of a much larger body of experimental writing.

Marinetti himself—professional rabble-rouser, polemicist, and artistic ringleader—"produced" futurism's reputation. He did this by disseminating his manifestos in art journals at a furious international pace and by organizing brilliant happenings and "futurist banquets" throughout Europe. The publicist in Marinetti worked at being remembered either as a highbrow clown or, as the saying went, as "the caffeine of Europe." He did his work so well that, today, futurism's reputation is as a strictly aesthetic affair, concerned with shattering literary tradition and whisking the activity of art onto a new playground of signifiers. This view is so dominant as to belie, in advance, any serious political work a critic might attempt on it.[1] Nowhere in my own work have I felt more "ridiculous," more "embarrassed," about connecting art and fascist politics than in my work on futurism: how can you connect something so funny with something so dreadful? This is where I begin my analysis: futurism is funny, but it is dangerous in its funniness because it has the power to make me stop thinking about its effect.

The power is most evident in the manifestos, the purpose of which is to clear a path for a new art by decimating and ridiculing the old ones. The manifestos are, in a sense, defenses against anyone who would refute them. When I feel like a joyless, stuffy critic trying to criticize the futurists, I take it that the manifestos are doing their best work. To understand futurism politically, I decided to begin by reading the writing of a less defensive Marinetti, a Marinetti less concerned with his critics and with a school of writing than with his own desires.

I have found a text relatively unencumbered by the prerogatives of an institutionalized avant-garde; a text that seems to be about ambition and leadership rather than about performing that ambition (like the manifestos). It is Marinetti's *Mafarka le futuriste, roman africain*, which was first published in Paris in 1909, the same year the Founding Manifesto appeared in *Le Figaro*.[2] The author of *Mafarka le futuriste*, we might say, plunged so deeply into his futurist fantasies that he forgot, momentarily, about the mechanics of avant-garde organizing. With all of its desires and ambitions nakedly displayed, *Mafarka le futuriste* seems to many critics to be the most ridiculous Marinetti text of all: intellectual historian James Joll called it "a tedious rhetorical tale of rape and battle in a mythical Africa."[3] But dismissals like this one proved, in the case of Sorel, to be signals or clues that some misunderstood fascist writing practice was at work. I'll continue to take these texts seriously.

Let me express my own reading strategy another way. *Mafarka* exists in juxtaposition to the manifestos as Freud has described a daydream existing in relation to a work of art.[4] The daydream is a relatively blatant version of the ego wishes, which in successful artistic activity are disguised by what Freud calls "the aesthetic bribe." The futurist "bribe" might be best understood as a series of stylistic innovations and iconoclastic dogma by which critics link futurism to surrealism, dadaism, and other avant-garde art movements. The link is real and important, yet it places futurism in an anarchic tradition that obfuscates its eventual sympathy to a highly constructive brand of fascist nationalism. Recovering the paradoxically constructive aspect of futurism through a reading of *Mafarka le futuriste* is a way for me to understand the fantasies that lead to futurism's fascist affinities. I've talked about the fascist "slogan effect"; with *Mafarka* I will be able to talk about a somewhat larger unit—the fascist fantasy narrative. I hope that this work will prove to some of my readers to be a useful starting point for thinking politically about the fantasies of other avant-gardists.

Though *Mafarka le futuriste* was the first futurist novel, it presents to its readers a willful "incest of genres," inconsistently primitive and modern. It

F.-T. Marinetti (center) at a convention of writers. Photo Collection Viollet.

echoes with self-conscious strains of every contemporary literary style from romantic-exotic to late decadent, while hearkening back to the most ancient epic forms. Its setting is African—not exactly the Egyptian desert of Marinetti's youth (he was born and raised in Cairo), but a dramatic combination of safari jungle and Sahara, inhabited by black soldiers, copper-colored warrior kings, hyenas, giraffe war machines, mad dogs, and decorated with hypogeums, medieval castles, and even a whale-belly amphitheater under the sea. The different episodes appear foreign to each other. In this way the novel marks a move from the exotic historical Carthage of Flaubert's *Salammbô*, or even the airy mythic evocation of place in Mallarmé's *Hérodiade* (postromantic works to which *Mafarka* has been compared), to an almost adolescent vision of the primitive, reminiscent of contemporary science fiction: synthetic and archetypal at once. Trying to compare it to standard exotica of the romantic or symbolist world would be like putting an overly ferocious le Douanier Rousseau next to a Delacroix. The two worlds don't mix.

Marinetti himself called his book "polyphonic": "It's a lyrical song, an epic, an adventure novel and a drama all at the same time" (p. iii). By his own admission, then, the futurist project involved the use of a multitude of literary voices; not merely for a leap into the literary future, but for a conquest of the literary past. His other prefatory announcements make clear, in standard "épater-le-bourgeois" style, the supplemental erotic pleasures of literary conquest. Here he is at his most "obnoxious," his most "adolescent": "my creator's pride is satisfied herein"; "I am the only one who would dare write this masterpiece"; and, right to the point, "I announce to you that the spirit of man is an untrained ovary: we [the futurist brotherhood] are the ones who fertilize him for the first time" (pp. ix-xi). The stories inside the book rival these prefatory promises with their own obsessive force.

*Leadership*

> [H]e let loose his great war cry: "Mafarka-Allah!" with such a thunderous voice that he made all the faces, all the pupils of that crowd turn towards him, just as the sun which punctuates the horizon of the sea brusquely draws unto itself the gazes of all the waves. (pp. 29–30)

Mafarka the warrior is a supernature. Source of echo, of sound, he is also a sun that captures its own rays back from the waves.

The granting of supernatural powers to him is countered throughout the work by the granting of human characteristics to the landscape: rocks are "hostile and taciturn like crouching negroes" (p. 263); the sea is a "feeble planter [*semeur*]" (p. 228); the winds have "agile thighs" (p. 261). This exchange of natural and human phenomena creates a pantheistic atmosphere in which Mafarka's effects on the earth are as inevitable as the effect of weather on human beings. Mafarka's face has the tint of "beauteous baked earth"; his body is "painted with the colors of luck and victory, like the hull of a beautiful ship" (p. 7). The proliferation of metaphors thus extends from the natural to the manufactured. Mafarka the sun, controller of waves, is also Mafarka the ship, rider of the waves—just as in Greek mythology, Apollo, god of the sun and ruler of the sky, is himself both sun and carrier of the sun across the sky.

## The Story-Teller

Thus, overdetermined by a supernatural landscape in which power and nature are equivalent, Mafarka is portrayed both as an aesthetic interpreter of nature's powers and as a natural power in his own right. He studies the sun for some signal to action and then decides that in order to trick his enemy, the warrior Brafane, he must disguise himself as a beggar, ride into Brafane's camp, and tell provocative stories that incite Brafane and his men to great orgies and ultimate destruction. He decides that the story most likely to excite them would be one of his own undoing. He calls it the story of the horse dealer, the stuffed fish, and the devil.

Mafarka the Warrior, he begins, was once a horse dealer. One day a demon disguised as a rich merchant admired one of the dealer's stock, a black stallion with a red mane and tail. Here, the enemy warrior Brafane wants to get in on the act of storytelling, and so he asks about the horse's phallus—his "zeb," he calls it—and his men roar with laughter. Brafane has declared his intention to control the direction of the narration.

Mafarka the beggar complies, answering the question with what seems to be a total reorientation of his story around the horse's phallus. The zeb of this horse, he answers with a smile, is purple, its point encrusted with sapphires: this is the kind of zeb that the girls of Tell-el-Kibir dream of before their marriage. It should come as no surprise to you, he tells his audience, that the demon-merchant purchased the horse without even bargaining. But the result was tragic. Even as the demon rode away, he discovered that when the red mane made contact with the wind, it caught on fire and set fire to everything in sight. Because it was spring, the brilliantly zebbed horse also insisted on copulating with all the animals of the forest, continually unsaddling and injuring the demon-merchant. In order to take vengeance against Mafarka the horse dealer, the demon castrated the horse, stuffed its phallus, and served it to Mafarka at a dinner party in his palace. He called his entrée a stuffed fish—a most concrete example in the text of the play between fiery phallic imagery and maternal sea imagery!

Having eaten this magic stuffed phallus, Mafarka the horse dealer grows insane, kicks the demon out of his own palace, and proceeds to behave exactly as the horse had in heat, reenacting his ritual of supernatural masculinity. Finally exhausted, Mafarka creeps to the seaside to rest. His own penis has grown so enormous that it is mistaken by some sailors for a rope and attached to a sail. Mafarka, happily still attached to his "rope," was thus carried by sea to the city of Tell-el-Kibir, where he entertains that city's king and then captures his throne. Ever since, Mafarka the beggar concludes, a castrated horse in search of his lost part has been running through the countryside carrying pestilence and death.

Mafarka the beggar then frames his narrative by announcing to his audience that the only way to guard against the curse of the castrated horse is to drink and dance. Brafane, now well under the power of Mafarka's story, obediently demands dancers and liquor, and an orgy begins. As soon as everyone is sufficiently inebriated, Mafarka the beggar announces that he sees the horse of his own story: the story is true! Brafane's army takes off in a drunken stupor to kill the horse, and Brafane lends his best war horse to Mafarka the beggar, so that he can help in the hunt. Mafarka creeps ahead of the drunken mass and carves wounds onto Brafane's war horse, soaking its mane and tail red with its blood so that it resembles the red-marked horse he had invented. In their frenzy at seeing what they think is the horse of the story come true, one flank of Brafane's horsemen mistakes the other flank, composed of black soldiers on white horses, for a pile of black rocks emerging from the sea and madly charges in its direction. The two groups end up destroying each other. Meanwhile, Mafarka and Brafane's favorite beast, magically unaffected by bleeding, escape. The beggar's story has ended.

This willfully confusing, and willfully ridiculing, tale within the novel acts as a "performative" in the most perverse sense of the term: it becomes true merely because it is believed, although it is "about" nontruth. Its various forms of disguise—disguise of the phallus as fish and as rope, disguise of the story as the truth, disguise of the warrior as beggar—are so many codes for fiction and for fiction's own phallic power. Although at the most obvious level the story is about watching out for a castrated horse, at the narrative level it is about an enemy castrated by a story, about the penetration of an audience's psyche by the most outrageous sort of tale. Mafarka the beggar has internalized the power of the absent zeb in his role as storyteller. By believing that Mafarka the beggar actually sees the horse, his enemies grant him all the powers of his main character, Mafarka the warrior—that is, his own powers. They, poor artists, pathetically imagine their comrades as "rocks": their fiction destroys them. Mafarka rides away from Brafane's camp as a victorious artist, and hero of what may be the first spaghetti western.

Then his role in the novel changes. He eschews the life of the warrior altogether for that of the free-floating artistic demagogue. He begins to pursue this new career as a manipulative plastic artist. In the third chapter, "The Sun Dogs," Mafarka builds "war giraffes," "great machines in the form of hugely sculpted animals," on the turrets of his fortress. The innocent-looking creatures project large pouches of boiling pitch onto an advancing enemy with their hidden metal wings.

*Training the Male Ovary*

The establishment of Mafarka as supernarrator and sculptor serves as a prelude to Mafarka's ultimate creative act: the building of a son, Gazouramah. The construction of Gazouramah extends on the level of theme a preference for the mechanical qualities of humans—a rendering of the mechanical as "second nature"—which occurs throughout the novel on the adjectival level as a desire to characterize and define all human beings by means of a technological vocabulary. As we have seen, this desire is strangely countered by the granting of human qualities to landscape: rocks are hostile, and winds have agile thighs; Mafarka has a "sharp metallic brain" (p. 218), and his brother Magamal a flexible body of rubber (p. 16). Thus, in an implicit satire of romantic pathetic fallacies, landscapes receive decidedly "leftover" human qualities. The human and plant metaphors clash: this is not merely an exchange, but an *uneven* one, a linguistic instance of what marxist economists call "unequal development."[5]

In other words, the technological man must oppress someone in order to exist. He is born, in futurism, not only at the expense of standard "human" qualities, shunted onto nature, but with the specific exclusion of woman. Technology gives its hypothetical master the ability to reproduce without the help of the female: to fertilize the male ovary, the futurist fraternity must somehow do away with female ones. Male procreation, in letter and spirit, is thus constantly buoyed up by attacks on female fertility, which is represented over and over again in the novel, as it is canceled out, in the form of muddy spaces, decay, and death. To his mistress, who attempts to interfere with the creation of Gazouramah, Mafarka cries: "Your body has nothing but famished mouths! . . . If I offer you a heroic idea, admit it, you are taken by the desire to suck it like sugar cane!" (p. 248). Woman devours and kills good ideas and is therefore aligned with death itself, which is personified elsewhere in the novel as a female seductress who, like Mafarka's vampire-lover, sucks at the heroic male: "Death holds you between its purplish lips and sucks your blood, and its caresses marble your body and its kisses voluptuously strip away your flesh" (p. 220).

The fantasy of a male body as a metal machine effectively fills in possible "feminine" gaps in the male by covering them with a shining reflecting material. How close we are, here, to the futurist poet of the *Founding Manifesto*, passing through the "maternal ditch" in his metal automobile and, once having escaped the old myths and ideals, undergoing his own "violent spasms of action and creation." Gazouramah is a particularly well functioning futurist: he needs neither sleep nor dreams (he ostensibly "lives" them), and his greatest skill is that of taking flight. He offers no clue of a secret inward self, but moves outward, symbolically protected from conflicts by his rigid surface.

Like the projection of pitch by the war giraffes, creation in the futurist credo is always a violent launching outward into a watery female world, a "mer(e) mystérieuse" of phenomenon. Artistic creation is an opportunity to combat the murky creation of first nature with a second male nature, a perpetual motion machine that, like Gazouramah, never rests.

## The Origin of Gazouramah

It's hard to see, once machinery has been fetishized, that the vehicle—the alibi—for the phallic energy in futurism remains, at some level, science and industry. In examining the actual construction of Gazouramah in *Mafarka*, I am trying to understand how a futurist narration manages to erase the industrial base and leave industrial products erotically and aesthetically intact.[6]

While Mafarka fights off his concubines in order to save his sexual energy for the creation of art, two crews of workers are actually building the son: the Herculean blacksmiths, who construct the foundation and the cage for Gazouramah, and the weavers, who supply the finishing touches. Production is thus divided into three levels: hard labor, light industry, and pure creation (the work of the father, Mafarka).

Mafarka must defend the weavers against the brutally jealous blacksmiths, who ridicule them as "reprehensible little women [*femmelettes*]." An orgy of destruction breaks out between these two camps, and eventually the ingenious "feminized" weavers win when they remove the support for Gazouramah's cage so that it crushes and kills the blacksmiths. The blacksmiths—the proletariat, in other words—are overcome by the product of their own labor. And, yet, the fate of the weavers isn't much happier—Mafarka sends them away without pay for having impeded the progress of his work (there's no easy light labor-heavy labor allegory here). Mafarka, alone at last with his machine, mysteriously brings it to life without the help of either group of engineers.

Thus, though futurist creation would substitute male science for murky female procreation, the actual industrial agents of scientific production—the workers responsible for the engineering of the mechanical son—are banned from the novel. The disappearance of the workers from the scene of creation is much like the disappearance of Mafarka's lusty concubines: both workers and women are destructive elements who cannot be allowed to interfere with the final duet between the artist and his creation. The power of will alone, rather than the power of work or of sexuality, is deemed sufficient for creation. Marinetti lauds the machine, but abhors the factory.

Though the birth of Gazouramah will occur without the interference of workers, it does not take place entirely in utopian form—that is, devoid of "the collusion and the putrid complicity of the uterus of woman" (p. 215). Mafarka discovers his lover spying on the scene of birth and establishing an incestuous maternal relationship with Gazouramah through eye contact. The mere glance of a woman is enough of a threat to enrage him, and so he hurls a rock at her to remove her. She responds by confirming his fears—her glance alone has made her a true mother:

> Oh! I forgive you, Mafarka, for wanting to smash the mother of your son under the rocks! . . . He is my son, you know it, since the moment that his first glance was for me! . . . I melted in pleasure under the rude caress of his eyes! . . . He is also my lover, and I gave myself over to all his caprices in that first glance. (p. 283)

She then warns him that even if he murders her, he cannot destroy her influence over Gazouramah: "If you kill me, I'll be born again, incessantly, in the heart of your son, like a poison of terror and of love!" (p. 285).

Mafarka responds by crying and wandering through an obviously uterine landscape in search of his own mother's spirit. His mother's voice then warns him of the despair of creation. She orders him to destroy himself for the sake of his son, and he complies: "Oh, caressing breath of my mother! You push me into the arms of my son! You order me to annihilate my body in giving life to him! . . . I obey you! In haste!" (pp. 290–91). From this moment on, Mafarka, by his own definition, is a feminized, martyred mother. Science has failed as a model for creation, and so, finally, has pure will. Gazouramah is rather the creation of a "total woman," Mafarka, who offers all his life and his desires to his progeny: "Oh my son! Oh my master! . . . I have given everything for you" (p. 291).

This is the most surprising and most crucial moment of the novel: the place where Marinetti's authorial intentions, as stated in his preface, appear to break down through some involuntary return to the maternal. Yet, at this very moment, Gazouramah emerges. Nothing less than a corrective version of the two unhappiest sons in Greek mythology, Oedipus and Icarus, will do to rescue the narrative from feminization. Gazouramah throws Mafarka into the sea at Mafarka's pathetic cry "You are killing me! and I am dying of jealousy for you!" (p. 293), flies to the sun to demand its worship, and leaves the earth quaking and exploding below him.[7] Gazouramah is an Icarus whose daring is rewarded, and who kills his father *because* he is not a father (a master), but a mother.

In his final flight upward, Gazouramah is surprised that he can no longer hear the earth exploding. The explosions are muted by the sound of his wings making their own ecstatic music. His parent dead, Gazouramah is nonetheless a happy Oedipus. Rather than groping, he sings and flies, discovering "the great hope of the world, the great dream of a total music." In a draft of the novel, Marinetti wrote that he intended to sketch "the great clacking of Gazouramah's wings from distance to distance, like a refrain."[8] Here is the refrain, as he completed it:

Now Gazouramah, still rising, was surprised by the inexplicable silence that enveloped him in spite of the violence of the earthly battle growing at his feet. All of a sudden, as his flight changed course, a suave and strange melody charmed his ears. He soon understood that it was being given off by his wings, more vivid and sonorous than two harps, and, drunk with enthusiasm, he entertained himself by modulating these harmonious cadences, slowing down the vibrations one by one and pushing still higher their exalted returns. This is how the great hope of the world, the great dream of a total music, was finally realized in the flight of Gazouramah. (pp. 305–6)

Thus, the great battle between a maternal creation and a male artistic production, a battle that Mafarka seems to have lost, is deflected onto the fantastic, utopian figure of Gazouramah. The "total music" in the last moments of the novel offers a final corrective to feminine truth. Ideal sound can now originate not from a hole (the feminine "hungry mouths," corrosive to meaning) but from a flapping wing (an emblem of phallic motion instead of vaginal stasis). Mafarka's disturbing fall into femininity has been transcended by Gazouramah's dehumanized phallic flight upward; Gazouramah's total self-absorption is a final mark of the successful abandonment of a crumbling earth and of the irresolvable conflicts that lie there smoldering.

## Gazouramah's Legacy

With all this fantasy in mind, we can now return to the more abstract manifestos and political tracts, in which we see Gazouramah's rigid transcendent perspective repeat itself at even airier heights.

The basic Mafarka principle surviving in the manifestos is this: a futurist artist must be a leader; and in his double role, he must destroy in order to create. In the 1911 *Against Amore and Parliamentarianism*, Marinetti alludes explicitly to Mafarka's fantasy as the collective wish of the entire futurist movement: "We have even dreamed of one day being able to create a mechanical son, the fruit of pure will, a synthesis of all the laws that science is on the brink of discovering."[9]

The deeply sentimental passion of the novel, the desire it expressed to create progeny mechanically — that is, to bypass motherhood — coupled with its radical fear and disgust of women is corrected here with a hyperrationalist discourse on speed and machinery. The discourse remains phallic, but willfully disinterested. Marinetti will say it best in his "Technical Manifesto of Futurist Literature": "We are not interested in offering dramas of humanized matter."[10]

We can historicize this antisentimental strategy, first, as a reaction against the more feminized rhetoric of certain late nineteenth-century poetry and, second, as an appropriation of science into the realm of art. Whereas romanticism, and, to some extent, symbolism, had taken refuge from industrialization in fertile landscapes and pathetic fallacies drawn from nature, futurist poetry must embrace and aestheticize industrialization, render it—through intensely phallic metaphor—a tool of male will. By investing industrial objects with libidinal energy, futurism attempts to bridge the gap between private and scientific reality. The old symbolist poet is weak in the minds of the futurists because he is a-utopian: the futurist desires revealed in *Mafarka* project a program for utopian behavior both forward, to the creation of an immortal mechanical son, and backward, through a precapitalist epic setting. But the melodramatic fears and wishes of the novel—the tortured expression of everything that will be lost in the postindustrial world—are erased in the manifestos just as efficiently as they were burned, at *Mafarka's* end, by Gazouramah. Few clues remain of that narrative of unequal development.

Marinetti would claim *Mafarka's* language as a model for the future of futurist poetry, a precursor to the more syntactically adventurous futurist aeropoetry. In *Les Mots en liberté*, Marinetti quotes *Mafarka* to recommend, in all futurist writing, the use of what he called its "nets of imagery": "To catch and gather whatever is most fugitive and unattainable in matter, one must shape *strict nets of images or analogies*, to be cast into the mysterious sea [*la mer mystérieuse*] of phenomena.[11]

Futurist language, therefore, intends to "trap" the referent and then to throw it back into a sea of phenomenon. As opposed to the surrealist ideal—to Breton's emblematic "dissolvable fish," for example, which indicates a willingness to plunge into magical waters, into those places where language dissolves reality—futurist doctrine demonstrates a desire to control nature by means of language. Language, for the futurist, is a trap to use and not to fall into. Language is a net; nature is a dangerous, mysterious sea of phenomenon: a murky maternal force. That language itself must fight nature with speed, immediacy, and disruptiveness and that it must form the world—capturing and reproducing the very stuff of creation—are the two major dicta of the futurist credo that pass from the novel to the polemics and the most experimental futurist poetry in more and more successfully phallic form.

The following passage from *Les Mots en liberté*, for example, takes us back to Gazouramah's last flight:

The profound intuitions of life, juxtaposed word by word according to their illogical birth, will give us the general lines of an *intuitive physiology of matter*. This was revealed to me from the height of an airplane. Looking at the objects from a new point of view, no longer from front or back but at a vertical [*à pic*], that is to say shortened, I was able to break the old logical shackles and the plumb lines of the antique understanding.[12]

It is, thus, a real object—the airplane—that allows for the "imagination without strings"; and it is the airplane that makes possible the nets of images or analogies and that promises the real possibility of illogical narrative births like Gazouramah's. The new point of view is extremely powerful because it allows the poet to encompass the entire universe in one coup. It is not that Marinetti's discourse on technology brings him back down to earth, but rather that the airplane allows him to remain a distant poet, while "seizing" the earth all the better from his total perspective. We might say here that, with the help of the airplane, Marinetti has forged a total artistic practice from Bergson's dynamic intuitions and their politicization in Sorel. He is recapturing the spirit of engineering for the world of art. In the sense that the air view gives him a powerful new perspective, he feels paradoxically quite earth-intimate. Thanks to technology, he writes, "finally the earth gives its full yield. Held close in the vast electrical hand of man, it passes out all its rich juices, lovely orange so long promised to our thirst and finally won!"[13]

Here, as in *Mafarka*, the aeropoet must feminize the earth to take it and to leave it behind, just as he does the old logic, the symbolist poets, the parliament. In a futurist utopia, man replaces woman, noise replaces talk, and immediate hygienic violence replaces the implicitly filthy mediation of the law. But we also discover that categorical distinctions blur upon an examination of the actual descriptions of the futurist world, clothed, as above, in male fantasies of fornication starring the female. The earth is played by woman—so is war, the machine, the sea, and, in fact, nearly every possible thing except woman herself, who, having given over her essence to everything around her, is completely void of intrinsic meaning. Womanhood is foremost among the "leftover" human qualities that futurism relegates to nonhuman objects in the course of its metallicization of man. War, in particular, as we saw in *Mafarka*, creates desire for orgy—war rallies erotic feelings. Here, it is rape: "See the furious coitus of war, gigantic vulva stirred by the friction of courage, shapeless vulva that spreads to offer itself to the terrific spasm of final victory."[14]

The most successful transvestite of all, war ties man to a chain of signifiers—to lust, to possession, then to orgasm and creation. By means of a rhetoric of pleasurable rape resulting in procreation, ideologies of militarism and social upheaval combine forces in Marinetti's work with social reconstruction. War can destroy Italy and at the same time bring about its rejuvenation. Indeed, war "rescues" the female image from the murk and restores it to active duty.

It is in the nationalist writings that the political implications of Marinetti's aesthetic perspective, his industrial referent (the airplane), and his love of destruction become clear. In this unpublished, undated letter to *La Revue Bleue* (written in French on *Poesia* letterhead and therefore probably composed late in 1909), Marinetti thinks about Italy as seen from an airplane:

We have here in Milan a group of 30 young writers, all profoundly
animated by an energetic will to clear out, cost what it will, as quickly
as possible, our radiant, fertile and intelligent peninsula, which has, as
you know, the form of a *raised foot*. On *the march*, therefore, and
with good kicks to the right and to the left, against the great rising
army and talking fogies and old monotone monkeys who govern our
cowardly politics and our twaddling literature. . . . We're tired of living in an atmosphere of prison or boarding school and we voluntarily
[illegible word] our old masters, who keep us from striding over our
ruins to follow at top speed the blossoming azured flight of beautiful
airplanes.[15]

Here, Marinetti implies, the static statues who inhabit Italy have failed to
realize the dynamic destiny inscribed in its shape – a marching foot. True intelligence is on the side of geography, the organic factor. The old right-left politics
have been rewritten and vitalized as "kicks." This personification of the nation
by its human form bears a strong resemblance to the many human metaphors
used to describe the landscape in *Mafarka le futuriste*. And with a similar result:
as man "humanizes" nature, he reinvents it in a form he can control. Yet only
the distance permitted by modern technology allows this foreshortened
perspective – this visual version of uneven development – whereby countries become feet, and boulders become crouching natives. Technology gives to man the
impression of having created nature, but also of having killed it. This is where
misogyny comes in:

You will certainly have watched the take off of a Blériot plane, pant-
ing and still held back by its mechanics, amid mighty buffets of air
from the propeller's first spins. Well then: I confess that before so in-
toxicating a spectacle we strong Futurists have felt ourselves suddenly
detached from women, who have suddenly become too earthly, or, to
express it better, have become a symbol of the earth that we ought to
abandon.[16]

The discourse on airplanes is more fully politicized in the 1930s when, in the
journal *Futurismo*, a page entitled "Aerovita" is devoted to the regular idealization of flight. By this late date, futurism is highly institutionalized, its favorite
forms weary from overuse. The manifesto is an automatic seal of approval for
anything new, including a newspaper column. Here is an excerpt from the
November 12, 1933, manifesto of "Aerovita":

Futurism is inherent in the soul of all the ingenious patriotic, heroic
youth: the fascists. "Airlife," created by Marinetti and myself,
epitomizes the past activities of futurism and directs those to come toward a greater understanding and valorization of the great sublime
conquest: flight. Flight represents under its various artistic or political,

economic or scientific aspects, *the clear-cut edge between the past and the future* which no backward looking "power" will ever be able to put back in the margins [*remarginare*].[17]

The airplane, that industrial carrier of Mafarka's sexual fantasies, is the prime mover in the translation of a futurist spirit into a fascist one.

On February 1, 1934, the futurist hero and the political leader finally become one. The "Aerovita" section of *Futurismo* consists of a pictorial essay entitled "Il Duce Aviatore," complete with photos of Mussolini in full flying gear and inserts of various war planes.[18] Lending its most clever graphic discoveries to fascism, the futurist newspaper will establish color-forms as background for polemics: a futurist reduction of Mussolini's face, done in bright red and blue, supports the headline's claim that the fascist is a futurist genius; the border print on the page balances a string of "duces" (a printed chant) with a lower left-hand "Marinetti." Another issue of *Futurismo* sets its message on the front page against giant orange airplanes—"Fascists, be futurists in art!"—and includes a serious philosophical article on "the political function of art."

The real-political connection between futurism and fascism is complex, partially because Mussolini eventually dropped the futurists to secure a wider base of support among Catholics and other traditional Italians. Futurism, fine for the young warrior, was an embarrassment to the postadolescent bureaucrat. This does not cancel out the extent to which Mussolini owed the futurist avant-garde for their revolutionary methods of disseminating propaganda and for their use of aesthetic and sexual criteria in analyzing social issues. One of his often-quoted lines is pure Mafarka: "War is to man what maternity is to woman."[19]

I can offer several examples of similar links between Marinetti's futurism and generalized European fascist topoi, with one important proviso. There are not always "intentions" signaled by an author or movement when futurism is recycled into fascism. At the same time, once you have read Marinetti it's impossible not to see a stylistic imprint in later fascist culture. The connections thus appear both as accidental—as culturally unconscious—and as perfectly obvious.

Futurism traveled by cartoon. I discovered this when I tried to find French accounts of Italian futurism. They are conveyed almost exclusively in comics. The obscenity trial of *Mafarka*, noted in a 1910 issue of the French theater magazine *Comoedia illustré*, is generously illustrated with the childlike cartoons of André Warnod. In 1931, *Comoedia* features caricatures of a flying Marinetti to illustrate a "Futurist Manifesto of Aeropainting." These caricatures are the work of Ralph Soupault. Soupault will continue illustrating futurist pranks at *Je Suis Partout*. He was one of the intimates of what Brasillach and Rebatet liked to call the "gang" or "soviet" there—a flamboyant excommunist with a taste for loud suit jackets, jazz, and the Marx Brothers.[20]

Indeed, Soupault makes the Italian futurist–French fascist connection for us.

The front page of *Futurismo*, 1932. Photo Beinecke Rare Book and Manuscript Library, Yale University.

He recorded, on the one hand, the futurist banquets that followed the publication of the famous "Manifesto of Futurist Cuisine" (also known as the "Manifesto Against Pasta"), but he also stylized the anti-Semitism of the 1930s with his grotesque caricatures of the Jewish millionaire, the shtetl bum, the hook-nosed parliamentarian. When *Je Suis Partout* printed excerpts from Céline's racist pamphlet, *Bagatelles pour un massacre*, the illustrations in the margins were Soupault's. The passage he took in visual terms from futurism to fascism transmuted caricature into scapegoat; in literary terms, we might think of it as parody entering the cutthroat arena of the pamphlet.[21]

Soupault's affinities aren't entirely personal. The translation of both the futurist and the anti-Semitic spirit into cartoons was guided by developments in the French press at large. The cartoon industry was booming in the France of the 1930s. It may have started with the introduction of American comic strips in 1934; it may, as in the United States, have been connected to economic depression. People needed to laugh at their worries and, perhaps, to ridicule their enemies. At any rate, 3 million comic books were selling each week in 1939, and more than 1.7 million of them were foreign-drawn. In 1939, Mickey Mouse, in his French format "Le Journal de Mickey," sold 400,000 copies: I imagine that his admirers included adults as well as children.[22] *Je Suis Partout* used three illustrators, one of whom had debuted in the "child-press." It also reprinted political cartoons from great papers all over the globe. Indeed, the favorite complaint of the *Je Suis Partout* writers about the Popular Front Government was that it had no sense of humor, no energy, no joy, and that they did.

And what could travel better, in this age of cartoons, than Marinetti's fictive heroes? With laughable indestructibility, they are smashed and stretched in fantastic machines, bullied by natural forces, and ambushed, only to reemerge for a new round of adventures: they beg to be cartooned. There's a cliché about Italian fascism that's worth noting here: this is the idea that Italian fascists weren't violent, because they didn't have an efficient standing army as did the Nazis. But the view changes once we consider that the history of violence in Italy revolves not around the standing army but around the ambush.[23] This is exactly the tradition that the Mafarka character captures so well. His storytelling techniques, like his war games, were of the sneaky kind—the result is more comic, more ridiculous, than epic.

But it is as epic that the Mafarka story, or more precisely the Gazouramah story, will reemerge out of Germany. The year is 1936, and Leni Riefenstahl is using aerial cinematography in the service of the fascist revolution. In the opening scene of *Triumph of the Will*, she places the camera in the position of a pilot flying through the cloudy heavens. For the soundtrack she uses a "total music"—the "Horst Wessel" song combined with the sounds of the airplane's engine. The plane makes the shadow of a giant eagle as it passes through clouds over a group of orderly humans marching below. When the plane lands, the

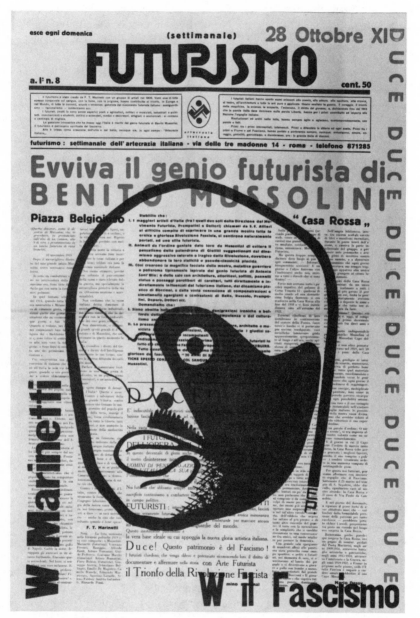

The front page of *Futurismo*, 1933. Photo Beinecke Rare Book and Manuscript Library, Yale University.

spectator learns that the "camera eye" is none other than Adolf Hitler, arriving in Nuremberg to lead his famous 1934 rally. The rest of the film will insist that the man Hitler, the party eagle, the air perspective, and the camera eye constitute one total principle of leadership.[24]

The spirit of Gazouramah, made concrete in camera and air technology, comes through to French audiences in the screening of *Triumph of the Will* at the 1937 Expo Nazi pavilion. Lucien Rebatet files this report for *Je Suis Partout*:

> Triumph of the Will . . . introduces us immediately into an epic atmosphere. The plane of the Führer, surging in the clouds, surveys [survole] Nuremberg, while a brass orchestra slowly intonates the grave and powerful music of the "Horst Wessel Lied." . . . . There is, in effect, no better initiation to Hitlerian Germany, to this sort of nascent lyricism of a gigantesque uniformity, to the spiritual unanimity of these crowds seized by the film. . . . Leni Riefenstahl "humanizes" the cult which often disconcerts by its gregarious and mechanical aspect, the spectator lost in one of its festivals. It's cinema which is in the right, thanks to its well employed ubiquity—and not the reporter armed only with his legs and his eyes.[25]

Doubtless Riefenstahl could have had no idea what an immense synthesis her film was performing of the abandonment of the earth in futurism with the return-to-earth populism of a triumphant Hitler. Even her sound is on a double track: the archaic sentimental strains of the "Horst Wessel" were voiced over an airplane engine's mechanical asides. The cinema has replaced the reporter's arms and legs with its wings: everyone can be a Gazouramah. Has the Italian ambush comic hero faded into a futurist past, only to be born again in the filming of the staid mechanical festivals, in the Nurembergs and Olympiads of the fascist imagination?

## Drieu la Rochelle

We might well assume that new economies and social structures have a way of writing themselves into new forms of literature; but to show how this happens, we must find homologies or structural relationships between lexical and political events. I suggested in the previous section that Marinetti's violent modernist prose bears some of the weight of "uneven exchange." How much can such a technical expression mean to the noneconomist?[26]

The history of capital is the history of growth. Capitalism fails unless it can expand—it must look for new sources of profit, new methods to increase production. The explorations of the Renaissance and the great technological discoveries of the nineteenth century helped move the European economy into new locations, at new rates. With the invention of the steam engine, then of electricity, came more and more authoritative machinery and less and less need for manual labor at even the most elemental stage of production—the search for raw materials. Furthermore, different parts of the world have always grown at different rates, and capitalism has depended on this unevenness for its success as much as on its advancing technologies. This is the rule of uneven development: the economy of the metropolis can only expand as long as there are less-developed places to be exploited.

By the beginning of the twentieth century, industrial machinery has grown so expensive that small businesses have concentrated into monopolies. Once the European factories are equipped, these industries cross national boundaries, colonizing foreign soil in their search for growth.

Unevenness is so pervasive that, within the realm of capital investment, there is a good deal of transfer—one kind of capital depending for its progress on investment money from another kind. In the 1870s, extra money made from the sale of consumer goods is poured into heavy industry and serves to pay for the great factory machines and railroads, which gradually come to be used in the place of manual labor. At first people produce machines; then machines produce. Purchasing machines requires an enormous capital outlay for any enterprise, but the outlay is a "one time only" investment. After they are secured, there is extra capital with no place to go. So it is poured back into the area that funded it in the first place—the consumer goods market. Economists observe a drastic upswing at the turn of the century in the production of electric equipment for individual use: they are talking about the same individually operated machinery celebrated by the futurists. That power has become electric is evident even in the prose of a back-to-the-soil writer like Barrès. Here Barrès describes the effect of a charismatic Parisian lycée teacher (and dangerous republican) on a group of provincial male students:

Ah yes! They were certainly Frenchmen, these excitable adolescents! One only had to see them, their ink-stained fingers, their humble work clothes, their chins covered with untended hairs, totally moved— electrified—by the beloved eloquence and by the great authority of the young schoolmaster: "Vive la France! Vive la République!" they cried, of a unanimous voice.[27]

Authority is electric, and electricity is metropolitan: first it takes the factories, then it enters daily lives in the cities, the provinces, the colonies.

But something unexpected happens to economic growth around the time of World War I and continues until the second war. Capital takes a dive, or rather a nap. Economists cite two factors: first, the interruption of international trade brought on by the war, and second, the removal of Russia from the world market after the revolution. Colonial profits stagnate. One compensatory maneuver is to concentrate investments even more heavily in the consumer sector. This works better for the United States than for older industrial nations like England and France. The lowering of wages by fascist governments and the propping up of production lines everywhere through arms manufacture will provide an eventual solution to this dilemma at the end of the 1930s. Meanwhile, the world economy is in crisis: for the first time since the beginning of the industrial revolution, capital has contracted.

We can infer, then, at least a historic difference between the manic verbosity of a prewar Marinetti and the frantic, gloomy backwardness and forwardness of Drieu la Rochelle, citizen of the world depression. Marinetti is determined — in manic fashion — to be on the winning end of every production, every technological arrangement. Like Sorel, he is utopian where the possibilities of machines are concerned, though unlike Sorel, he has initial affinities with the flamboyant captains of industry rather than with the workers. He exploits natural landscapes and female bodies. He is a lexical imperialist, strip-mining the exotic to empower his consumer goods.

What is extraordinary in the writings of Drieu — beyond his gloom, perhaps, but encouraged by it — is his awareness of this world economy. He is one of the few of the French fascist nationalists to look beyond the boundaries of Europe and react to a world picture. He translates an awareness of himself as an unhappy transitory figure into a study of France caught between a world of classical imperialism and one of stagnating production. He is obsessed by internationalism, what it will cost France, what France's place can be in a world economy. He slides — in melancholy, now, rather than in mania, like Marinetti — from thinking of himself as a machine or a statistic to thinking of himself as a hero. Whereas Marinetti can fantasize Italy as the center of the world, Drieu can only imagine various deaths for France and for himself. In the worst of deaths, he is a number; in the best, a martyr. He constructs fantastic homologies between his personal and political life in order to dismiss the possibility of normal happiness in either. Alienated even by his own reactions, he ties himself into painstaking ideological knots.

At the most obvious level, Drieu is a writer who can't get out of the trench. His literary career began with a small book of war poems, *Interrogation* — odes to the body of the warrior and to German, as well as French heroism.[28] A later autobiographic work, *Etat Civil*, might be seen to represent a partial renunciation of that heroic stance.[29] Drieu tries to describe himself as a statistic, as data, as the result of a certain class background and a certain time. The young Drieu liked too much to bask in the ancient-regime atmosphere of his grandparents' sitting room, pouring over illustrated books about Napoléon. Feeling tied to their France, rather than his own, he decides that he has been "born too old."

It is Drieu's melancholy, his constant sensation of unevenness with the world, that has saved him from being dismissed quite as severely as the other fascists have.[30]

First, there is the question of his friends. He consorts with the surrealists, then breaks with Aragon over his communism. He joins Doriot's PPF in the 1930s, quits in disgust, then joins again. He is anti-Semitic, yet maintains a life-long friendship with his first wife, who is Jewish, and saves her from deportation. He is committed to ambivalence. Daniel Halévy called Drieu "infinitely nuanced":[31] there is always that self-consciousness in his prose, that hint that he understands his error; that, despite his desires, he can watch himself, make himself into a statistic from a lucid outside. In the midst of a gloriously overdramatized battle scene at the end of *Gilles*, the narrator interrupts himself when he is most intensely impassioned to remark, "There will come a moment when, despite all my exorcisms, I'll still regret those movie houses on the Champs-Elysées where the view of such adventures as these is so effervescent [*émoustillante*]."[32] Critics like to point out that Drieu's fascist warrior *was* pure fantasy; that, indeed, he did enjoy the Spanish Civil War from the cushy seats of the right-bank theaters. A weakling, then—too ambivalent to live out his dreams—Drieu is for those he interests most something less than an all-out fascist.

A recent critical debate over his fascist bildungsroman *Gilles* has centered on whether Drieu "testifies"—whether he gives us information about his conversion to fascism—or whether he manipulates—giving us the information in such a slanted way that we are forced either to conclude naively that we, too, should be fascists or to conclude more sagely that the manipulation is so blatant as to be ridiculous.[33] The title of a recent biography, "The Mystified Seducer," puts this dilemma another way: Is it Drieu who is blinded—is it *his* problem—or are we blinded by him? The fact that Drieu couldn't decide between fascism and socialism and that he flirted with surrealism and enjoyed an intense male friendship with the communist writer Aragon sells books in the age of the gulag. It is more grist for a widespread suspicion about the committed literary career. Between Drieu and Aragon, between the gulag and the camps, it is possible for the critic to "cancel out" an entire generation of committed writing, to write off the connection between literature and politics as a doomed risk, as formal and personal failure.

But before writing off critical activism, shouldn't we explore the specific conditions under which instances of it have failed? We can start with the homologies in Drieu's prose. The personal is political; geography is always allegorical; even his orgasms are willfully sociological. It is nauseating. Homologies are manipulative, and they are totalizing. They convince us that "everything is part of the the same" (they are fascist). But they are also, and I think, inevitably, the incentive behind every progressive piece of literary criticism: we can't understand the text unless we read it in a larger world. Reading Drieu, then, the challenge is to demystify the homologies.

### War and Peace

The First World War, starting point of so many of Drieu's narratives, is also the posited origin of Drieu's career as a writer. The war, for Drieu, was not a fight between France and Germany but between two worlds—his grandparents' and his, between heroic deaths and statistical ones. *Interrogation*, which Drieu will later describe as "fascist without knowing it," tries to combine old world and new by celebrating the new soldier as best it can—as heroic engineer: "The new soldier will be an athlete and specialist in mechanics, not an ignorant and fearful domestic. Or he will be vanquished."[34] The restoration of the body through war, as well as the voluptuousness of wartime death, and the love of German force as well as French are proffered to convince the reader that heroism can exist in technological realms. Drieu begins his career as a futurist: the failure of that project is recounted on the eve of yet another world war in *Gilles* (1939), Drieu's account of a conversion to fascism.

At the start of the novel, Gilles leaves the trenches to come to Paris for an operation. A poetic project akin to *Interrogation* is described in the novel as a convalescent's bodybuilding exercise. In the no-man's-land between the trenches and the salons of Paris, Gilles writes voluptuous war poetry. "Far from books for three years his thinking unbound and muscled itself. He meditated on his war experience and saw that it composed a figure of life for him" (p. 65). War and death are the ultimate poetic principles for Gilles: the realms of nature, sensation, force, joy—of that one absolute death, that great expansion of everything into nothingness.

Peace, women, cities, modernity are the principles of prose, of intrigue, of parliamentarianism, and of everything else the narrator abhors. Peace is the realm of alcohol, words, money: the possibility of exchange, the spasms of orgasm—unacceptable "little deaths." And peace is "above all the kingdom of women" (p. 29).

The major driving force of *Gilles* is prosaic because it is organized around its hero's futile attempts at loving women. The search for women is not merely psychological. No political position, no narrative movement, no emotion can take place in this book without passing through an allegorical female. At the center of the allegory is the raw material of the female body. Entire narrative sequences are announced anatomically. Rebecca—"ugly legs, a low slung ass" (p. 413)—will betray his dear suffering friend. Alice—"perfect bone structure" (p. 210)—will send him soaring like a plane. Mabel—"a long stem, without thickness, ending in a face" (p. 95)—will bore him to distraction. The most veterinary exactitude of all is reserved for Dora. "This American, with her mixture of Scotch, Irish, Saxon blood, crossed and multiplied several characteristics of the nordic peoples. . . . Long legs; long thighs; long thighs atop long legs. A powerful thorax, dancing on a supple torso" (p.271). This body promises him escape out of France into a new world of animal potency.

Gilles's subsequent anxiety over the dominant female function is signaled in the novel by the appearance of *teeth*: not vaginal teeth, just oral ones.[35] Seeing two women acquaintances engaged in conversation, Gilles "felt something akin to a toothache" (p. 319). Women never want men without money and power, that is, unless "they truly have nothing to sink their teeth into" (p. 402). An angry fiancée "didn't bare her teeth at first" upon hearing that Gilles wanted to return to the front. Gilles himself is described as having an overly rounded nose—but, thank god, "blue eyes, white teeth."

Why this anatomical obsession? The clenching of teeth is both a signpost for the invasion of the narrative by female chatter and intrigue and a last-minute barricade against the inevitable—a miniscule flexing of the facial muscles against loss. And it is also, for Gilles, an attempt to remind himself of his own body, which—in spite of his numerous sexual adventures—he is not sure exists. Gilles is a character in search of a body because, as he tells us, the only body he's ever really felt was left behind on the front.

Gilles marries Myriam, the wealthy sister of one of his fallen comrades. With her, he tries desperately to abandon the trenches, to operate as an urban consumer rather than a fighter. He buys clothes compulsively. As the war rages on, Myriam tries vainly to distract his attention by involving him in furnishing their apartment. She buys him a particularly cunning armchair: "They imagined an interior together" (p. 87). An interior so different from the trenches that it bears no trace of the color of blood: "He spoke of his passion for blue. Forgetting his maneuvers, Gilles suddenly thought of nothing but visiting the decorator who had furnished the armchair" (p. 87). But the appeal of the new decorations is short-lived. Domesticity with Myriam fails because of a lack of physical passion. And with Mabel, the nurse he starts to see on the side, passion is destroyed by her own trashy American domesticity, by too much décor. Her room is filled with ridiculous childlike trinkets that cut his desire. Sitting in it, he imagines a speech he would like to give her: "You are mediocre. But you don't have a shadow of an idea of what there is in me. You don't know what *depths* I reached in myself, in the war" (p. 99).

All interiors are shallow after the trench. Even sex, especially sex, becomes a doomed attempt to wage war on higher ground:

His body expressed that furor of sacrifice which, by force of circumstances, he had asked of his own body in war. He obscurely sought its counterpart in love. Perhaps the soldier, who is not very strong, needs

Drieu la Rochelle at home, 1928. Photo Harlingue-Viollet.

to see the woman's body humiliated and hurt as his own was. (p. 103)[36]

Fearing impotence with Myriam, he tries to think of sex as "annihilating her." It doesn't work, so he returns to the front as to a better mistress, to the "imperceptible sigh of the eternal in the bosom of being," to the "beatitude of the trenches," the "hours of ecstasy" (p. 112).

It's not surprising, given Gilles's proclivity for finding bodies that designate his every strategy for mental health, that the front also houses a literal war mistress. Her name is Alice. "She was all he had sought among soldiers and girls." Just when we thought women represented the same thing—peace, prose, compromise—the poetic woman appears. A total warrior, a perfect bone structure, a pure line, her hair seems made of nets of silver (chain mail?). Tragically too old for him to be a mere wife, Alice is a grenade mother, exploding all Gilles's cynicism and remorse, reviving his "war force." The vocabulary describing their relationship, her body, and their sexuality is entirely military. She says very little, but about the war, she offers, "You love all this—so do I." When they finally come to discussing the "trivial specifications of their civilian state," Gilles discovers, in total admiration, that Alice is completely unmoved by the compromised city life: "money was a phantom for her" (p. 237). Alice is Gilles's most successful fusion. At the same time, if he were to stay with her, his story would be ruined, since its guiding narrative principle is that there really is no body for Gilles to find—that the French body, and the French soul, are dead.

The narrative principle of *Gilles* is that negative. The novel depends so much on the unsuccessful passage from woman to woman, we could argue that even the most despicable of female characters is desperately needed to breathe life into its male character; that Gilles is dead without his women to bounce off of. Their personalities completely control his attempts at existence: Myriam, the modern moneyed life; Alice, the eternal front; and then Rebecca, the bad nurse, a negative Alice who "invades" the second part of the novel in the role of lover to the neurotic son of the president of the republic.

## Against Plot

The story of Rebecca is contained in a section of the novel called the "Elysée" (the French presidential residence). It is devoted to the triumph of prose in Gilles's life. Drieu has taken the most exaggerated kind of nineteenth-century melodrama, flattened it *ad absurdum*, and used recognizable artistic and political figures in France in the 1920s with a gossip columnist's meanness to express the meaninglessness of both the artistic and the political activism of his times.

Some punks of the communist-surrealist type plot against the government. They decide to use Rebecca, a communist nurse, to seduce the president's son and persuade him to steal some important government papers from his father, thus discrediting the entire regime. Rebecca, as I said, invades the narrative: she shows up at at Gilles's apartment, his habitual restaurants, among the communists, at the scene of every petty crime and domestic shuffle. But for her occasional prompting, Gilles can hardly follow the complications of the dreadfully complicated plot line that Drieu has created. "I know everything from Rebecca," Gilles tells a friend. "Who is Rebecca?" he asks. " A little Jewish communist." That Rebecca is ugly, Jewish, Freudian, Russian, communist, and thick-legged is certainly, as Suleiman has shown so well, all too obvious proof of Drieu's attempt at manipulating his readers into coming to similar conclusions about any communist.[37] Would Drieu be trying to convince us that Jewish, Freudian communists are in control of our plot lines?

But from another point of view—from Drieu's—we can say that a man of such habitual ambivalence must have struggled quite intently to create so complete, so clear a threat as a Rebecca. Rebecca is a monster against which he must organize an equally unambivalent defense. To understand his fascism, rather than his success or failure as a novelist, we have to look at the the systems he tries to build against his own habitual unevenness.

In reaction to Rebecca, Drieu will invokes Maurras, force, and a more general principle of his responsibility as a writer, as though to say to his reader, "isn't this ridiculous story boring you too? How can we stop such petty intrigue and get on with a better novel?":

> What did this story have to do with his life? How could he possibly be involved in this . . . in such stories and people? What grotesque respect for humanity had prevented him from kicking out the door this frightful Jewess who had come to remind him of a little world he hadn't chosen, a little world of hideous weakness. Certainly he hadn't gotten involved with all that crowd except for lack of anything better, perceiving absolutely no one outside it. On the side of tradition, no one knew how to draw a decisive force from the teachings of Maurras. The Catholics were coming up with something rather unsavory: each had a more or less secret and convulsive complicity with the devil. He had vaguely hoped in moments that Galant, Caël, and their friends would succeed in fomenting some catastrophe. And low and behold, all that miserable agitation prefigured its abortion in Paul's crisis: all that the group could produce was a *fait divers* of this genre. (p. 426)

The first defense is thus "generic": Gilles must get out of the "fait divers" and into more interesting forms—catastrophe, or "apocalypse," as the following section of the novel will be called.

A second defense extends to the structure of the entire novel. Drieu's favorite rhetorical gesture is always analogical; he harnesses body, soul, and party together in individual personalities, and the personalities offer stable, tangible proof of the evils of the world. To coin an old expression, Gilles needs to feel things in his bones: fascism has to be a bodily cure against parasites. The politic is always a body politic.

Finally, when the surrealist plot fails, the son of the president kills himself, and the surrealist gang blames Gilles, Gilles will wander the streets in search of a definitive new position. He remembers his childhood under the foster care of a right-wing mystic named Carentin. His memories turn quickly to Carentin's teachings, principles of primal energy and sexual speculation.

> These little debilitated intellectuals, full of the most meaningless blather [*jactance*], were the last escapees from the villages with closed windows that he passed by when he went to see [Carentin in Normandy].[38] The old man had taught him to embrace them in all their horror. These little intellectuals were the last drops of sperm yanked from those stingy old men. If a rare door still swung open, they kept busy (with landlordly agony), by closing it off. (p. 487)

He remembered a Carentin slogan: You understand, men used to think because thinking was a real gesture for them. To think was, in the last analysis, to give or take a blow of the sword. . . . But today, men have no more swords. . . . Grenades flatten them like passing trains. (p. 487)

Being "on the right," according to Gilles's early education, means being able to think with your body instead of just with your mind. (No wonder Gilles is looking for his!)

From the insufficiency of parliamentary intrigue, Gilles returns to the basic obsession: the possibility of true combat in mechanically waged war—and the possibility of true sexuality among the machines, the possibility of truly vital thought. The only thing close to vital thought—to poetry—that he knew came from war, but according to Carentin, modern war wouldn't do. Old war, yes, was virile, swashbuckling. New war, new weapons, castrate—flatten—men. Castrated and bodiless though he may be, armed with this analysis, Gilles is at least not alone. At last, in this thought, he can belong to something, since not just Gilles, but all of France, is losing its body with him.

Gilles then remembers visiting the tired villages of postwar Normandy with Carentin. In his memory, the old man is reciting the statistics to which Gilles feels so vulnerable:

Here, you see, there were three sons killed in the war. . . . Here a cripple with two kids, a son and daughter who work in Paris. The son is married, but has no children. The daughter is living with a guy in Courbevoie, and dying with him. . . . They had children, all dead young: alcoholism and syphilis. (p. 492)

Carentin goes on to explain that war victims don't want to have children. They don't even like planting crops anymore, but do it for money, like Parisians. Gilles asks his mentor where it will all lead: "They'll be invaded. They are already. Poles, Czechs, Arabs [bicots]. But their vice immediately devours the invader. There's a syphilitic power in France" (p. 494).

Here Gilles remembers that he, too, married Myriam for money and that he has no child. What he has just called an "aborted intrigue" in the Elysée section of the novel is starting to grow into a giant abortion mill that will dominate the rest of the narrative.

### The Politics of Abortion

Abortion anxiety means that Gilles, however desperately he may try to construct a body in war poems and sexual adventures, may not really exist—that he, like France, was aborted by the war. And even if he does exist—indeed, if his problems are a lot like other people's—it may be that he can never create, that any attempt to produce a child, a relationship, a political party is doomed.

Bystanders in the novel consider Gilles a "neither nor." An old priest remembers him at school as "a man of our western provinces lost in your terrible Paris." A Catholic writer answers him, "But no, Monsieur l'abbé, he's the most perverse of Parisians" (p. 606). The exchange sounds a lot like the critical debates over Drieu in the 1930s: people couldn't pigeonhole him at all.[39]

It is interesting that Drieu's abortion anxiety surfaces with even more clarity in political discourse than in narrative. When declaring himself a fascist in *Socialisme fasciste* (1934), Drieu la Rochelle described his political reputation as that of a stillborn: "In the A. F. [Action Française] they consider me rather more abortive than devious, at *Commune* [a left publication] more devious than abortive."[40]

A 1927 series of political essays entitled *Mesure de la France* is devoted specifically to the abortion theme: it is remarkable for its global reach.[41] Indeed, of all the fascist nationalists, Drieu is the only one whose anxiety carries him outside the boundaries of France and Germany. He is the only world economist of the bunch, the only geographer. We read in his account of France's failing prestige an extended version of Gilles's personal failures. France, he argues, is no longer a great economic power, a true first world, when compared with the great producers in Russia and America. Neither do the French know the natural beauty, the pure savagery, of the third world. Economically and demographically sterile, France has filled up with other peoples' children. The demographic and the economic weaknesses work together: the French colonial empire is suffering because there isn't enough new manpower to send to the third world. Not having enough people means, first of all, filling its space with "flesh produced by the mothers of other countries. Behind us in each house in the place of he who died or he who hadn't been born was a foreigner. He was alone with the women" (p. 26): "And then, not having enough people means anxiously seeking out allies, to be no longer self sufficient and to be but part of a whole. Before . . . we gave birth to a world that enclosed all that was human" (p. 56).

Abortion anxiety, depopulation woes, fear of weakening colonies: all this discourse on abortion is not uniquely reactionary. One finds variations on it in dictionaries, and in the high school history and geography books used in France throughout the 1930s and 1940s. The discourse on depopulation and the ensuing fear of waning colonial supremacy persists from Popular Front editions well into the textbooks of the Vichy and liberation years, proof of an anxiety that surpassed even such a monumental event as the fall of France. Indeed, for the right, sterility *explains* the fall of France.

What follows is an exemplary quotation from Etienne Baron's *Géographie de la France et du monde,* a standard scholastic text of the 1930s and 1940s.[42] A passage immediately preceding this one, on the subject of French national unity, is rendered in a dry descriptive third person. Then Baron switches abruptly into a first-person plural:

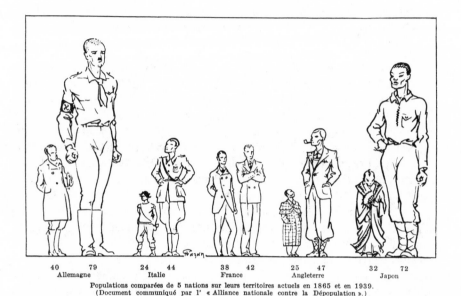

40      79          24      44          38      42          25      47          32      72
Allemagne           Italie              France              Angleterre          Japon

Populations comparées de 5 nations sur leurs territoires actuels en 1865 et en 1939.
(Document communiqué par l' « Alliance nationale contre la Dépopulation ».)

"L'Alliance Nationale Contre la Dépopulation," comparative population graph for five nations from 1865 to 1939, published in the May 1939 *Larousse Mensuel Illustré* in an article on "Dénatalité." Reproduced courtesy "L'Alliance Nationale – Population et Avenir" (formerly "L'Alliance Nationale Contre la Dépopulation").

The declining birthrate [*la dénatalité*] is a *grave danger, which risks killing our country.* Let us reflect: a) a nation where many children are born has many inhabitants, thus many soldiers to defend her frontiers. Consequently, her enemies hesitate to attack her. She then has a greater chance than another to stay at peace. If war breaks out, she has greater chance of being victorious. On the contrary, a nation which is depopulated becomes *a tempting prey for its enemies . . .* c) a nation which has many young people itself has the characteristics of youth: force, élan, the ability to get enthused over an ideal, the spirit of initiative, the taste for risk, the necessary audacity to dare and succeed in difficult enterprises; a set of qualities that we designate to-day with the word *"dynamisme"* . . . . d) A nation which counts many young people among her own will not only be able to conquer the colonies, but people them. . . . On the contrary, a depopulated nation is *invaded as soon as there is peace by foreigners* who establish them-selves in it as farmers, workers, businessmen, and her colonies, if she has any, know the same invasion. e) A depopulated nation *can not send emigrants to foreign countries*, they who spread her language and augment her prestige, etc. France already suffers from several of these evils. She *doesn't send emigrants to foreign countries* (except a few

Basques to Argentina) *nor colonizers to her colonies* (only a few thousand a year to North Africa). On the other hand, *foreigners are establishing themselves in France.*

In the childish world of the geography book, simply making babies would offer France a solution. But for a cynical Drieu, a postwar France can no longer be a glorious whole, only a partial object, condemned to federate with foreigners or die. Perhaps the most devastating aspect of his global analysis is the way it interferes with his patriotism and forces him to revise his understanding of the First World War effort. The war, Drieu decides, had very little to do with Germany and France. Their age-old quarrel was used by the English to help test English hegemony against an eventual threat from the new Russian, Japanese, and American superpowers. Drieu then needs to rewrite *Interrogation* as a Franco-German exercise in masochism: "I resent the democracy for having flagellated my fantasy for four years" (p. 64). The blame lies not with England but with England's ability to pass off its defense of imperialism as a defense of democracy. Uneven exchange strikes again.

Still the alienated spectator of *Etat civil*, Drieu will try to transform his masochism into his own perverse version of "human geography." The machine society (of which British imperialism is a symptom) enforces negative genetics: instead of producing children, Europe produces machines and discovers, too late, that what they do best is kill. Germany is even more a victim of the new mechanical illusions than France: "produce, produce, no matter what (and take pleasure [*jouir*] no matter how, in lost moments)" (p. 79).

Hence the double bind that Baron's book dare not mention. Colonialism is an outgrowth of production and requires new population for its labor, but there aren't enough babies because the world of overproduction is a masturbatory world: "jouir n'importe comment." The old sword phallus has been, as it were, squeezed out by trains transporting produce to the colonies. There is only time for orgasm in lost moments.

In the time of Napoléon, writes Drieu the historian, the production of babies was a joyous business. Now, babies are doomed to empty assembly-line production. However much he is morally opposed to sterility, Drieu finds himself here taking the Malthusian position—overpopulation in the colonialist era is going to be overpopulation of the "lowest forms of life." Making babies these days is indistinguishable from making machines: because production and reproduction have ceased to be different, it is better not to reproduce at all. "We are not coolies. We can't produce workers and soldiers indefinitely. Someone had to stop first, and we're a logical people" (p. 85). Again, Drieu has written himself into a bind, a kind of intellectual abortion: the zeroes on the population figures for Asia and Africa are meaningless. Civilization "doesn't count" there. But at the same time, how can France fight these great virgin lands, these infinitely expanding capital resources, these enormous chunks of populace, without its own babies and its own war machines? Drieu whips himself again: isn't it the very surfeit of French logic, as he is demonstrating, that is responsible for zero growth, decadence, sterility, and a total lack of that vital imagination that France needs? In a desperate recuperative effort, Drieu works up some last-ditch futurist affection for machines:

> Certainly human activity seems without goal and differs little from the machines decried here. I've caressed motors that were beautiful beasts. If the objects that they produce are still-born, miserable abortions, the machine itself is a living masterpiece. . . . Its movement intoxicates me and leaves a trace of regret. (pp. 112–113)

France has to figure out its "wedding" [*épousailles*] to the machine. It must understand the general worship of production (in Russia as much as in the United States) that is threatening to reduce everyone, middle class and workers, communists and capitalists, to "stockholders of modern industrial society": "There is no more *peuple.*"

The leveling of the classes in modern production gives Drieu an idea, a tentative answer: couldn't the classlessness of the world of production be turned into an advantage for a new populism—neither capitalist nor communist, but some third spiritual party that might resuscitate the people? The fantasy involves the victims of capitalism finally putting their suffering to good use:

> All we can imagine is that capitalism would become so tyrannical, so blindly anarchic, that the whipped masses react and throw themselves into the arms of certain bourgeois who, by wisdom, have separated themselves from their own class affiliation. (p. 109)

Returning to the novel with this train of thought as a guide, we aren't surprised to find that its conclusion involves first a retreat from parliamentary Paris to the production vortex of the French colony, and then a euphoric bout with the populism of "whipped" veterans.

Drieu's Gilles goes to Algeria looking for spiritual and sensual renewal. There, of course, waits a woman embodying colonial purity, and colonial availability—Pauline, a little bit Spanish, virgin and "poule" at once. She has "the élan of savages," the passion of Spain, and a refreshing lack of taste. He takes her to Paris as his wife and impregnates her. "How," writes Drieu "could [Gilles] think about the depopulation of France? What was a thought next to a child?" (p. 565)

But Pauline, like the Czechs, the Poles, the Arabs of Carentin's warning, also becomes impregnated by the bourgeois putrefaction of Gilles's metropolis, which soon seeps through to her internal organs. Gray tones shadow her amber skin. She is extremely ill. The doctor diagnoses a fallopian inflammation and warns that the fetus will have to be sacrificed. The operation-abortion reveals worse—a fatal cancer. "Cases of cancer in a 30 year old are rare and mortal," concludes Drieu, thus tying Pauline's death to the year 1934, and to the fate of the nation in the subsequent narration of the riots of February 6.

So as the parliamentary world, more and more sterile, ambles toward the Stavisky revelations, Pauline takes morphine and takes Gilles back to his less ennobling memories of Verdun. As she dies, the Stavisky riots offer him a last flow of life. He is "dead for women," but alive for fascism. When his sometime ally, Clérences, fails him, France dies for him too. February 6, the early heart-beat of an authentic French fascist populism, ends in a national abortion.

To remain a fascist, Gilles must leave the country. The epilogue of *Gilles* is nothing less than a rebirth, though it is so cutoff from the gloom of the preceding chapter, so religious, as to smack of a pastiche, or at least of a self-consciously "stillborn" attempt to conclude. Gilles reappears as a character named Walter, a secret agent fighting for Franco in the Spanish Civil War. He is finally himself; above all, he is finally creative. His happiness is just as he imagined it in his most fervent moments of nostalgia for the first war. He is able to extend war's voluptuousness throughout his own body. Consequently, he no longer desires women. "Madly himself," Walter's body is a grenade, "projecting, smashing him against a savage death" (p. 686). Citing Dionysus and Christ as his models, Walter faces death prepared to be reborn. A final religious allusion says it best: Gilles hears the cry "Santa Maria" and chants to himself "the mother of God, the mother of god made man"(p. 687). Since killing is the ultimate creative male act, killing makes man a mother.

But let's not forget that odd phrase from this section with which I began, that reminder from narrator to reader that Gilles is not so easily removed from his own ambivalence: "In spite of all my exorcisms, I shall still regret the cinemas of the Champs-Elysées, where one has such an exciting view of just such adventures" (p. 682). The phrase is like a prick of the balloon to the solemnity of this entire end narrative; the writer's warning to the reader not to "believe" in his newfound commitment. And it is also a clever device to keep Gilles's fascism from being too slick, a way of maintaining some continuity with the earlier, ambivalent character. Drieu la Rochelle had written in *Mesure de la France*, "I feared that the [first] war was a cheap spectacle, like the movies" (p. 24); he has decided to write the fear into the character of Gilles.

One way to read the Champs-Elysées quip is to contend that Drieu was never *really* a fascist, since he only sat back and fantasized the action. But isn't he telling us, too, to pay attention to fascist fantasy, to the way he sat back? His ability to experience the voluptuousness of war depends upon a *real* institution—the movie theater. He enjoys war more when he thinks of himself as the hero of a war film. So a second interpretation of Drieu's relationship to fascism, and the one to which I subscribe, is the following: the very things that make Drieu's fascism interesting—his distance and ambivalence, his alienation from his own image—also *found* his fascism as a spectacle.

## Céline

It is possible to write brilliantly about Céline's style without mentioning his on-again, off-again enthusiasm over Hitler or even his anti-Semitic pamphlets. Or one can quote his most clearly racist ravings without acknowledging or caring about what is most "radical" in his style. When you try to read Céline criticism, you discover "critical pluralism" and "critical specialization" at its most intense: the syntactical Céline of the linguists, the mad Céline of the psychoanalysts, the hateful Céline of the moralists rarely meet. Or one can choose to write about Céline by writing like him. Unlike the writing of Brasillach or even of Drieu, Céline's writing is in and of itself, and at the level of syntax, an important cultural event recognized by his earliest readers. This intense literary recognition of Céline by critics differentiates him from the other repressed and abandoned fascist writers we have discussed, and presents a number of complex problems for an ideological analysis that have not been encountered thus far in our study.

The biggest problem in writing about any of the critically recognized Célines is figuring out what technical languages to call upon and which passages to call up in support. If you quote an anti-Semitic passage, chances are you can find another sentence in the same paragraph or chapter, or certainly in the next book, that will contradict it.

In *Bagatelles pour un massacre*, for example, Céline states that Jews pervert direct emotion.[43] This seems near enough to the standard racist attack on Jews as hard-hearted, rootless intellectuals. But as one reads on, Jews become indistinguishable from the surrealists, and even from the Soviets. In the course of the text's long lists, everyone becomes "jewified" until the identification of Jews is impossible. "Jewification," in *Bagatelles*, takes place "up the ass"; Jews are excrement incorporated—the "ex" become "propre"; the dirty, clean. The play on the polarity "propre/sale" describes the insidious contamination by the Jews; those to whom nothing truly belongs must ap*propri*ate. The repetition of the word *juif* throughout the text, accompanied by differing, even contradictory, modifiers is quite typical of Célinian "délires." Céline has a talent for cancelling out his most meaningful errors, in self-ridiculing repetition, before you can safely categorize them. This is not the self-deprecating distancing of a Drieu but an apocalyptic verve closer to the spirit of orgy than to that of suicide. Hopping around from one statement to another, spreading the possible culpability of the Jews so that it covers the entire metaphoric range between "clean" and "dirty," his ravings declare their own ridiculousness, their own eccentricity. Céline puts the reader in a state of confusion as to the seriousness of the claims at the same time that he presents them—gives them voice, noise, energy. This kind of spread renders Céline's pamphlets impervious to thematic political analysis *at the same time that it constitutes their persuasive ground.*

Julia Kristeva's recent work avoids the hyperspecialization Céline has tended to engender in critics. Céline belongs for Kristeva to a larger crowd of modernist revolutionaries who explode paternal meanings and "de-center" the speaking subject, revealing all the wondrous energy and rhythms that poetic language does not owe to those constructs. This explosion corresponds to the great institutional crises of the twentieth century—drugs, the youth culture, the women's movement. If, however, such poetic energy passes over into the realm of action, Kristeva believes that it is likely to nourish psychosis, or even totalitarianism or fascism. In the twentieth century, she writes, you can't describe these dangerous truths without falling into their errors. Suffering from the truths they liberate, Artaud and Mayakousky commit "big errors," live with "big madnesses." Céline's error is fascism: "Do not all attempts, in our own cultural sphere at least, at escaping from the Judeo-Christian compound by means of a unilateral call to return to what it has repressed (rhythm, drive, the feminine, etc.), converge on the same Célinian anti-Semitic fantasy?"[44]

The picture is transhistorical. Using Georges Bataille's anthropological term *abject* (a term for excess of excretion that remains undefined within the subject-object structures of Western philosophy), Kristeva traces the leftovers of Western reason from the Bible, through Freud, and up to the twentieth century, in which abjection enjoys a special dominance in literature. "Since at least Hölderlin, poetic language has deserted beauty and meaning to become the laboratory where, facing philosophy, knowledge, and the transcendental ego of all signification, the impossibility of a signified or signifying identity is being sustained."[45] If we think about Céline in these large icon-philosophical categories—the destruction of reason, preoedipal truth, the impossibility of the signifier—it is then impossible to call Céline a fascist without also thinking of him as a champion of our Western dilemma—as the person who explains the dangerous rigidity of empirical thinking, and whose style might liberate us from it. It is impossible not to love this Céline. Indeed, Kristeva suggests, people who don't like this kind of modern literature are resistant to many wonderful preoedipal rhythms and pleasures, resistant to a certain kind of energy that is ultimately revolutionary.

The steps of Kristeva's argument lead us from preverbal sputter to the modernist canon. Thus, in her recognition of an abject primitivism on the part of Céline and the various experimental modernists with whom he is placed, we find a highly sophisticated critical reenactment of the same alliance forged by the modernists themselves in their various homages, copies, quotations, and appropriations of primitivist art forms. Kristeva's rescue of Céline depends on an appeal to his primitivism—this has, for her, an aesthetic value that the political culture of the 1930s (read fascism) inevitably misuses. By distinguishing modernist from fascist culture, by lauding a literary expression of the primitive or abject, Kristeva has temporarily rescued modernism from its own historical misadventures in the service of bad politics.

Canonizing Céline with the modern primitivists, Kristeva saves him from fascism without having to deny his fascism or apologize for it. She thus makes him readable for a new generation of theoretically oriented intellectuals interested in exploding various forms of meaning. And because Céline really does have specific historical ties to fascist politics, it is a good thing that the Célinian writing forms canonized in that theory are stripped of a coherent ideological subject. The aesthetic links in *Powers of Horror* are specifically to prehistorical, authorless forms of language production: individual human and chronological variants of the newborn, preoedipal childhood and prehistoric mythologies. Historical context drops out of the picture with the modern-primitive equation, and Céline can resound with universal aesthetic value.

The primitivist-modernist link she makes, however valuable for having made Céline readable in a very new sense, entails nonetheless several problems for the understanding of Céline's fascism. First, its obvious ahistoricity: when one leaves the canonized modernists in order to study the fascist readership of Céline, one learns that the fascists' pleasure, too, was as deeply tied to Célinian syntax as to his reactionary themes.[46] Second, its core of mystery: fascism is evoked in Kristeva's text as philosophic inevitability. Modernist writing is granted a kind of compensatory universal value; its occasional links to fascism are introduced as "error," dissociable from a modernist agenda assumed to be aesthetically radical.

Is Céline a modernist? He explodes the sentence, fragments the story line, exaggerates and distorts temporal and spatial perspective. This is not the "clean" fascist modernism of a Marinetti, merely resituating the subject from atop a skyscraper or in an airplane, but rather a willful disorientation of reader and writer. Céline wants literature to "stink," to "ooze": he wants to reconstruct it. His characters—how much, one can argue, like the Jews of a more traditional anti-Semite's worst fantasies—are continually wandering, obsessed with death, destruction, and failure. Yet at the same time they are received by their readers as embodying something deeply national: the eternally disgruntled Frenchman, full of complaints, argot, and the occasional literary aside—the wandering *rouspeteurs*. There is a subject being built in Céline's early novels, a speaking subject, living in the impoverished peripheries of the city, the *Zone*, or in some imaginary *îlot insolubre*. The subject is not at home; he is out slumming, "hanging out in the suburban slums, his 'genre."[47]

The link to institutionalized fascist nationalism is not obvious at the level of style. Unlike a conventional fascist ideologue who posits a whole, healthy body, an authoritarian voice-body alliance, Céline is constantly digging away at the body in these texts. He is taking swipes at it, concentrating on its excrements, its losses. His characters are either diseased or in the process of contaminating themselves. Céline's society is built on disease. Disease, he lets us know, is the only thing that levels all society's classes to the same base. A base unto death. Ferdinand Bardamu, the narrator of *Voyage au bout de la nuit*, says that when he has trouble with rich people—and he often does—he undresses them. Then he can look at them for what they really are, what they will be—maggots. In fact, we learn from him that an attentive person can even perceive this rotting principle at work just by listening to people speak:

> When you stop to examine the way in which words are formed and uttered, our sentences are hard put to it to survive the disaster of their slobbery origins. The mechanical effort of conversation is nastier and more complicated than defecation. That corolla of bloated flesh, the mouth, which screws itself up to whistle, which sucks in breath, contorts itself, discharges all manner of viscous sounds across a fetid barrier of decaying teeth—how revolting! Yet this is what we are adjured to sublimate into an ideal. It's not easy. Since we are nothing but packages of tepid, half-rotted viscera, we shall always have trouble with sentiment. Being in love is nothing, it's sticking together that's difficult. Feces on the other hand make no attempt to endure or to grow. On this score we are far more unfortunate than shit; our frenzy to persist in our present state—that's the unconscionable torture.[48]

The important moment in Célinian language is the moment of loss; the separation of words from the mouth being reminiscent of the body's daily losses. Speech casts doubt on the body's integrity even as it offers proof of the body's existence. But this moment of loss is also the great moment of leveling—the ultimate basis of human sociability and, as far as Céline is concerned, the real "raw material" for storytelling.

Storytelling in Céline begins as a diagnostic activity. When Ferdinand's patients describe their illnesses, they do so with an extraordinary energy—a kind of total expenditure: "ça gémit . . . ça rote . . . ça titube . . . " What the original French shows better than the English [rendered by Manheim, "they moan . . . they belch . . . they stagger . . ."] is that their cries are indistinguishable from their diseases.[49] The "ça" here can refer to the patients' bodies—pustulating, belching, staggering—to the equally pus-like words they "belch" as they report their illness to their doctor, as well as to the doctor-narrator's own manner of description. You can't attribute the verbs either entirely to speech or entirely to disease. Just as the work of voice is excremental, so is the work of the body. Céline's constant verbal ritual is to recover the lost connection between the two. In social terms, this means letting the body talk by indulging in that age-old form of popular entertainment: complaining about illness. The neighborhood doctor, the medicine man, the midwife know that storytelling and symptomatology are linked. Céline belongs to their tradition.

Disease and loss are what is most socially and linguistically "alive" in Céline's stories. People are so entertained by their own slow deaths, we learn, that they don't need to go to the theater. But death becomes entertaining only through the institutional function of the sentence. In *Voyage au bout de la nuit*, Ferdinand makes fun of his American lover, Lola, for spouting "Coué method" rhetoric. The Coué method was a popular positive-thinking cure of the 1930s. You chant to yourself: "Every day in every way I'm getting better and better," and you do. Gustin Sabayot of *Mort à crédit* announces his rather different motto to its narrator: "Ah, getting a kick out of his death while he's busy manufacturing it: that's Man for you, Ferdinand!" (p. 25).

In *Voyage*, Ferdinand Bardamu's pal Robinson gets himself hired by a couple to kill their old mother. "A hundred francs for the wood and two-fifty for my work and a thousand more for the idea" (p. 264). The thousand-franc plan is to plant some firecrackers on a rabbit cage in the garden so that they will explode in the old lady's face the minute she opens it. But as Robinson is completing his deathly installation, the rabbit moves, and the bomb explodes in his own face. The old lady runs to fetch Ferdinand to make a house call: for the first time in years, she is vital, energetic. Ferdinand points out that she no longer believes in her own death; what has taken over that belief is her constant babble. The moment of recognition in Céline—the only really constructive moment—is always both a recognition of death and a breach of silence that violates death by the telling of a "phony" story—the story of catching death in a trap, seeing and saying one's death over and over again:

> "My death!" Grandma Henrouille was shrieking now. "That's some-thing I want to see! Do you hear! I've still got my two eyes! I want to get a good look at it!" She never wanted to die! Never! That was defi-nite! She had stopped believing in her death. (p. 279)

Céline's characters will never tire of recounting their own death. That this simple fact quite literally inaugurates Céline's style can be seen by studying a text he composed before he took his literary pen name, a medical essay signed "Dr. Destouches."

## Tripe Talk

In 1924, Céline-Destouches completed the thesis requirement for his medical degree with a biographical study of a medical hero.[50] Philippe Ignace Semmel-weis (1818–65) was a Hungarian physician who discovered how to prevent puer-peral fever, ordinarily called childbed fever. The extraordinary part of the dis-covery was that Semmelweis had no knowledge of germs—this was left to Pasteur. Nonetheless, by careful observation of his surroundings, Semmelweis was able to conclude that childbed fever was being transmitted to women by "something" on the hands of the doctors who were helping them deliver. Women whose deliveries were assisted by midwives simply didn't contract the fever as often. Semmelweis's hypothesis was confirmed by a tragedy. One of his doctor friends, Kolletchka, cut himself during an autopsy and died of the same disease as the cadaver. Semmelweis was then able to connect the women's death to the hands that touched cadavers. Wasn't Kolletchka's open wound as vulnerable as an open womb? Following his intuition, Semmelweis tried to persuade his fellow doctors to scrub carefully between leaving the autopsy table and delivering babies. His idea was met with hostility, and he was ostracized from the hospital where he worked.

Céline's interest in Semmelweis's life is highly romantic. He admires the doctor for rejecting the conventional scientific "truths" of his age and listening to his intuitions. His Semmelweis is not so much the discoverer of the truth as he is someone who suffers for his truth. Even Semmelweis's genius is attributed to a passion for humanity rather than to conceptual skills:

> As far as he was concerned, he had no ambition, nor did he have that worry over pure truth that animates scientific researchers. One can say that he never would have gotten onto the path of research if he hadn't been lead to it by an ardent pity for the physical and moral distress of his patients. (p. 51)

The idea of a Semmelweis uninterested in method seems extremely odd today, when philosophers of science use Semmelweis's work on childbed fever as a major illustration of modern scientific inquiry.[51] Semmelweis's thought process supplies the philosophy of science with a model of hypothesis testing.

Destouches concludes from his analysis of the Semmelweis discovery something rather different: that finding the truth leads to rejection, to madness, and to death. (This is the part of the story upon which the science manuals, though they refer to the "martyr of modern medicine," don't dwell.) In his final days, writes Destouches, Semmelweis occupied himself by wandering the streets and posting notices warning families against using doctors to deliver their babies. He dug at the walls of his room, looking, he said, for secrets buried there by a priest he knew. He turned against all his former friends.

Employing unusual narrative technique for a dissertation, Destouches describes Semmelweis's downfall as though it had just been told to him by someone at the scene of the crime:

> Around two o'clock, he was seen roaming through the streets, pursued by the horde of his fictive enemies. Raving, disheveled, he managed to arrive at the Medical School's anatomy amphitheater. A cadaver was there, on the marble in the middle of a class, for a demonstration. Semmelweis, grabbing the scalpel, broke through the circle of students, and knocking over a few chairs, approached the marble, sliced

the skin of the cadaver and before you could stop him he was digging into the putrid tissues, detaching in shreds muscles that he threw into the distance, by chance impulses. He accompanied his maneuvers with scrambled exclamations and phrases [d'*exclamations et de phrases sans suite*]. . . .

The students recognized him, but his attitude was so menacing that no one dared interrupt him. . . . He didn't know what was going on. He took up his scalpel once more and dug, with his fingers at the same time as with the blade, a cadaverous cavity dripping its humours. With a gesture more brusque than the others, he cut himself deeply.

His wound bleeds. He cries out. He threatens. They disarm him. They surround him. But it is too late. . . .

Like Kolletchka before him, he had just infected himself mortally. (p. 90; ellipses are Destouches's/Céline's)

Destouches's first Célinian narrative didn't go entirely unnoticed in the medical community. Reading an abstract of "Semmelweis" in a medical journal, the Hungarian editor of Semmelweis's complete works wrote in response that the entire scene around the cadaver was "purely imaginary." Semmelweis, it seems, had died because a tiny undiscovered wound that he contracted while performing surgery went untreated. This was discovered long after his institutionalization.[52]

Destouches was thus so interested in constructing a self-fulfilling diagnosis that he modified the facts of the Semmelweis biography. In Destouches's mind, Semmelweis had to inflict a wound upon himself in public, rather than merely contract a wound accidentally. He had to announce in this way that his truths were deadly, and he had to die from what he had discovered.

It is this martyred man, punished for knowing the truth of death, who is championed in Céline's powerful language and convincing scenery. More important, perhaps, in accounting for the transformation of Dr. Destouches into writer Céline is the fact that the situation of martyrdom produces what we will come to recognize as the characteristic Célinian sentence, the technique. He accompanied his maneuvers "d'exclamations et de phrases sans suite [with scrambled exclamations and phrases] . . . ": confrontation with death in Céline always produces a language (already marked here by the characteristic three dots) akin to those germs whose existence Semmelweis understood without ever proving, except by his own death. The three dots represent here—perhaps for one of the first times—physical and vocal guts and muscles. As Semmelweis lay dying in the asylum, tripe-talk continued. Semmelweis indulged in "incessant verbiage. . . . His shattered head appeared to empty itself in long dead phrases. . . . Death seized him at the throat" (p. 77).

In *Mort à crédit*, we see the development of tripe-talk into something funny and fantastic. The principal raver here is a curate or "padre," as Céline's translator dubs him. He comes to visit the shop of inventor Courtial des Pereires (to whom the narrator is an apprentice), hoping to sponsor a contest for an invention that can suck up hidden treasures from underwater shipwrecks. The initial description of his verbal style echoes the images of the guts that Semmelweis flung from the cadaver. This is so much the case that when the translator of the American edition looked for an American equivalent of the narrator's contention that the curate is "bullshitting" [*il déconne*], he chose the phrase *Some tripe!* to introduce the following description: "He spoke in long bursts. . . . You had to catch his words in full flight, the sentences came out in tangled bundles . . . . full of knots garlands, and throwbacks . . . and loose ends that went on forever" (p. 426).

The curate's sentences come out something like the treasures he wants to recover. It is not precisely that he speaks his desire, but rather that his desire bursts from his body in neverending succession, in contorted shapes that imply the intestinal confusion of his needs, as well as their goal. Courtial, a conman in the tradition of the late nineteenth-century medicine show, proves to be up to the curate's game and manages to construct an elaborate on-the-spot verbal treatise on the subject of deep-sea divers: names, dates, and bibliographic sources that cause the curate to *burp* with joy. This is the gist of the scholarly gesture in Céline; it will surface again in *Bagatelles pour un massacre* in the stringing together of tens of anti-Semitic quotes, themselves already pilfered out of context by other anti-Semitic writers.[53]

The curate returns several weeks later to inspect the progress made on his proposal. Because of the enormous crowd of consumers that has been flooding Courtial's office with regard to his "perpetual motion machine" contest, the place is a shambles: "torn papers, disemboweled books, putrid manuals, manuscripts, memoranda, all reduced to streamers . . . clouds of flying confetti. . . . The bindings all ripped, thrown in all directions (p. 441).

It is not the intestinal images per se that are important in the juxtaposition between *Semmelweis* and *Mort à crédit* and between these texts and *Bagatelles pour un massacre* as much as what we might call a decaying positivism, that obsessive interest in disintegration that keeps the writing close to the body. The curate is fascinated by so much disconnected text in the same way that Dr. Semmelweis was fascinated by a cadaver, and Ferdinand the pamphleteer by his quotes. He takes his own papers out of his briefcase, adds them to the mess on the floor, and proceeds to rub himself in them:

> Plunging his head into the papers. . . . He sniffs at the piles. . . .
> He grunts, he puffs and blows. . . . He picks up a whole armful
> and . . . whoops! . . . he tosses them up in the air. . . . He flings
> them at the ceiling. . . . It all comes raining down . . . papers,
> folders, plans, pamphlets. . . . They're all over. (p. 441)

And it goes on and on, as the curate "howls with joy." Meanwhile, an enormous crowd — a real vaudeville audience — is collecting outside the window to the office. Several police inspectors arrive, pin down the priest, and cart him away, explaining that although he's a real priest, he's an insufferable *escroc*.

The curate disappears from the story until the day after Courtial's suicide. Courtial, disgruntled at the failure of yet another scheme (a farm-camp for children) has run into the woods and shot himself in the mouth in such a way as to spill parts of his body outside himself, leaving the narrator to collect and arrange his corpse underneath a blanket.

The curate appears out of nowhere as if to celebrate this dissolution. He insists on inspecting the body and treats it in the same crazed manner as he did the papers in the shop; sniffing at it, rubbing his hands and face with it, digging into it, and throwing pieces of it against the wall of the barn where it was being kept. The description is nearly an exact repetition of Semmelweis's death scene, with an even greater complicity on the part of the narrator. The narrator describes the actions of the curate with the same frenzy with which they are being executed:

> He plunges both hands into the meat . . . he digs into all the
> holes. . . . Crack! . . . He tugs. . . . He struggles like in a
> trap . . . some kind of pouch bursts. . . . The juice pours
> out . . . it gushes all over the place . . . all full of brains and
> blood . . . splashing. . . . He manages to get his hand out. . . . I
> get the sauce full in the face. (p. 560)

The curate is someone who can only glimpse pieces of himself, scattered on the outside. Starting with his body, which he loses in constant emission and convulsions (even burps), this subject, as hero of Céline's text, seems only to exist as a kind of smear across the page, and thereby joins with a perfect consistency the rhythms — fragmented but repetitive, disparate but rapidly multiplying — of the sentences themselves. The curate's ecstasy is like the writer's; he "smears" Courtial, making Courtial's fate similar to that of the narrative. By violating the cadaver, the curate does not succeed in "killing death" (old lady Henrouille's fantasy); he merely extends it throughout his world — he amuses himself by playing with it.

Céline complains in *Bagatelles pour un massacre* that literature has become an odorless corpse, more "deceptive" than the greenest "charogne" (literature now looks as dead as an oozing carcass looks alive): "Literature, in sum, deader than death, infinitely" (p. 172). Céline has made the corpse of literature "ooze" again — he has brought it to life. It is not the death of the traditional French sentence that is at stake in this new style but the death of "dead letters," "deadening forms." The curate sniffs at his papers hopefully, just as Semmelweis rummages in the cadaver's guts. In the interpenetration of the body of the text with the human body, there is an implicit demand that language recuperate the lost body behind expression. Death, in the form of the cadaver or the rotten papers, is confronted only somehow to be saved from its incomprehensible finality in the spreading and smearing of the dead thing's entrails, guts and words, its leftovers and traces. Céline posits death as "truth," and yet by insisting and digging at whatever is leftover after death, by refusing the finality – not just of death but, in strictly textual terms, of narrative endings and of the break between sentences (and, in the pamphlets, between quotation and comment) – by dressing most of his tableaux with excrement, smells, blood, and sweat, he is demonstrating the lack of satisfaction that "every body" feels with the boundaries between life and death, possession and loss. For a sixteenth century Rabelais, excretory functions were life-affirming.[54] Here we find loss circulating as the lifeblood of the text. Roudiez has pointed out that Céline's interest in childbed fever is an interest in an event by which life is destroyed at its origins by the living germs of cadavers – death, as it were, actively punishes the bearers of new life.[55]

In Céline's stories, death must be repeated because it is not understood; but because it is not understood, it is repeated as something else – as a refusal of death itself, as the repeated denial of death by the offering of death's remainders – guts, blood – as loss recuperated by the narration as a nourishment for the crazed subject.

### The Big Lie

We discover something else about Céline's narrative strategy by comparing the medical martyr Semmelweis with the more purely fictional Courtial. We know that both Destouches and Céline are interested in moments of invention. Scientific discovery in Semmelweis is both joyous and deathly. The Courtial character is an inventor too, and he is based upon a real fellow, Raoul Marquis – alias Henry de Graffigny. But Marquis-Graffigny was no icon in the history of science. He was a people's scientist, director of a review of scientific vulgarization called *Eureka: The Magazine of Invention*. The magazine was full of harebrained schemes and suggestions, just like Courtial's *Génitron*.[56]

Courtial, then, belongs to a tradition held dearer by the writer than the doctor. His twentieth-century being marks a transition from an age of tinkers and popular showmen to one of entrepreneurs and entertainment engineers. Clothed in the garments of the nineteenth century medicine man, Courtial is in a sense both ahead of his time and already obsolete. He invents lies about technology and offers to his crowd of followers dreams about the mastery of the universe. He ends up creating only chaos and destruction. He offers only products that don't work – houses that move and collapse with the wind, pamphlets for the assembly and repair of bicycles he's never seen – with all the good faith of the prophet. Courtial's own life is overspent: for every lie that brings him the trust and pennies of the public, he spends double at the races, placing himself in such preposterous debt that each of his promised inventions must be even more earth-shattering than his last. He finally devises the series of contests for the invention of a perpetual motion machine and a diving bell. While his machines are quaint, his manner is already modern: he teaches his followers to do the lying for him; he fosters a society of liars.

Courtial, Ferdinand of *Voyage au bout de la nuit* and *Bagatelles*, and Semmelweis thrive on the ethnographic-diagnostic idea. Once the defecatory reality of human existence and of language have been assimilated into the rules of narrative, it no longer matters whether the idea is "true." Lying is, in a sense, true. It needs only to be set off by a search. It needs only the trappings of authenticity to flourish.

The "big lie" is thus the weighty responsibility of narration, or, as Ferdinand complains in *Voyage au bout de la nuit*:

> there seemed no possibility of my ever managing, like Robinson, to fill my head with one single idea, but that one superb, a thought far stronger than death, and of my succeeding, just with my idea, of exuding joy, carefreeness, and courage wherever I went. A scrumptious hero! (p. 431)

Courtial's last grand idea, the one he dies from (the one worth death), has to do with the death of the individual and the energy of a new force, the pseudofamily. The pseudofamily is made up of those people who gather in huge bunches any time there's good show in the streets: an arrest, an act of violence, a fight. In a sexual fantasy at the beginning of *Mort à crédit*, a mob fight has to be cleared away by 250,000 policemen on the Place de la Concorde (the locus, we remember, of the February 6, 1934, riots). The point is that the curious crowd exists, ready to gather at a moment's notice: it's only a question, for Courtial, of convincing them of their family resemblance. "The individual is washed up!. . . . You won't get anything out of individuals. . . . It's to the family, Ferdinand, that we'll have to turn! Once and for all, to the family! Everything for and by the family!" (p. 496; ellipses are Céline's). The scheme that follows this revelation is, interestingly enough, not a family romance but a parody of a fascist youth corps. Courtial grows "radio-telleric" vegetables by wiring potato fields and invites city children to a camp program called "Renovated Familistery for the Creation of a New Race." His publicity attracts a crowd of tough urban youngsters—escapees from the Zone—who soon organize into a successful band of truants, pilfering food throughout the countryside while pitiful radio-telleric potatoes rot in the field. Here Courtial has finally understood his times. He has made the transition from individualist chicanery to demagoguery, from romantic to futurist, from shaper of machines to people mechanic. After several of the children are arrested, he commits suicide. Semmelweis found a truth and died of it; Courtial died of a big lie. Both kinds of death produce goodly amounts of tripe-talk and social diagnostics.

## The Political Sentence

How might the reader of Céline historicize this body of work?

First, by recognizing that along with all the death and excrement in Céline's novels, within the abject, there is something being built. Céline is a raconteur, a comic, a grand storyteller. Always the practitioner of "social medicine," he lets people tell what ails them. Consequently, the stories, long diagnoses, resemble each other. In the construction of his sentences, as of his characters, we get an unusually vivid idea of a modern urban "mass"—bodies squished together in the modern city, living too close to each other and to each others' deaths. Though war plays a role in death (especially in *Voyage*), death takes place more often than not in the little enclaves of Paris; death resides in the kinds of neighborhoods where stories are not generally deemed worthy of being told.

Second, with the stated goal of communicating sentences as he might have heard them in those drab streets, Céline radically alters written French syntax. And does it in such a way that the sentences don't end up resembling recorded dialogue so much as they build a new kind of language that exudes, from within its planned anarchy, the authority of a masterpiece. And he is a success. He writes in a way that makes it desirable for generations of writers after him to do the same. He "discovers" a way of writing as surely as Semmelweis discovered the cure for puerperal fever, and as surely as Courtial discovered the radio-telleric vegetable. And that way of writing is profoundly national: it is nearly impervious to accurate translation in other native slangs.

This Céline was welcomed onto the literary scene as a grass-roots literary populist. Intellectuals on the right and the left alike (people unusually prone to feeling alienated from the streets) welcomed the opportunity to relearn the language that their university training had denied them. Simone de Beauvoir writes that she and Sartre memorized passages from *Voyage au bout de la nuit* and chanted them to each other, much as the fascists I discuss in the next chapter chant passages from *Bagatelles*.[57] In other words, there was something in Céline's writing that led to its being learned and "told" to others, which resuscitated an age-old oral tradition French letters had lost. Let's retain the gist of the appeal: that explosive modernism and street sense work together in Céline's writing. What makes him avant-garde is the same thing that makes him national; this is precisely where his populism verges to the right.

This assessment is not entirely dependent on biography, although it can be supported biographically. Céline definitively rejects communism after a trip to the Soviet Union. But he never is much of a fellow traveler anyway. He simply

The Big Lie: Céline at a lecture in the Institut Anti-Juif, 1941. Photo Roger-Viollet.

doesn't like the left establishment in Paris, any more than he likes the rich. At the same time that the Popular Front is building low-income housing in Clichy, Céline is rebuilding his fictional *taudis* in *Voyage*. He's attracted to the martyrdom of the angry common man more than to any party or doctrine, left or right. He constructs races, then picks them apart. He makes as much fun of Doriot and de la Rocque as of Blum. But this is not to underestimate his usefulness to the right, despite his own masterful political incoherence. Céline makes available to right-wing culture its first real twentieth century alternative to the Action Française. When Céline collapses Maurrasian classicism with Jewish style in *L'Ecole des cadavres*, Brasillach groans that he's finally gone too far: "We find it in extremely bad taste that *L'Ecole des cadavres* asks Maurras—someone who is guilty of too much moderation—whether or not he's a Jew."[58]

But what Céline is offering the fascist right (and it would be up to an intellectual historian to gauge the extent to which the right took him up on his offer) is a chance to differentiate itself from that lucid, classical Maurrasian right, from right-wing aristocracy and right-wing lucidity. With Céline, the right can reject the aristocracy for "the people" and still stay on the right. A right ready to embrace Céline can gain countless ideological privileges. It can be earthy; it can speak with the voices of the people; and, at the same time, it can ally itself with forces of regeneration in French prose: it can be culturally avant-garde. Losing Maurras, it loses its stuffiness. Being a racist à la Céline is not the same as being a blue-blooded snob. It has the very different cachet of desperate revolt, the heroic edge of a lifesaving measure taken against a deadly parasite. Céline's fascism, read in the novels of the 1930s, lies in his populist combination of the ethnographic and diagnostic gesture: the discovery of the low life, the production of the germ.

Partly because of the authority of Kristeva's reading of Céline, we have come to think of him primarily as an international writer, a prophet of apocalypse.[59] Does this picture change when we concede how deeply his modernism is tied to the Frenchness of his sentences? You can come out of reading Céline celebrating the marvelous materiality of language, the liberating effect of the rhythms of the avant-garde, or you can come out of it convinced of the vitality of France, of the Frenchman in the streets. Imagine, for a moment, a right-wing populist reader's response: Whereas Drieu warns him that the French body is sterile and dying, a quick read of Céline can reassure him that it isn't quite so. The Frenchman, he decides, is simply not going to die without a fuss. He'll go down screaming, and the screams will entertain the world. Our reader may feel too stubborn to join any party. Nonetheless, he's got his voice, his right to complain. Aren't they in his literary family, these characters whose speech has blood and guts, but who are too just-plain-French ever to have been sung in any body politic? Here's the voice in *Bagatelles*:

> I never microphonized, macrocosmized [*micronisé, macronisé*] in meetings! . . . (. . .) I've never signed a petition . . . for the martyrs of this . . . the torture victims of that. . . . They're always about a Jew. . . . from some yid or masson committee. . . . But if it were about "tortured" me, poor simple jerk of an indigenous Frenchman . . . no one would cry over my fate . . . no petition would circulate to save my bones. . . . (p. 45; ellipses in parentheses are for deleted material; other ellipses are Céline's)

It's hard to separate the pulsing joy of Céline's neverending sentences from the resentments that fuel them. It's hard to disengage the whiny "what about me?" from the more cosmic pleading, calling, and crying—from the magisterial force of everything that voices and bodies can do. Does this mean that identity is somehow exploded here? The force of a single one of these sentences might well convince a fascist reader, contrary to the suicidal pronouncements of Drieu or the theoretical claims of Kristeva, that "the people" really do exist, that in the face of great odds they are livelier than ever. An ideological reading need not ignore the fact that Céline's poetics are anything but spontaneous or crude; they are all the more extraordinary given their effect.

In the next chapter I'll take a look at a specific reader who is "buoyed up," who is, in fact, "micronisé," in just this way by the Célinian sentence.

## Notes

1. See Marianne Moore's *Futurist Art and Theory, 1909-1915*. Moore's discussion of Marinetti's fascist enthusiasm is limited to her contention that Marinetti upheld an avant-garde spirit in the face of Mussolini's dreary traditionalism *in spite of his fascism* (see note 3, p. 33). Marinetti's American translator and editor, R. W. Flint, believes that "the Futurist cult of 'synthetic' verbal violence, of 'war, the world's only hygiene . . .' is the greatest obstacle to the understanding of Futurism" (p. 7).

But if this American critical position appears reactionary, it is not "simply" reactionary. On one account, American critics who defend Marinetti are fighting on the progressive side of an "in-house" culture battle with their Italian colleagues. Some critics believe Marinetti was repressed by the postwar Italian literary establishment not so much because he was a fascist as because he was experimental. That his fascism was used largely as an "alibi" for a repression of his modernism seems apparent to the extent that adherents of fascism in the traditionalist camp (such as Pirandello and Umberto) continued to be read throughout the guilt-ridden 1950s. When the complete works of Marinetti were edited and published by De Maria in 1968, they were attacked by the conservative right as neo–avant-garde, and attacked by the left as fascist. See Flint's introduction to Marinetti's *Selected Writings* for an account of futurism's current cultural standing in England, France, Italy, and the United States.

2. F.T. Marinetti, *Mafarka le futuriste*. Page references to the novel will appear in parentheses following the passages cited. "The Founding and Manifesto of Futurism" is reprinted in Marinetti, *Selected Writings*, p. 41. The manifestos will be cited according to this edition, hereafter referred to in the notes as SW.

In an earlier, rather different version of this study of Marinetti entitled "Futurism and Fascism: Reflections on the 70th Anniversary of the Trial of *Mafarka the Futurist*," pp. 39–56, I discuss the fact that *Mafarka* earned Marinetti an obscenity trial in Milan in 1910 and that Marinetti used the occasion to outline the political and literary goals of the futurist movement.

3. James Joll, "F.T. Marinetti: Futurism and Fascism," p. 142.

4. See Sigmund Freud, "The Relation of the Poet to Day Dreaming (1908)," pp. 44–54.

5. See my more extensive use of this term in the section of this chapter on Drieu la Rochelle.

6. This is the question that Turner asks of Nazi culture. See Chapter 1 ("Theoretical Voices,").

7. In the Icarus myth, the daring son fell to the sea, and the father, Daedalus, survived.

8. Folder 3, series 4, box 16, "Mafarka," in the Marinetti archives.

9. SW, p. 75.

10. Ibid., p. 87.

11. Marinetti, *Les Mots en liberté futuristes*, p. 18 (Marinetti's emphasis). Translations from this text are mine.

12. Ibid., p. 22.

13. "Electrical War" (1911–1915), p. 106.

14. Ibid., pp. 53–54.

15. An undated, unpublished letter from F.T. Marinetti to *La Revue Bleue* (probably a draft) beginning "Je me hâte de vous exprimer. . . " Quoted by permission of the Beinecke Rare Book and Manuscript Library. My translation.

16. "Against Amore and Parliamentarianism," p. 75.

17. Mino Somenzi, "Aerovita," p. 6.

18. Anacleto Tanda, "Il Duce Aviatore," p. 7.

19. Quoted by Max Gallo in an epigraph in *L'Italie de Mussolini*, p. 308. Gallo dates the quotation May 26, 1934.

20. An interesting selection of cartoons depicting the futurists is reprinted in Giovanni Lista, *Marinetti et le futurisme*. Lista's anthology also contains several short essays on Italian futurism's committed fascist phase.

21. Pierre-Marie Dioudonnat, *Je Suis Partout*, describes the strange careers of *Je Suis Partout* cartoonists Soupault, Hermann-Paul, and Philippe Larquier (who signed, à l'américain simply "Phil").

Soupault's first drawings appeared in the official communist paper *l'Humanité*. In the 1930s, he broke with the communists and joined the ranks of Action Française, illustrating a number of royalist and extreme right publications. He joined *Je Suis Partout* in 1938 and supported its fascist line until the very end of the war. He was an active member of Doriot's P.P.F.

Hermann-Paul was the oldest illustrator of the three, part of an earlier generation of painter-engravers. At the turn of the century, he had been an antibourgeois Dreyfus supporter. World War I is said by Dioudonnat to have converted Hermann-Paul to a right-wing posture of anti-German, anti-Semitic nationalism: however strange this double hatred of Jews and Germans may seem, it is characteristic of an Action Française style of nationalism.

Of "Phil," Dioudonnat notes only that his political drawings retained some of the spirit of the children's publications in which he had made his debut.

22. The circulation statistics come from *Histoire générale de la presse française*, pp. 600–603. The comic strip is referred to in this volume as "the revolution of 1934" (p. 602).

23. My perception of an ambush tradition came to me through helpful discussions with Paolo Valesio.

24. An excellent print of *Triumph of the Will* is available for study at the Museum of Modern Art in New York. See also Richard Meran Barsam's *Filmguide to Triumph of the Will*, an analysis of the film followed by a translation of its script.

25. François Vinneuil [alias Lucien Rebatet], *Je Suis Partout*, August 20, 1937, p. 2.

26. What follows is my attempt to transpose some of the theses of Ernest Mandel's *Late Capitalism* into the simplest of narratives. I hope that curious readers will consult this brilliantly nuanced work.

27. Maurice Barrès, *Les Déracinés*, p. 34.

28. Pierre Drieu la Rochelle, *Interrogation*.

29. Pierre Drieu la Rochelle, *Etat civil*.

30. See Dominique Desanti, "Remerciements," in *Le Séducteur mystifié*, pp. 439–45. In the guise of an annotated chronological bibliography of work on Drieu, Desanti gives an excellent account of Drieu's rehabilitation in postwar letters.

31. Daniel Halévy, preface to Pierre Andreu, *Drieu, témoin et visionnaire*, p. 12, quoted by Frédéric Grover, *Drieu la Rochelle and the Fiction of Testimony*, p. 26, and by Robert Soucy, *Fascist Intellectual*, p. 4.

32. Pierre Drieu la Rochelle, *Gilles*, p. 682. Subsequent page numbers from the Gallimard/Folio edition will be noted in parentheses in the body of the text.

33. Susan Suleiman, "Ideological Dissent from Works of Fiction," reads *Gilles* as unreliable narration. The opposing viewpoint is asserted in Frédéric Grover, *Drieu la Rochelle and the Fiction*

*of Testimony.* Grover, writing in 1958, had the arduous task of making a political *persona non grata* acceptable on literary merit. Suleiman's task in 1976 is rather to make political narratives like Drieu's formally interesting to a theoretically oriented audience.

34. The retrospective comment on *Interrogation* is from Drieu's *Socialisme fasciste,* p. 220. The passage cited is from *Interrogation,* p. 62.

35. I thank Phil Watts for first pointing out to me the surfeit of teeth in this novel. They are so obvious as to be almost invisible.

36. Drieu's sexual fantasies are closer to those of the German Freikorps officers studied by Klaus Theweleit than to those of the other French fascists in this book. His conventional writing fits the patriotic and anguished postwar genre better than does fellow veteran Céline's. Notice, however, the careful, clinical interpretative distance that Drieu as narrator takes from his character's problems—as though to assure a readership that his most irrational needs are well under control, or at least that he is appropriately disgusted by them. "Every time that Gilles tries to be sincere, it turns into a manipulation" (p. 134). Drieu, unlike the freikorps officers, is always performing for an intellectual audience.

37. I refer the reader to Suleiman, "Ideological Dissent," for a useful close reading of the descriptions of Rebecca.

38. Gilles's denunciation of "jactance" echoes Sartre's line on Sorel's "bavardages fascistes." I've been tempted from time to time to argue that "discretion" is an aristocratic right-wing value and that "idle talk" is a left-populist one. The Drieu and Sartre quotations would argue against me by demonstrating how an "empty language" accusation can be put to work by any ideological camp against any other.

39. See Marc Hanrez, ed., *Drieu la Rochelle,* for a broad assortment of prewar and postwar positions on Drieu.

40. Drieu, *Socialisme fasciste,* p. 241, in a chapter entitled "Itinéraire" (pp. 219–245).

41. Pierre Drieu la Rochelle, *Mesure de la France.* Subsequent page references to this edition will be noted in parentheses in the body of the text.

42. Etienne Baron, *La France et ses colonies* (Paris: Magnard, 1936) contains less frantic passages on slow population growth and rising immigration (pp. 201–5). The passage quoted here is from Etienne Baron, *Géographie de la France et du monde* (Paris: Magnard, 1943), pp. 79–80; the same argument occurs in his *Géographie générale* (Paris: Magnard, 1942), p. 167, and *Histoire de la France* (Paris: Magnard, 1941), p. 416. Baron, professor at the Lycée Rollin, directed a successful collection of geography books for the Editions Magnard, a publishing house of primary and secondary school textbooks founded in 1933. In a publicity brochure for the publishers' fiftieth anniversary, Louis Magnard describes Baron as "a delicious man, great pedagogue. . . his expositions flowed like limpid water. A friend of Anatole France, he shared his alert, evocative style" (Harold Portnoy, "Entretien avec Louis Magnard," p. 36). I am most struck by Baron's ear for fashionable (and ideologically overdetermined) neologisms: according to the *Petit Robert,* the word *denatalité* didn't come into the language until 1939. Baron's remark that *dynamisme* is a word in vogue is probably a reference to the trickling down of Bergsonism. *Élan* is another Bergsonian buzzword.

43. Louis-Ferdinand Céline, *Bagatelles pour un massacre.* Subsequent page references to the 1937 edition will appear in parentheses in the body of the text.

44. Julia Kristeva, *Powers of Horror,* p. 180.

45. Kristeva, *Desire and Language,* p. 145: "Since at least Hölderlin, poetic language has deserted beauty and meaning to become a laboratory where, facing philosophy, knowledge, and the transcendental ego of all signification, the impossibility of a signified or signifying identity is being sustained."

46. This is the subject of my next chapter.

47. Céline, *Journey to the End of the Night* (originally published in 1932 as *Voyage au bout de*

*la nuit).* Page references in the body of the text refer, if not noted otherwise, to the Manheim translation, though the title will be given in French. Here the translation is my own and refers to *Voyage au bout de la nuit* (Paris: Gallimard/Folio, 1952), p. 203.

48. *Voyage,* p. 291.

49. Céline, *Death on the Installment Plan,* p. 24 (originally published in 1936 as *Mort à crédit).* I will refer in parentheses to page numbers from Manheim's translation; the title will occur in the text in French.

50. Céline, *Semmelweis.* Page references will appear in parentheses in the body of the text.

51. See Carl G. Hempel, "Scientific Inquiry," pp. 3–18.

52. This 1924 letter from Tiberius de Györy, Professor at the University of Budapest, is reprinted in Céline, *Semmelweis,* pp. 94–95: "Everything having to do with Semmelweis's last days must also be modified. The whole scene around the cadaver is purely imagined. The truth is that Semmelweis carried with him into the asylum a little wound, nearly undiscovered, which came from the operating table and whose consequence was the fever of resorption, pyoemie, the same ill against which he had fought all his life."

53. For a documentary study of Céline's use of quotations in *Bagatelles pour un massacre,* see my forthcoming "Citations et sources dans L.-F. Céline, *Bagatelles pour un massacre.*" Publication schedule did not permit me to include my findings here.

54. See Bakhtin's gloss in *Rabelais and His World,* p. 317: "eating, drinking, defecation and other elimination . . . all these acts are performed on the confines of the body and the outer world. . . . In all these events the beginning and end of life are closely linked and interwoven."

55. Leon S. Roudiez, "On Several Approaches to Céline," pp. 94–104.

56. Céline contributed a translation to *Eureka.* He and Marquis joined the Rockefeller commission together, touring Brittany in search of tuberculosis. Destouches was lecturer and interpreter, Marquis a mechanic. See Dauphin and Boudillet, *Album Céline,* pp. 54–55.

57. Simone de Beauvoir, *La Force de l'âge,* p. 142: "The book that counted the most for us that year was Céline's *Voyage au bout de la nuit.* We knew a bunch of passages by heart," quoted in the annotated bibliography of Le Roux, "Louis-Ferdinand Céline," p. 328 (the translation is mine).

58. Brasillach reviewing *L'Ecole des cadavres* in *Je Suis Partout,* February 17, 1939.

59. An additional quote from *Powers of Horror,* p. 207, demonstrates in how broad a context she places him: "On close inspection, *all* literature is probably a version of the apocalypse that seems to me rooted, *no matter* what its socio-historical conditions might be, on the fragile border (borderline cases) where identities (subject/object, etc.) do not exist or only barely so — double, fuzzy, heterogeneous, animal, metamorphosed, altered, abject." Since this text on Céline was completed, several important books have appeared in France which have served to complicate and enrich the critical picture of an apocalyptic Céline. Philippe Muray's *Céline* (Paris: Seuil, 1982) is a convincing account of Céline as the inheritor of both nineteenth-century positivism and racism. As this manuscript goes to press, Henri Godard's landmark *Poétique de Céline* (Paris: Gallimard, 1985), shows us a Céline who skillfully manipulates the various and distinct registers (archaic, popular, oral, bourgeois) of the French language, and who sets into play, with increasing intensity, the miniscule details, references and *fait divers* of his epoch.

# Chapter 5
# Broadcasting: Rebatet

The cult of Céline was led by the most unequivocally fascist of the "tempted" intellectuals of the 1930s, Lucien Rebatet.[1] Rebatet was a professional journalist who got his start, like his better-known colleague Brasillach, as a culture critic at *Action Française*, and who went on to write film and theater criticism cum anti-Semitic diatribe for *Je Suis Partout*. Rebatet's other affiliation was relatively uncompromising—he wrote for *Radio Magazine*, "the great weekly of the wireless," which was founded in 1922 and which, with several other periodicals that had sprung up around the new medium, served radio listeners with program schedules and light criticism. Of the two journals to which Rebatet contributed, *Radio Magazine* reached more people. Its circulation was, by 1933, 200,000 — approximately twice that of *Je Suis Partout*. Although *Radio Magazine* advertised regularly in *Je Suis Partout*, connections between the two journals are far from evident. What follows is an attempt to make a broader ideological link not only between Rebatet's work in radio and in fascism—between his two journalistic affiliations—but between the circulation of two kinds of "talk": fascist talk and radio talk. Together they constitute a translation of fascist ideals into technological action.

Colleagues at *Je Suis Partout* as well as friendly rivals in their respective literary columns at *Je Suis Partout* and *Action Française*, Rebatet and Brasillach are said to have raced one another to see who could print the first review of *Bagatelles pour un massacre*.[2] Brasillach won, and this first statement of his on the pamphlet was far from being overwhelmingly enthusiastic. Rebatet's one-upmanship with Brasillach consisted of Rebatet quite cleverly choosing not to

(Dessin inédit de Lortac.)

**INDUBITABLE !**

— *Papa ! encore un conférencier proboche, qui parle français avec un accent nasillard...*
— *Un accent... « nazillard » ?... Pas d'erreur possible : c'est Berlin !*

Cartoon by Lortec; father and son listening to a broadcast's "accent nas(z)illard." From *Radio Magazine*, 1933. Photo Bibliothèque Nationale, Paris.

describe the book but to describe reading it. In a January 21, 1938, review, he explains the book's effect on a group of writers at the paper:

> There are a certain number of us on this paper who, for the last two weeks, have made a Baruch out of Céline's latest—*Bagatelles pour un massacre*. To say that we have read it signifies nothing. We recite it, we proclaim it. If we haven't already sold 500 copies of it, it is then the case that we don't exist, that no one is listening to us.[3]

Céline's pamphlet has become the occasion for a collective, oral reading—a blessing—and a sales "jingle": "let us read Céline in chorus. . . . I want to make you hear . . . this joyous and formidable voice" (Rebatet's review, p. 8).

Five weeks later, *Je Suis Partout* actually reprints a number of passages from *Bagatelles*.[4] An introduction explains that the deed is being done upon the urging of readers of Rebatet's review. The reprint starts with the phrase "You are going

The first visitors to the 1937 Exposition. At left, Nazi pavilion; at right, Soviet pavilion. Photo Collections Viollet.

to see anti-Semitism," the phrase that *concludes* Céline's own saga of the genesis of his anti-Semitism.[5] Céline's story goes something like this: a Popular Front administration refuses to accept the narrator's ballet-drama for production in the 1937 exposition. The martyred narrator then screams to his Jewish agent, "You are going to see anti-Semitism," and the raving begins. The phrase is both a simple "entrée en matière" and a guarantee of the "visibility" of the racist invective that follows. In the pages of *Je Suis Partout*, it becomes an editorial promise.

What is dropped out of *Je Suis Partout's* quotation is Céline's use of the Exposition of 1937 as the "breeding ground" for his reactionary anti-Semitism. And no wonder: Céline's exposition prose "exposes" the difference between his understanding of France's ideological dilemmas and that of *Je Suis Partout*. *Je Suis Partout* gains polemically by omitting Céline's reference to the exposition in its excerpt from the pamphlet.

The 1937 exposition itself looked like an ideological map of the 1930s. It housed Picasso's *Guernica* in a pavilion of the doomed Spanish republicans; it introduced to the French public Riefenstahl's *Triumph of the Will* on the oversized screen of Albert Speer's Nazi pavilion; its Soviet and Nazi buildings, an architectural anticipation of Arendt's "twin" theory of totalitarianism, faced one another from either side of the Eiffel Tower. From its inception, the exposition was a favored topic for political journalists of all persuasions; there was probably not a single ideological alternative in the France of 1937 that was not worked out in some statement about it.

*Je Suis Partout* was obsessed with the efficiency of the exposition, complaining that the French workers—members of the Confédération générale du travail (C.G.T.), the union supporting the Popular Front—were incapable of opening the exposition on time and that the Exposition of 1937 would be the Exposition of 1938. To their delight, the Germans and Italians brought their own (fascist) workers, and their pavilions opened before the French ones. In the pages of *Je Suis Partout*, one can find endorsements of the Nazi pavilion as against the French ones, ridicule of Blum's organization of the exposition; but nowhere does one find (as one will in Céline) a radical critique of the *notion* of exposition. Indeed, a well-mapped space full of oversized ideological marker-monuments, banners, slogans, and every conceivable visual demonstration of nationalist spirit was exactly what Brasillach admired in his visits to fascist Germany and Italy. For *Je Suis Partout*, the exposition would fail only by not exposing enough.

The "official" posturing on the exposition, as exemplified in an introduction to a photographic account of the event by Albert Laprade (general inspector of Beaux Arts and chief architect of state buildings and national palaces), reveals some interesting ideological anxiety about the stylistic and political influences being exerted on the French through other participating nations.[6] The French national aesthetic has assumed in the Exposition of 1937 a position somewhat like the spatial one of the Eiffel Tower. Although Eiffel's child of the Exposition of 1889 remains, in 1937, the geographically central emblem of French sponsorship of the expository space, Laprade notes (and Céline will complain in *Bagatelles*) that the tower is the marker of a distant exposition, a dated technology, an old (republican) nationalism. The new nationalisms represented by the Soviet and Nazi buildings confront the French just as they flank the old tower. And they confront the French not so much with a choice between communism and fascism as with their either/or-ness, their inevitability as models: "Above all, French architects fear that they'll be reproached for copying their neighbors" (Laprade). What new space could the French create which wouldn't look either embarrassingly Bolshevik or fascist?

Laprade goes on in "La Trop Belle Exposition" to describe the general mood of the exposition in a manner that inadvertently "quotes" each dreaded building's ideology:

> The 1937 Exposition is the very precise reflection of our "state of the soul, circa 1937." In it, in the midst of a generalized lack of discipline, one can discern a very vivid sort of aspiration toward "some-

thing else," as yet vague. Toward the grandiose, the off-the-scale, toward order and heroism, toward the ideal—toward solidarity and social consciousness . . . As a consequence of economic and political troubles, one can see mixed in with the currents of "pure technique," explicit currents of nationalism. . . . The world, divided into teams, is acquiring a taste for a life of danger, egoism, intensity. (Laprade)

Order and heroism on the one hand, solidarity and social sensibility on the other; this combination of a nationalist and socialist rhetoric suggests that, for Laprade, the Popular Front exposition that failed to expose a specifically non-Bolshevik socialist aesthetic may instead have exposed a nation caught, like the Eiffel Tower, between two untenable alternatives. The immanent synthesis of these rhetorical poles is, of course, none other than a national socialism or a fascist socialism—a "state of the 1937 soul" far from what Laprade had in mind.

Céline is anxious about the exposition, not because of what it projects (which is what bothers Laprade), but because of what it hides. The only thing he shares with the *Je Suis Partout* group is his view of a Jewish-dominated exposition administration. There the similarities stop. For Céline, the exposition is not a successful ideological space but a pathetic attempt to blind the city to its real economic woes. Céline cannot look at the exposition without thinking of another commercially defined, restricted space, the "Passage Choiseul" where he grew up. With the memory of that commodity cathedral, he starts to associate the city, the crowds, the immigrants, the bad air, the rot beneath the exposition's lies. The exposition becomes for him a perverted celebration of the hyperurbanization, the internationalization, and the resulting denationalization of France that he holds responsible for the rot: the city is his *antipatrie*. It is on the subject of the responsibility for this *antipatrie* that Céline's discourse swerves from a hyperreal description to a racist reification of blame. The exposition is a Jewish internationalist cover-up, a spatial equivalent of the Jewish assimilationist newspaper *L'Univers Israélite*, the society columns of which Céline starts to quote in pagelong chunks because, he says, the paper is an extension of the exposition. He fantasizes his own exposition. No pavilions, only a simple engineering feat: the extension of the Seine to the sea. The sea is the only suburb that can purge the overcrowded city of its evils. Then, in a moment of identification with the enemy, he remembers that the Jews understand flight, just as they understand the need for social reform: "They're the ones who should be thinking about dismantling Paris . . . The Sozial! The Sozial! . . . it's easy enough to say. But the 'sozial,' first and above all, is a question of air and of corpuscles" (p. 240). The problem with the socialist exposition is that it has absolutely no social benefits. It exposes the socialist officials at their hypocritical worst.

Céline on the exposition is thus at his most sympathetic and his most offensive at once: the disappointed radical, the tired slum doctor, the city-living countryside nostalgic, the racist. The exposition is a fantasy machine that manages to refigure his disappointment as racism.

So by erasing the exposition from its quotation of Céline, *Je Suis Partout* erases the suggestions in the midst of Céline's racist text—however associative those suggestions might have been—of historic factors at work in aggravating his anti-Semitism; of anti-Semitism as a complex reactive social structure nourished in a conceptual neighborhood, serviced by fear and loss; a structure that Céline's language practically begs the reader to map as symptom, as displacement, as need, and that Rebatet's review of the book, so intent on "using" *Bagatelles* for oral pleasure, must deny: "For my part, I greatly appreciate that Céline, faced with the Jew, superbly refuses discussion. The christian is not a Talmudist" (p. 8).

The cartoon caricature of the Jew in *Je Suis Partout's* March excerpt from *Bagatelles*, then, has an important function. It is the token substitute for the repressed context of anti-Semitism. It replaces those ravings that might give the attentive reader some sense that anti-Semitism, like other diseases, has what public health officials call "etiology": causes, origins, and reasons that can be studied. Instead of reasons for hatred, it offers exaggeration of the hatred itself. By distorting the image of the thing hated, it offers a reward to those who hate in the form of pleasure and laughter.

The satiric political cartoons in fascist Paris move slowly but surely in the direction of racial stereotyping and voodooism. A few weeks after the Céline excerpt is published with illustrations by Soupault, more drawings star in Rebatet's special issue of *Je Suis Partout* entitled "Les Juifs et la France." In 1941, and now under a Nazi administration, the same genre of images is institutionalized—and proffered for its scientific value—in a section of the Palais Berlitz Exposition "Le Juif et la France" entitled "Comment reconnaître un Juif" (How to recognize a Jew). That title was already familiar to the intimates of Parisian anti-Semitic circles via the pseudoscientific musings of "ethnologist" Georges Montandon, author of a 1940 pamphlet entitled *Comment reconnaître le Juif,*[7] which included numerous quotations from *Bagatelles pour un massacre* and *L'Ecole des cadavres* in an attempt to give a "moral portrait of the Jew." In 1943, Montandon became the official racial theorist for the Commissariat général aux questions juives and was paid both by officials and by potential victims (in bribes), for examining citizens suspected of being Jewish.[8] The same year that Montandon ascends to officialdom, an occupation edition of *Bagatelles* appears announcing a supplement of twenty photographic illustrations (actually issued with sixteen).[9] Among the photographs: a caricature of Anatole France from *Le Cahier Jaune* (an anti-Semitic periodical published by the same group responsible for the Palais Berlitz Exposition); a photo of a rabbi attributed to a 1940 *Paris Match*; portraits of two "typical Asians"; two Hassidic Jews labeled "two Polish Gaullists 1943"; and so on. A veritable racist scrapbook, carrying

C'EST UNE NÉCESSITÉ POUR TOUT FRANÇAIS DÉCIDÉ
A SE DÉFENDRE CONTRE L'EMPRISE HÉBRAÏQUE
QUE D'APPRENDRE À RECONNAITRE LE JUIF

FAITES RAPIDEMENT VOTRE INSTRUCTION
EN CONSULTANT CES DOCUMENTS.

Display at the Palais Berlitz Exposition, "Le Juif et la France," Paris, 1941–1942. Photo courtesy Centre de Documentation Juive Contemporaine.

the often self-ridiculing parodies in the text of *Bagatelles* even closer to the kind of pseudoanthropology so dear to Montandon and company.

Empirical traces of solidarity between Céline and the racial professionals are easy enough to locate. In an undated letter to Sézille, director of the Berlitz Exposition, Céline asks why his pamphlets aren't for sale at the exposition book-shop.[10] Céline's signature (along with Rebatet's) is noted in the exposition's dedication book.[11] Indeed, as early as 1939, Céline's interest in a racial cause emerges in an exchange of letters between the director of the Welt-Dienst (or Service Mondial—an anti-Semitic press agency financed by the Nazi party of Er-furt) and Georges Montandon.[12] Montandon is uninterested in subscribing to the Welt-Dienst newsletter until he is informed that he is being solicited upon the recommendation of L.-F. Céline. He then responds with a flourish, "Since it's my friend Céline who recommended me, I'm going to go over to the bank to buy my subscription to the Welt-Dienst." Céline, then, in a worldly rather than a textual sense, is responsible for putting a German racist organizer in cor-respondence with a French one.[13]

Along with this provocatively literal correspondence, however, we must note the symbolic ones: the communication of racism from genre to genre (mad pam-phlet to political cartoon to journalistic endorsement and back to the actual exhi-bition of racial images in the pamphlet) and from milieu to milieu (artistic to journalistic to pseudoscientific to institutional). So many flexible "recognitions" of a Jewish enemy.

In this atmosphere of racist escalation, Rebatet keeps thinking about

Lucien Rebatet, autographing *Les Décombres* at the Librairie Rive Gauche, 1942. Photo Harlingue-Viollet.

*Bagatelles.* His next comment on the text appears in his memoirs, *Les Décombres*, published the year of the Palais Berlitz Exposition. Rebatet now understands *Bagatelles pour un massacre* as a monument to what he names elsewhere in the book a fascist "golden age of invective" (1942, p. 52; 1976, p. 54) during the Popular Front:

> For two years, we had been talking at *Je Suis Partout* about the Jewish, democratic war. We were marvelously well acquainted with its doctrines [*nous les connaissions*], its agents, its preparation. We had welcomed Céline's *Bagatelles pour un massacre* with a joy and with a limitless admiration. We knew pages of it [*nous en savions*], and 50 of its aphorisms by heart. (1942, p. 72; 1976, pp. 74–75)

What has changed from Rebatet's spontaneous reception of the pamphlet in the 1930s to his monumental reading here? First, he accounts for the long term effect of his reading experience. When the text is committed to memory, it is transformed from battle cry to aphorism. Aphorism, in turn, is set against a degraded, ostensibly Jewish notion of "doctrine," synonymous in this idiolect with parliamentarianism, sophism, rhetorical inflation. On the level of the sentence, the transfer of credibility from "doctrine" to "aphorism" actually takes place by the shift from *connaître* to *savoir*—knowing Jewish doctrine is tantamount to recognizing a Jew, while knowing the pages of Céline is an empirical advance. (This difference between *connaissance* as habitual knowledge and *savoir* as fact is a nuance in the French language that every American student struggles to learn.)

By using *connaître* for his acquaintance with what he deems a false Jewish doctrine and using *savoir* for his knowledge of the writings of Céline, Rebatet has mimicked, in a single sentence, the essential achievement of fascism: *he has placed invective on the side of science.*

And very literally so, for Rebatet, who soon after the fall of France is busy expanding his work from writing about radio to radio broadcasting. He is the critic who often signs "Vinneuil" in homage to Proust's musician Vinteuil—who likes to read out loud, loves simply to talk, to play his voice: "I always loved to speak in public, I was ignorant of stage fright, my golden voice carried a long way" (1976, vol. 2, p. 143). (In French, "ma voix cuivrée" suggests a voice with the power of a brass instrument, not at all the pejorative American sense of a "brassy voice.") Rebatet takes his technical radio training in 1940 and describes it in somewhat Delphic terms: "I was ardently initiated into the little secrets of radiophonic style, into its shortcuts and its necessary simplicities" (1942, p. 488; 1976, p. 546). In August of that year, Rebatet joins the Vichy Journal de la Radio. Though he soon quits the station in disgust and leaves Vichy to pursue a less compromised style of collaboration in occupied Paris, his method tells us much about his longing to project an authentic fascist voice in France:

> We forced ourselves not to let a single quarter of an hour go by without recalling the exact causes of our defeat, the ravages of Israel, the democratic dupery, the cynical egoism demonstrated by the English in multiple proofs . . . [We set out to] break the French of the habit of ignoble paraphrases, the "it is believed to be known that . . ." the "it could be the case that . . ." with which our toxic predecessors were accustomed to enveloping their venom. (1942, p. 488; 1976, p. 546)[14]

Like any new technology, radio created a need for what it could satisfy—in this case, amplified, telephonic invective. As it unleashed an uncritical social fascination with the transmission of voice, it encouraged an individualism of linguistic groups—it fostered a notion of the nation as a group of like speakers. In the France of the 1930s and 1940s—the France that has received masses of immigrants from eastern Europe and Germany—radio is an available interpretive instrument for xenophobic diatribe, for the protection of one imaginary tribe against another.

Anti-Semitism is expressed through social critique of the radio as a sonar interference–a disruptive voice. (And, by a bizarre morphological, or should I say phonological coincidence, the word *parasite*–the traditional anti-Semitic trope for the role of the Jew in the host country–enters the French language of radio transmission in 1928 to mean, figuratively, any noise or static that prevents reception of a radio broadcast.) "Radio had a Yiddish accent," Brasillach complains of the Popular Front stations in his memoirs written in the 1930s.[15] Rebatet raves in a pamphlet called *Les Tribus du cinéma et du théâtre* that the Jews, "all these Mittel European Ashkenazim, jargonizing the horribly bastardized German that is their Yddish [*sic*]" have falsified and trivialized the magnificent invention of the film sound track.[16] Interest in a French national voice is thus constructed with the help of this notion of an encroaching foreign one.

One notices the dependence of exclusive nationalism on the excluded–that is, the dependence of the host on its parasite–in Rebatet's humor, which appropriates the very speech that threatens him. Céline's pamphlet is Rebatet's *baruch*, and Rebatet's own writings are riddled with Yiddish words and with transcriptions of accented immigrant French. In his memoirs, Rebatet describes hearing a family of Berlin Jews shout "Fife le Vront Bobulaire" during the July 14 parade of 1937 and reacting to their accent by chasing them up the Champs Elysées, screaming in German "Shut your mouths [*maul zu*]"–a linguistic exercise he calls "a very slim diversion for an enervated sort like myself" (1942, p. 40; 1976, pp. 40–41). (The 1976 edition describes the same incident but omits the actual German words.)

Behind the anti-Semite's notion of the Jew as parasite lurks what might be called a "telephonocentrism." "Because there was so much talk about remaking the French soul, it had to be recognized too, that those of us facing our microphones counted among the directors of the French conscience," writes Rebatet (1942, p. 495; 1976, p. 554). It is the *reproduced* voice, rather than the voice itself, that conveys the archaic values demanded by so-called antimodernist fascist rhetoric: nothing less than the *soul* of the French could be reformed by microphone or by sound track. For the fascist critic, listening, often highly mediated, is the privileged means of conversion. Consider Rebatet's description of his conversion to Hitler. He is in a restaurant in Germany; the restaurant owners put on a Hitler broadcast, and he feels obliged to stay. Before the broadcast, he insists, he's thought of Hitler in the most ordinary of terms–"more or less like my concierge, that is to say, like everybody" (1942, p. 23; 1976, p. 27). Yet after the radio speech, which he has scarcely understood, Rebatet finds himself telling a waitress, "He is a marvelous man"–"and I really think," he muses, "that I was starting to be sincere" (1942, p. 23; 1976, p. 27). The "alibi" he has inserted in this conversion description is not the charisma of Hitler himself, nor the content of his speech, but rather the exigencies of behavior in a crowd. The pressure of the crowd prevents him from leaving the restaurant, the enthusiasm of the crowd determines his enthusiasm for what he hears. It is the crowd who elevates the petty bourgeois individual, this universal concierge of a Hitler, to the status of a marvelous hero.

But it is also a *listening* crowd. Through the magic of radio, listening to Hitler's voice coming out of a Bakelite box can be much the same experience as seeing him at a party rally or on a newsreel of a rally. "I remember having heard Hitler often on the radio or at the movies during his 1933 election campaign," writes Brasillach in *Notre Avant-Guerre* (p. 274). Listening is his chosen memory from both the audio and the visual events.

Much of the writing for radio in the 1930s is marked by a similar confusion of the senses, reminiscent of the visual-auditory sensorium that emerged in our analysis of the slogan in Sorel. An article on radio law in the French *Almanach de la T.S.F.* of 1934 explains that French law deems a radio broadcast a "spectacle": the proprietor of any public place who uses a radio broadcast owes copyright fees. The article then goes on, however, to describe an interesting counterexample: the owner of a shoe store that played phonograph records and that had an "entrée libre" sign on its door was tried and acquitted of unlawful mechanical reproduction in 1931.[17] This new understanding of radio and records—not as spectacle but as ubiquitous "mood music"—is an equally important precondition for radio's ideological penetration. As Rebatet put it, "One imposes everything on crowds by the force of habit" (1942, p. 495; 1976, p. 554). Fascist listening did not have to be planned, just repeated.

The administrators of fascist radio stations sometimes connected their broadcasting success to real crowd-gathering. In the Italy of the 1930s, Mussolini organized a radio show called the "Worker's Ten Minutes" that interrupted all activity in factories, unions, and public squares. But there were other ways to spread the consumption of sound. In Germany, the government imposed mass production of a seventy-six-mark Volksradio, then sold 100,000 of them in one evening at a nationally organized Radio Fair.[18]

What about radio in the house? As of 1933, and in the same month that Le Poste Parisien (a French radio station) initiated the first daily "wake-up" weather and news program directed at the private listener, that station also began, as part of its morning diet, a translation of the radio speeches of Hitler, the new chancellor.[19] By 1937, the Popular Front government was aware of radio's fascist potential. In an effort to democratize its own stations, it organized radio elections in 1937 whereby each listener could vote for administrators in charge of programming.[20] Two major "radio parties" sprang up, each of them proposing its own candidates for administration of the radio. These two were "Radio-Liberté," the Popular Front coalition, and "Radio-Famille," a coalition of right wing leagues and religious groups that wanted to "depoliticize" the radio in order to make it more faithful to the spiritual goals of the nation. At the time of the elections,

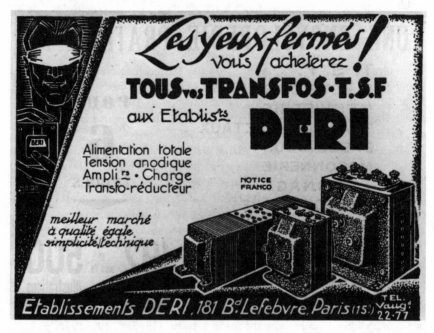

Ad, *Almanach de la T.S.F.*, 1934. Photo Bibliothèque Nationale, Paris.

French radio had a larger audience than France's best selling newspaper. Ironically, even though the Popular Front proposed the idea of radio elections, its own party in the elections lost.

The tension between the radio experience as a private experience and as a public one is at the heart of radio ideology. Radio and telephone were the first electrical "personal appliances," the first electric machines to leave the factories and become "part of the furniture."[21] Radio gave people a sense of intimacy with electricity, a sense of control over technology: at the same time, radio's "wirelessness," the invisibility of its method, made it subject to the greatest mystifications. By 1937, the year of the Popular Front exposition, radio had been broadcast from the Eiffel Tower for fifteen years, and more than three million people were registered radio owners. The box was thus no longer in the realm of electricity experts, nor was it as banal as the broom. While the Popular Front pushed state radio and even spoke of eliminating the few privately owned stations, profascist opposition in *Je Suis Partout* and *Gringoire* lobbied for independent stations, while professing great admiration for the concept of the radio crowd. Hence, the fascist position on radio was figuratively, not literally, collective: the ideal fascist broadcast, whether monitored individually or in a crowd, should extend the listener into an imaginary crowd spirit.

Ad, *Almanach de la T.S.F.*, 1937. Photo Bibliothèque Nationale, Paris.

It is into this radio world, this ideologically vulnerable space of listening, that Rebatet, as fascist reader, receives the texts of Céline. Rebatet, for whom the famous three dots in Céline's text are not, as Céline himself would have it, the "brush strokes" of an impressionist pointillism[22] but the traces of a wireless communication; an extended subjectivity, a voice that won't stop. The three dots represent, for Rebatet, the ideological—and erotic—superiority of sound, the same kind of superiority suggested in radio ad slogans of the 1930s: "With eyes closed! [That's how] You'll buy all your wireless transformers from the Déri Company" and "Make nations parade across M.J. radios."[23] Céline is received—and broadcast—by the fascist reader as a radio script. For Ezra Pound, the broadcast is literally acted out, as in this homage to Céline on his Roman radio program of May 11, 1942, entitled "A French Accent":

> no fuzz on the blighter's tongue. Voice of France, as when France was young. . . . It is not only that spoken French, the French of the mechanics is at last put down on the page. It is that it takes hold of the page; it is alive on the page.[24]

In a prophetic misreading, the American Federal Communications Commission officials who monitored and transcribed the Italian broadcasts didn't recognize the word Céline and recorded it as Stalin, thus substituting a political totalitarian label for what is now recognizable as the quite specific telephonocentric phenomenon of a French fascist aesthetics.

For the team of writers at *Je Suis Partout*, the pleasure in reading Céline—the audio version of male-bonding—is created out of the sense of vocal power made possible by radio. References to broadcasting also emerge unintentionally in many supportive definitions of fascism, so that what is customarily read as merely a fascist aestheticism might now be understood as "the insistence of the radio in the fascist unconscious."[25] Or, to return to Albert Laprade's anxious description of the "state of the soul, circa 1937," that aestheticism might also be understood as "the pure technical current intermingled with very explicit 'national' ones." Rebatet, on fascism: "not an ideology, but a method." Drieu, in *Gilles*: "it will be a century of methods, rather than of doctrines"; and in an essay: "It's useless to judge a political party on its doctrine. One must merely ask: What is your human value? What is your potential for youth and energy? What is your creative force?" Rebatet, on the failure of an authentic French fascist movement: "We had no catch phrase [literally, "word of order," *mot d'ordre*] to throw to them." In Brasillach, wherever there is fascism, there is broadcast of all kinds: "radiating," "shining," "mirroring," "pulsations of a vast heart," "a 'pre-fascism' already in the air."[26]

None of these statements have anything to do overtly with a discourse *about* technology. It is easy to understand, then, how they might both suggest an ahistoric account of the fascist sensibility and contribute to an inability to define the *content* of fascist ideology. Such sentences, in effect, veil technology's political potential in purely aesthetic terms. Fascist aesthetes intentionally borrow the vocabulary of literary romanticism, but it is nascent technology that inspires them to put their vocabulary to political use.

Brasillach's 1941 *Notre Avant-Guerre*, for example, might be read simply as the diary of an aesthete gone wrong. In my analysis, it becomes the seasonal account of vocally defined male-bonding, from the student camaraderie through "key phrases" and "pass words," to the early 1930s, when, "in the evening, we used to read old World War I magazines out loud" (p. 152), to the institutionalization of oral reading at *Je Suis Partout*, where secretary Henri Poulain is described as someone who "can recite long pages of *Bagatelles pour un massacre* and who has a delicious spirit" (p. 153), to the defensive fascist orality of 1939, stirred by the censorship of "prophet" Céline's *Bagatelles*.

In tribute to the fathers of his fascist orality, Brasillach's 1942 review of the Rebatet memoirs simply repeats Rebatet's 1938 piece on Céline: "the manuscript of this mammoth work is bound in three enormous volumes that we steal from one another mutually, in order to read entire pages to one another out loud."[27] The broadcast has become a norm, a measure of a text worth reading.

Thus, the persuasive efficacy of radio was not merely a historic factor in the success of fascism. A discourse on radio, as well as a discourse *miming* radio, played an important role in the versions of successful social reality propagated by fascist intellectuals. Happiness, at *Je Suis Partout*, was connected to listening and speaking together. But listening and speaking together, circa 1939, were thrills already sustained and reproduced by the institutions of broadcasting. The role of Céline's *Bagatelles* in all this? Perhaps not, as Léon Daudet first called it, "an act," but an actor in a telephonocentric myth.[28]

## Post Scriptum

One question posed by this chapter is, of course, that of the role of radio in the imaginary arsenal of the French Resistance. Rebatet describes the Free French broadcasts as a Jewish drug by which the French people kept in touch with their true decayed selves, "their behind in an armchair, their door prudently closed" (1942, p. 646). Rebatet is thus firmly locked into his Popular Front era complaints of national passivity and refuses to recognize that people hid because listening to the BBC broadcasts was forbidden by the occupying forces. It would be interesting to study the extent to which de Gaulle developed his radio technique *against* a fascist model, including rallies and mass-listening. The following incident, recounted in Charles J. Rolo's *Radio Goes to War*, would surely enter such a study: On Joan of Arc day, May 11, 1941, de Gaulle staged a remote-control demonstration by suggesting on his radio broadcast that French people leave their houses between 3:00 and 4:00 P.M. and *reoccupy*, in *total silence*, the public streets, parks, and promenades. Silence was both a political necessity for the demonstrators and a symbolic blow against the reigning enemy voice. Not that the silence wasn't immediately understood as "noisome" dissent: Rolo reports forty arrests in Paris among the silent crowds. Silence, to conclude in more general terms, is every bit as much an emblem of resistance mythologies as broadcasting is of fascist mythologies.

## Notes

1. Known today, if at all, as a second-rate Céline—a Céline of "all ideology" and no poetics— Rebatet was a best-selling author of the occupation who, after the purge and after his release from prison, was reduced to writing pharmaceutical catalog (See chapter 7, "The Late Show".) The reading of Rebatet is complicated for the student of ideology by Rebatet's own revision of his 1942 bestseller *Les Décombres*—a revision published in 1976 by Jean-Jacques Pauvert under the new title *Mémoires d'un fasciste*, a two-volume work with *Les Décombres* in volume 1 and unpublished diaries and articles labeled 1941–1947 in volume 2. The 1976 books are no longer exactly fascist texts so much as the selective memory of them. Rebatet has edited his diaries from the perspective of 1970, and he has edited from the 1942 *Les Décombres* some 134 pages of compromising invective, especially those passages that now appear in retrospect as endorsements of a holocaust, for example, "a single form of politics would have been capable of getting us out of our fix: shoot a few thousand Jews and masons and deport just as many" (Lucien Rebatet, *Les Décombres* [1942], p. 32). Editor Jean-Jacques Pauvert implies in his 1976 preface to volume 1 of *Les Mémoires d'un fasciste* that the revised version of *Les Décombres* given to him by Rebatet's wife after Lucien Rebatet's death represents an attempt not only to correct stylistic faults but also to demonstrate an evolution away from anti-Semitism dating from certain articles published by Rebatet in 1967. Yet, in spite of the purging of the text, the publisher has pasted a "warning" to the book jacket, in which he argues that,

at most, the memory of fascism might guard against its reappearance ("let a new publication instruct and warn those who did not live through this drama"), or that, at least, the memory might educate modern-day ideologues about their fascist debts ("Does one combat ideas by burning books? We are in an age where many political movements, from the extreme left to the extreme right, are taking up the ideas and methods of European fascism of the 1930s, whether or not they appear to be aware of it. Isn't it precisely better to be aware?"). The publisher of the fascist text doesn't wish to appear an advertiser of fascist texts; but by editing—by refusing to publish what is most referentially damning—he is abetting forgetfulness. It is against this forgetfulness that I quote Rebatet.

Subsequent page references to the 1942 and 1976 editions of *Les Décombres* will be referred to by date in parentheses in the body of the text. References to volume 2 of *Les Mémoires d'un fasciste* will be referred to as "1976, vol. 2."

2. Dioudonnat, *Je Suis Partout*, p. 224.

3. Lucien Rebatet reviewing *Bagatelles pour un massacre*, *Je Suis Partout*, January 21, 1938, p. 8. Subsequent quotations from Rebatet's review of *Bagatelles pour un massacre* refer to this article.

4. Céline, "Morceaux Choisis: *Bagatelles pour un massacre* (Le Livre de la semaine)," *Je Suis Partout*, March 4, 1938, p. 8.

5. Louis Ferdinand Céline, *Bagatelles pour un massacre* (1937), p. 41. A subsequent page reference will appear in parentheses in the body of the text.

6. Albert Laprade, "La Trop Belle Exposition." This is a three-page unnumbered introduction to a book of photographs of the exposition. The passages quoted here are from the first page; the source is indicated subsequently in the text by "Laprade" in parentheses.

7. Dr Montandon, *Comment reconnaître le Juif?* (1940). The phrase "moral portrait of the Jew" is from the full title (see references). The book is first in a series of pamphlets entitled "Les Juifs en France", which includes Lucien Rebatet's *Les Tribus du cinéma et du théâtre* (1941). It was not available to me in time to offer a close reading of it here; Montandon's use of the Céline pamphlet certainly merits careful study.

8. For accounts of Montandon's career, see Pascal Ory, *Les Collaborateurs*; Michael R. Marrus and Robert O. Paxton, *Vichy France and the Jews*.

9. Louis-Ferdinand Céline, *Bagatelles pour un massacre* (1943). Copies of this illustrated edition are extremely rare. I thank Henri Godard for directing me to the copy at the Bibliothèque Céline, Paris.

10. Centre de Documentation Juive Contemporaine, archives of the Institut d'Etudes des Questions Juives, document no. XIg-119.

11. Ibid., document no. XIg-30.

12. On January 2, 1939, Director Oberst Fleischauer writes to Montandon (in French): "A friend of the 'Service Mondial' was kind enough to send us your address, informing us that our work would doubtless be of interest to you." No response. A second letter from Fleischauer to Montandon is dated February 16, 1939: "Upon the request of M. L.-F. Céline, I took the liberty of writing to you last January 2, sending to you under separate cover several examples of our bi-monthly information bulletin, as well as a circular." The prompt response from Montandon, quoted in the body of the text, is dated February 20, 1939, and is translated here from the original German. Centre de Documentation Juive et Contemporaine, Montandon archives, documents numbered XCV-47, and XCV-72.

13. Montandon, originally Swiss, was a naturalized French citizen.

14. The real radio star of the period was Philippe Henriot, who, unlike Rebatet, remained loyal to Vichy. Alfred Fabre-Luce wrote of Henriot: "with him, listening to the radio is as heart-warming as [being at] a public gathering. That voice, precipitous and fleeting (or else slow, with a sadness nuanced by irony) obtained a physical adhesion which precedes and determines the adhesion of the

spirit." (Alfred Fabre-Luce, *Journal de la France, 1939–1944*, vol. 2, p. 555). Henriot continued broadcasting the anti-Semitic message until his assassination by the resistance in June 1944.

15. Robert Brasillach, *Notre Avant-Guerre*, p. 167. Subsequent page references to *Notre Avant-Guerre* appear in parentheses in the body of the text.

16. Rebatet (François Vinneuil), *Les Tribus du cinéma et du théâtre*, p. 40. The phrase *jargonnant son yiddish* reappears in *Les Mémoires d'un fasciste*, p. 564.

17. Paul Roué, "Le Code de la T.S.F.," pp. 42–50.

18. See Arno Huth, *La Radiodiffusion.*

19. René Duval, *Histoire de la radio en France*, p. 131.

20. Tudesq and Cazeneuve, "Radiodiffusion et politique: les élections radiophoniques de 1937," pp. 529–55.

21. Pierre Sansot's *Poétique de la ville* describes the revolution in perception that accompanied the appearance of radios, telephones, and refrigerators in daily life. Reyner Banham's *Theory and Design in the First Machine Age* analyzes the effect of clean, lightweight, individually operated machines of the early twentieth century as against the "sooty, rusty, cast-iron" machines of the Victorian age. His distinction is crucial for an understanding of the fascist as someone excited by the extension of perceptual powers that comes with radio-hearing, aerial-viewing, and so on.

22. Louis-Ferdinand Céline, "L.-F. Céline vous parle," p. 934, quoted in Kristeva, *Les Pouvoirs de l'horreur* (Paris: Seuil, 1980), p. 236.

23. *Almanach de la T.S.F.* (1934), p. 94; (1937), p. 6.

24. Ezra Pound, *"Ezra Pound Speaking,"* p. 128. The FCC transcripts of the speeches are discussed in a preface.

25. Here I'm performing my own historicizing variant on the title of Lacan's "L'Instance de la lettre dans l'inconscient ou La Raison depuis Freud" (translated as: The Insistence of the Letter in the Unconscious).

26. Lucien Rebatet, *Les Décombres* (1942), p. 651: "Fascism as conceived by a Frenchman is not an ideology, but a method, the best known and the most modern to regulate the more than hundred year old conflict between work and money"; Pierre Drieu la Rochelle, *Gilles*, p. 537; *Chronique politique*, p. 42. Lucien Rebatet, *Les Décombres* (1942), p. 57. Robert Brasillach, *Notre Avant-Guerre*, pp. 204–44 (in a chapter entitled "Ce mal de siècle, le fascisme. . . " [This Malaise of the Century, Fascism . . . : notice that the three dots are part of the title]) and p. 37.

27. Robert Brasillach, "Espoir ou colère?" [Hope or Anger], *Je Suis Partout*, April 11, 1942. Patrick Modiano's fine-tuned parody of fascist intellectuals (*La Place de l'Etoile*) appears to borrow word for word from this review. The reading practice Brasillach describes is attributed by Modiano to the father of insane narrator Raphael Schlemilovitch. "He found *Bagatelles pour un massacre* very funny, and read it till all hours of the night. To my great stupefaction, he recited entire pages of the work to me" (p. 42).

28. Léon Daudet, "Un livre symptomatique, *Bagatelles pour un massacre*," *Action Française*, February 10, 1938.

*Modiano*

# Chapter 6
# The Movies: Bardèche and Brasillach

Perhaps the clearest result to emerge from my various textual investigations of fascist writing is that fascism is not a generic phenomenon within literature.[1] It is not simply to be located in a certain kind of text; say, in an autobiographical text "about" political belief, an ideological novel, or even in the traditional form of political writing, the pamphlet. This doesn't mean that fascism doesn't "take forms." In Céline's writing, something closer to diagnosis than pamphlet crosses over from the novels into the political writings. In Drieu's work, a discourse on population seems to surface whenever fascist anxiety is at a maximum. In Rebatet, dreams of a French fascism coalesce around the pleasure of speaking.

Fascism may have surfaced in unpredictable places in these writers, but once the place was found, it proved to be consistent. The task should be easier in the case of Robert Brasillach, a writer I've already quoted at length. From his description of the Nuremberg rallies to his ritualization of the sixth of February and his "radiant" vocabulary, what has emerged thus far is a picture of a man enchanted, and sometimes seduced, by political spectacle. A man well-disposed toward writing about films. Yet, ironically, it may be only for his work on films that Brasillach will be remembered as someone other than the French fascist intellectual executed on February 6, 1945. For Brasillach, with brother-in-law Maurice Bardèche, is author of what is probably the world's first attempt at a serious film encyclopedia.

Brasillach and Bardèche published their *Histoire du cinéma* in 1935.[2] The book soon came to the attention of Iris Barry and John Abbott, who had just founded a library for film studies at the Museum of Modern Art. Iris Barry took charge of its translation, which appeared in a Norton edition in 1938. Finally, Abbott wrote, there exists a book that "very properly attempts to survey the entire history of filmmaking in Europe and in America and to describe the exchange of influences to which the film as a whole has been subject."[3]

But the history of film continued to evolve, and Brasillach and Bardèche with it. They revised and updated their 1935 study during 1942 and published their second edition the following year in occupied France.[4] As the war dragged on, Brasillach compiled lists of the films he wouldn't be able to see until peacetime. He started to prepare a third edition from his prison cell in 1945, joking with Bardèche in a letter that he felt protected from evil spirits by "our fetish, the *Histoire du cinéma.*" The work, he said, had set the tempo for their lives [*il a rythmé notre vie*] for ten years: it mustn't stop. Another of his dreams was to have the *Histoire du cinéma* reissued in America: "Iris Barry will surely translate the new edition, because over there they don't give a darn about people's political opinions."[5]

This, however, was not to be. Brasillach's work in prison was completed by Bardèche after Brasillach's death, and a third edition appeared in 1948. Perhaps it is because of Brasillach's superstitious attachment to the project that Bardèche continued it by publishing histories in 1954, 1963, and 1964. The work has grown to two full volumes, one on silent film and one on talking film.[6] In a sense, Brasillach was right about America's relative disinterest in cultural politics. Barry's translation of the 1935 edition, *The History of Motion Pictures*, has fared rather well in America, albeit as a kind of innocent Gallic curiosity. *Cinema Booklist* called it "an important volume that belongs in all collections, along with the Ramsaye and Jacobs histories"; and *Film Research* described it, on the occasion of the 1970 reprint, as "one of the early and now classic motion picture histories which is still widely read, largely for a French view of the American motion picture. Despite factual errors, well worth reading for its frequently unique viewpoint."[7]

I wanted to know how this "unique viewpoint" would look once I filled it in with my knowledge of the authors' political views. One of the things that astonished me when I began my research was how little work has been done on right-wing reactions to film. Perhaps, I thought, Brasillach and Bardèche weren't modernists but were simply, as Georges Sadoul noted in his film history, "those 1930's aesthetes."[8] Then, I thought (returning to my preoccupation with "dismissals"), might not the fact that European film theory has been largely a left-wing enterprise be partly responsible for the assumption that the right isn't interested in so popular and modernist a medium? Or, if they are, that their interest is itself "uninteresting"? This seems especially odd given the degree of intellectual curiosity about links between the right wing and *literary* modernism (Pound, Lewis, Céline, and so on.) It turns out that the 1935 and 1943 editions of *Histoire du cinéma* have indeed something rather remarkable, and perhaps even unique, to offer: a textual record of Brasillach and Bardèche's passage from aesthetics to politics and, more specifically, an account of the metamorphosis of their right-wing nationalism into fascist populism—all expressed quite haphazardly through changing memories of different films. What follows is my account of that passage. Though I've organized my discussion around themes— the nation, the talkies, communities, the people—the encyclopedic organization of the texts I'm discussing will lend some of its fragmentary quality to my own arguments.

## The Nation

The 1935 edition is organized from the perspective of people who believe in the cultural integrity of nations. The book is divided into two major sections describing the silent era and the talking era, and within each era, films are classified according to the national film movement to which they belong. Films are often compared to the landscape of the nation they belong to, and filmmakers are perceived as representatives of a national character. I suppose it's not irrelevant that a special index (the title-author variety being already a rare item in a French publication) in the back of both editions records all the films mentioned by *country*. Approval is given to an uplifting cinema of current national events, to which the authors oppose a destructive cinema preoccupied with sadism, perversion, and death.

In the 1935 edition, they portray this latter cinema as a pernicious consequence of the experience of the First World War:

> Through these films the Germans found expression for that profound romanticism, that fascination with cruelty and fear and horror, that marrying of sex with death which were to intoxicate so many of her sons after the war.[9]

Though Brasillach and Bardèche use German expressionist film to criticize the eroticization of death in postwar culture, they might have launched their critique closer to home. Céline described the commonplace postwar attitude in *Voyage au bout de la nuit*, published in 1932: "Our youth has gone to the ends of the earth to die in the silence of the truth. And where, I ask you, can a man escape to, when he hasn't enough madness left inside him? The truth is an endless death agony. The truth is death. You have to choose: death or lies. I've never been able to kill myself."[10] The problem, as we saw in Drieu, is how to get out of the trenches in this world where any excitement is tantamount to fear of death, any escape a further entrenchment. We saw how Drieu's Gilles attempted to eroticize the truth in order to live.

It is interesting to see how Brasillach and Bardèche seek strength in the corrosive war experience through analysis of certain films. For example, they consider Renoir's *La Grande Illusion* (1938), generally recognized as an antiwar statement and swan song of the old European aristocracy, as a prowar statement in spite of itself. The 1943 edition reads:

> Jean Renoir became a communist, but he fought in the war. When he judges this war, and the fraternity of arms, he calls them "the grand illusion." But when he describes it, he describes it just as it was, with an admirable honesty and sang-froid. It isn't his fault, nor ours, if some men were able to experience in war what they would never experience afterwards. This could come as a surprise if we didn't understand that Jean Renoir's war, by means of the standard paradox, is the place of friendship, of youth, and perhaps of regret. Political opinions don't alter this fact in the least. If France has had her war film, she owes it to a man who, before returning to his errors, did not want to transgress the truth of his youth. (p. 346)

The war experience is collective; it transcends responsibility ("It isn't his fault, nor ours") and also transcends politics ("political opinions don't alter this fact in the least"). It is inevitably an experience of youth, friendship, and perhaps regret—that is to say, it brings inevitable nostalgia. But what differentiates Drieu's or Renoir's view of the war from that of these authors is the fact that Brasillach and Bardèche never fought in World War I. They were too young. They knew the war only through the book and film culture of their youth, through the work of the Renoirs and the Drieus. So it is in this highly mediated sense that the war was their truth.

The term *youth* alludes specifically both to the ideological truth of Renoir's precommunist youth and to Brasillach's most consistent locus of mystification: youth for him is always a time when error is impossible. A decadent, ambivalent fascist, Drieu kills off Pauline—and France—with literal and figurative cancer at age 30 ("cases of cancer in a 30-year-old were rare and fatal"), but Brasillach sees the coincidence as unequivocally hopeful. He devotes an obsessively romantic chapter of *Les Sept Couleurs* to "the 30's"—his, and the century's. The rise of fascism magically corresponds for his generation—that group of young men just too young to have had their idealism stilted in the trenches—to that last burning moment of youth (the age 30), that last possible moment of action. He saw his own celebration of youth and friendship reflected in *La Grande Illusion*, and it was very difficult for him to acknowledge the negations of war also depicted in the film. The unpleasant experiences of some soldiers in that war are neither Renoir's fault nor his.

Whose fault are they, then? *Histoire du cinéma* presents an ambivalent war story, since it both admires and regrets the sadistic beauty of expressionist films, and is admittedly a bit confused when faced with the edifying camaraderie of Renoir's vision. The question isn't answered until the 1943 edition, in which all the veterans' irksome problems are transferred conveniently onto "someone else":

> Germany satisfied her profound romanticism, and that taste for sadism, fear, shock, that junction of sexuality and death, which intoxicated so many of her *Jews* after the war. Because, like everywhere else, the Jews [in Germany] had thrown themselves into film.[11] (p. 150, my emphasis)

The real shock here, of course, is not in any change of attitude toward German expressionism but in the abrupt switch in the identity of the expressionists from native sons to Jews. The most severely internalized national problem—the veterans' war neuroses—has been transferred onto the proverbial outsiders. How does it work?

The substitution of the Jews in the 1943 text simplifies the dilemma in the first edition created by the "intoxicated sons" of Germany. The sadistic, destructive spirit of the German veterans is already a confusing factor to French nationalists like Brasillach and Bardèche in 1935, because the veteran spirit—the spirit of the "Croix de Feu" and the "Jeunesses Patriotes"—is the most visibly energetic form of nationalism around. That this same veteran mentality can also produce sadistic, perverted art implies that war might be destructive, rather than ennobling, to a nation—any nation. As long as such morbid preoccupations can be attributed solely to the Jews, nationalism is otherwise free to flourish untainted; the Jeunesses Patriotes can keep on marching in the name of the war experience. Thus, in the 1943 "occupied" edition, anti-Semitism has made it possible to recount the story of the First World War with the French and Germans as heroic comrades and the Jews as imaginary enemies.

What is most surprising, though, is that the authors have chosen something so "close to home" to "jewify." In the case of Chaplin, the 1935 edition reads:

> Volumes could be written about a certain toughness in Charlie and the suppressed resentment which often lends a strangely *human* note to his misfortune [*humiliation*]: he is less resigned than we sometimes imagine. (p. 220; Barry, p. 217, my emphasis)

However, the 1943 edition reads:

> Volumes could be written about a certain toughness in Charlie and the suppressed resentment which often lends a strangely *Hebraic* note to his misfortune [*humiliation*]: he is less resigned than we sometimes imagine. (p. 170, my emphasis)

The tribute to Chaplin's spirit and obduracy becomes in the 1943 text a warning: one must not ignore the Hebrew note. Again, something near and dear—one's own humanity—is replaced by a concept that denotes invasive foreignness. Especially important is the fact that a stance of resistance to humiliation is being transferred to the qualifier *Hebrew*. And that the French word *accent*, which in the first quote clearly connotes "note" or "tone," takes on a more literal sense of "foreign accent" when it is used to qualify "Hebraic." I'll say more about the authors' specific reactions to Jewish immigrants in the film industry later.[12]

The bargain that Brasillach and Bardèche strike with postwar fears is unsuccessful. Hoping to get rid of them, they "project" them onto the Hebraic outsiders. But the fear hasn't been disposed of: it merely returns to wreak havoc, now from the outside instead of from within. Anti-Semitism is introduced into the text in an effort to safeguard nationalism, and yet the Jews, "rués sur le cinéma," come to break down the nation and the old European values, and thereby indirectly disturb the book's encyclopedic categorization of films into discrete national entities. In 1943, the authors must do some fancy theoretical footwork to maintain that the foundation of film creation was in the nation, in spite of their admiration for some of the great German Jewish filmmakers who emigrated to the United States after 1933. Their 1935 text had lauded the prodigious play of light and shadow in expressionist film and had regretted the departure of the masters:

> If German films lose their passion for morbidity, so much the better, but it is to be hoped that the films of the future will retain the best things of Pabst, of Lupu Pick and even of Fritz Lang — especially their sense of pictorial composition, their rare mobile and plastic qualities. We must hope that they will forget neither *Variety* nor *Such is Life* nor *Maedchen in Uniform* nor — what was finest about the product of this country — their irreplaceable *humanity* (Barry, p. 353)

In 1943:

> Once they had left their country, the Jews who then worked in film suddenly lost these plastic qualities, as if those qualities had been attached not to themselves but to the soil.[13] (p. 154)

Uprooted Jews lose the link between art and soil, expression and location. Their ability to create with light and shadow, their sun, as it were, is attached to the soil. Before emigration, the Jewish artist is, oddly enough, not unlike the fascist hero who belongs totally to the nation — or, perhaps, who successfully feeds off it — so the minute he leaves, his talent must also disappear. Thus, the authors revise and deform the history of German anti-Semitism almost as though its condemnation of those Jews who stayed in Germany is the fault of those who fled!

## The Talkies

The history of film between the wars is inextricably linked to the instability of the filmmaker population. Among the masses of Jews who emigrated, at first out of Eastern Europe (before 1914) and later from Germany into France and the United States, were numbers of important film writers, producers, and directors. In Brasillach and Bardèche, this fact becomes a menace that threatens to destroy a national film culture throughout Europe. What is more interesting than their perception of a threat is the way they articulate it around what might seem to us a purely coincidental issue: the transition of silent films to talkies. Here, then, is another instance of the "projective" nature of their anti-Semitism.

In the 1943 edition, Brasillach and Bardèche develop their fantasy about an ideal national sound cinema: "may it become the epic [*chanson de geste*] of our new life" (p. 404). The *chanson de geste* recounts the adventures of an elite as its subject matter but is intended for the appreciation of the people. Unlike courtly literature, it cuts across class boundaries in a way similar to that in which a film about the rich and famous is intended for the anonymous poor. The *chanson de geste* speaks in a collective voice for a collective community and often uses a threat to that community, such as the Saracens, to spark the narrative. Brasillach and Bardèche's fantasy about the potential of sound film does not immediately entail a defense against a Jewish threat. In the 1935 edition, they object to the talkies as a degraded form of art but seem unable to explain why — their objections are qualified with phrases such as "we know nothing about it," "one isn't sure," "it might be that." Their concerns with the disturbance of national and linguistic unity in the film industry aren't explained politically until their 1943 analysis of the talkies. That analysis appears to be based on an unusual form of what I have called "literalization" — as when moral fortitude is measured by musculature, or the mystical notion of the *Volk* is reduced to those people with blond hair and blue eyes.[14] In 1943, Brasillach and Bardèche reduce and literalize the notion of a desired national voice in cinema to that of a mother tongue, properly enunciated on the sound track. Against this they posit an unstable Jewish accent, introduced by Jewish directors, producers, actors. The Jews are a particularly subversive enemy for the fascist nationalists because, unlike the medieval Saracens, they resist literalization. Vulgar anti-Semitic ideology has depicted their rootlessness, their multilingualism, and their mercantile economic role: it is from this unstable, "shifting" position that they seem to be undoing the desired harmony of national cinema.

The atittude toward sound film in *Histoire du cinéma* is profoundly ambivalent: possibility of a *chanson de geste* on the one hand, revelation of a fearful Jewish rootlessness on the other. In a less idealistic comparison between film and medieval art, the authors refer to Hollywood "stables" of writers as modern scribes. The ancient public scribe, often stationed in the forum or the town square for the purpose of helping citizens by furnishing them with public documents, was a figure who wrote essentially for others — a writer, yet not an author. The division of labor in Hollywood makes filmmaking both a collective and an anonymous enterprise: there seems a possibility of recuperating that collective feudal spirit admired in the *chanson de geste*. But what is absent in the modern film is that presumption of a common law to guide the community. Hollywood is scandalous because there the most vulgar public judges a film first, by means of a preview system, and the reputation of directors depends on their ability to predict public opinion. Cinema is thus condemned to a debased relationship with the everyday: "More than any other medium, it appears to be inextricably linked with the ideas and the ideals [*les moeurs*] of its time—and, moreover, with those which are the vulgarest, the most superficial, the most ephemeral" (1935, p. 391; 1943, p. 389; Barry, p. 372 ). Like a scribe who practices his trade in the company of illiterates, the filmmaker is condemned to reproduce the most meaningless paradigms of daily life, to advertise the commonplace.

Sound is thus a final debasement of film art, not merely because, by an accident of political history, it reveals Jewish accents, but because any sound renders the vulgar aims of the film industry more acutely than silence. "Speech [is] an awful avowal of this mediocrity that silence had had the decency to hide" (1943, p. 390). Presumably, silence might have left room for at least an imagined authority.

Technically as well, sound moves film away from the suggestive and closer to a realistic mode of expression. As André Bazin explains it, the early audio image was technically much less malleable than the visual one and did not accommodate the use of symbolic superimpositions and the collages of shots that flourished in the silent era; dialogue seemed to control and limit visual imagery to direct shots of the characters speaking.[15] If the sound film is going to overstep its commonplaces, it has to do so without recourse to willfully enigmatic imagery; it has to glorify its own synchronization of sight and sound to call attention to its own realism.

## Communities

It is important to keep in mind that in spite of their real nostalgia for the silents, Brasillach and Bardèche understand sound film as a potential *chanson de geste*; consequently, one of the first forms of sound track to excite their admiration is the newsreel, and more specifically, the political newsreel, which seems to them a perfect glorification of the real by means of sound. The importance of sound as a political vehicle received a sort of negative confirmation when liberal European and American governments in the 1930s found it necessary to censor sound tracks of demagogues and demonstrations: "To comtemplate a demonstration or a dictator still passes: it's when you *hear* them that it becomes dangerous" (1943, p. 246). Liberal governments rely on a written law, a constitution, that would necessarily be threatened by the vocal authority of a dictator; and so their censorship of sound reels only confirms a fascist suspicion: that the dictator is realizing the transcendent concept, a political "overvoice" by means of his voice and the voice of the crowd. Even a critique of parliamentarianism can be filtered through a discourse on sound.

One of the few early films to confirm their enthusiasm for the sound track was Van Dyke's *Eskimos* (1933), a story, perhaps not coincidentally, about the antagonism of races, in which the actors speak in the Eskimo language. The foreign sounds add to the pleasure of the film:

> A tale of murder and of race antagonism, it contains scenes like those of the walrus hunt and the attack on the caribou which are as touching as the finest things in the *Georgics*. Under a pallid sky each man or animal stands out in sharp silhouette against the great expanses of white snow. The actors speak Eskimo, which does not disturb us in the least, for the dialogue is not meant to be understood but, like the music of *White Shadows*, blends with the images. The important thing about the film is the way in which sounds and images are thus blended and combine to create a definite rhythm. Right at the start of the talkie era, Benjamin Fondane wrote in *Bifur*: "Dialogue and sound should be content to fulfil the function formerly entrusted to double-exposure and to take its place." With Van Dyke this is what happened. (1935, p. 321; 1943, p. 248; Barry, p.311)

In the case of Vidor's *Hallelujah* (1929), the authors admit that silent film could never have rendered the extraordinary emotions of the collective black spirit, as in a baptismal scene in which "the colored people adapt Christianity to the laws of their own hysteria through a succession of frenzied scenes in which the collective soul of a people is expressed as even the Russians have never expressed it" (1943, p. 249; Barry, p. 313).

The sound in Van Dyke's film and Vidor's film is understood as having a Dionysian mission: "The sound film has never come closer to its true function of creating a universe subject to the laws of music, where everything which is transitory and intangible (a flickering light, a sigh, a murmur) is caught for eternity." (1935, p. 321; 1943, p. 248; Barry, p. 313).

And ultimately, talking film has the possibility of transcending itself: "this sound film brought us silence" (1943, p. 249). The films strong enough to bring back the authenticity of silence are, not coincidentally, epics in the tradition of the *Georgics*, odes to ethnic origins and the calls of the primal community. Origins translate in these films as a nostalgia for and a mystification of exotic ethnic groups—such as the Eskimos and Southern Black Baptists—whose connection to nature and orgiastic communal life is to be revered and imitated. The other side of the coin of such nostalgia is racism directed against Jews, who come to symbolize the loss of such a life by their putative celebration of mediation and substitution (the exchange of money, country, languages, and so on). This double-edged racism is more sophisticated than the Ku Klux Klan variety, but it has its own cohesion.[16]

It is ultimately this natural process to which Brasillach appeals in his own translation of moviegoing into fascist politics. In *Les Sept Couleurs*, moviegoing constitutes a rite of friendship, an aesthetic experience against which political experience is later measured. The hero describes his conversion to fascism with a metaphor of the blossoming of a flower on a screen: "When we see the rigid flowering of nationalist youth on the silver screen, one must take a side."[17] There's an odd switch in subjects here that's very hard to translate. The aesthetic appreciation of the intelligence of nature is transposed here onto the nationalist youth corps; the individual romantic subject enjoys his own natural transformation on screen as he is swept into the group, and as he "hardens," it seems, he passes from a "we" into a "one." The young nationalist lobby of which he is now a part is a miraculously solid, yet blooming, flower, somewhat like what is shown in Painlevé's films of plant life which Brasillach and Bardèche admire, films in which days of plant growth are accelerated into a few seconds. The adjective *hard* [*dure* — as in the French fascist slogan, "les purs et les durs"?] ensures in turn the permanence of the image from nature, backed by the more substantial scientific guarantee of art on celluloid. The other implicit effect of this flower image on screen is that it is many times bigger than a real flower. The nature of the ensuing relation of the spectator to reality is evident in the following remark of a journalist in *Les Sept Couleurs* who meets Hitler for the first time: "A little man, smaller than one would think on screen" (p. 130).

Rebatet's concierge turned "*Ur*-speaker" appears again; now he is little man turned into a giant film image. Prepared by Rebatet for this faith in technology, we're no longer surprised that Brasillach is not disappointed in this acknowledgment of the insufficiency of the referent. The absence of a real Hitler as great as the cinematic one is not important compared with the fact of having experienced him in his plenitude on screen. What is recuperated in this little remark is not the lost authenticity or aura of existence but only the appeal of that meaningfulness, only its call.

It is as film that fascism calls for unmediated experience and only with film that men can follow *en masse*, as though creators; and yet the debt of fascism to film must be denied, because ideological activity must be understood by the fascists not as created but as the most natural, the most spontaneous, of experiences. Brasillach, for all his sophistication about film, finally believes that fascism enters men's lives like "lightning" or a "flame"; that it is a sun, an "immense red poetry." Only by forgetting its foundation in projection could a sense of proper mimetic hierarchy (ideology as given and not made) restore fascism to its important status as faith.

With such great expectations for the best of films, it is not surprising that most of the films produced only aggravated the authors' sense of a lost community. Brasillach and Bardèche describe cinema in the 1943 edition as an international business in which sound had ruined the careers of many silent film stars with language disabilities of one kind or another. Sound had also severely complicated the depiction of foreign nations: is a French film about Germany to be played in French by French actors mimicking German accents, or by Germans with "real" accents in French? Furthermore, once film importation got mixed up with translation problems, even subtitled films were not fully accessible, and certain national cinemas became opaque.[18]

Both editions mention a satire by Paul Morand on linguistic confusion in movie production, a small volume called *France la dolce*, which involves, in their words,

> what happens to a scenario by Joseph Bédier, when it has been rewritten by d'Annunzio, edited by a German schoolmistress, translated into dubious French by a newly debarked Ukranian, and from which all of a sudden it's necessary to remove every "b" in the dialogue, as one fillets the bones from a fish, because the leading lady from London pronounced them unpleasingly. Such things really do happen; they are actually a commonplace in every country, and if America indulged in them generously it was not without reason that Morand laid the scene of his satire in France, which, in films as in everything else, has become *the Good Lord's concentration camp*. (p. 336; 1943, pp. 264–65; Barry, p. 325, my emphasis)[19]

This use of the words *concentration camp* leaps out at today's reader, though it didn't mean quite what it sounds. Brasillach didn't visit Nazi Germany until 1937, and Hitler's policy of confining Jews and other undesirables to camps was yet unformed. The camps we speak most of today were built after 1939. What about the term as it was understood until 1934? It was originally used at the beginning of the century in connection with Lord Kitchener's civilian camps during the Boer War. But its pre-Holocaust meaning in the 1930s was eerily proleptic: it denoted — in figurative, often sarcastic, sense — any group of suspicious undesirables banded together.[20] The real anti-Semitic nuance is in the element edited out of the text by Barry, the qualifier "du bon dieu," which plays on the idea of God's chosen people (that is to say, the dispersed tribes of Israel). The suggestion, then, is that these dispersed tribes have once again banded together in France, now as God's suspects.

If anti-Semitism appears thematically in this film encyclopedia by way of a projective reaction to the incomprehensibility of the postwar experience; structurally, it works in the text as a desire to confine the dispersed. The 1943 edition of *Histoire du cinéma* demonstrates how many nations, many languages, and finally, a confusion about identity and nationality in general can be collapsed into the word *Jew*; the name functions as a kind of internment camp for the fear of multiplicity. Note the sentence tagged on to the description of the Morand text in 1943:

It must be added that all these nationalities [the Ukranian, the German schoolmistress, the London actress, and so on in Morand's satire] were but disguises for one and only one race, and that these are the years of the great jewification of the cinema. (p. 265)

The authors insist heavy-handedly that the problem of dispersion can be located and contained in the Jewish problem. Naming anything requires forgetting the differences within a thing or even between things. The anti-Semitic use of the word *Jew* is an exemplary naming inasmuch as it represents a radical refusal of difference and an attempt to compensate for a weakening of national and linguistic identity suggested to French nationalists in the 1930s by the geographic and linguistic mobility of immigrant Jews. By naming Jews as an emblem of dispersion, the authors have in fact denied the principle of dispersion, since fascist ideology, in a grotesquely exaggerated idealization of identity, insists on total mastery and containment of all problems. The phrase *il faut y ajouter* gives away the real need to edit multiplicity out of the 1935 text and to name one enemy for France.

The preceding textual analysis brings into evidence a peculiarly fascist perspective on cinema that is organized around the following premises: (1) cinema is a collective and public art that reveals to the spectators their regrettable everydayness; (2) behind this everydayness, there could be, but there is not, a guiding principle, or, as I have called it, an "overvoice". In fact, when many nationalities, many dispersed voices are heard on the screen, this everyday reality becomes meaningless and threatens to drown the spectator in meaninglessness. This process is understood by means of a false projection as the "jewification of cinema."

## The People

In an appendix to the 1943 edition, "Appendix for French Usage: Dreams of a Future Cinema," Brasillach and Bardèche describe cinema's essential failure to account for national sentiment and its epic mission, "which is to express the aspirations or the joy or the pain of an entire people" (p. 403):

Those weighty, trudging masses, the people's presence, the movement
and the lifebreath of an entire people: odes and poems have never
been successful either in rendering them tangible or, more important,
in rendering them awesome; legends sometimes approach it; cinema
evokes them at one fell swoop. (p. 401)

Cinema was to transform everydayness into legend or *chanson de geste*. The cinematic model of meaningful everydayness was Eisenstein's *Potemkin*, in which the crowd scenes and the overall depiction of unified multitudes resonated, for the authors, with an exemplary cinematic rhythm. Discussing the Odessa step sequence, Brasillach and Bardèche contrasted the visual pleasure of the "cadenced steps" of Odessa's soldiers with what they considered the fearful inorganic disorder of the flight of women and children before them. They admired *Potemkin*'s revolutionary power to orchestrate the march of history, to make it pulsate with meaning. For them, this pulse overrode issues of class struggle and the victory of the proletariat. Thus, their interpretation of the film empties it of its Marxist praxis by means of what seems to be a strict aesthetic preference for harmony over dispersal. But given what we already know about their desire to name and confine the dispersed, couldn't that fear of dispersal coincide here, as it does elsewhere, with their own historic dread of the massive emigration of the Jews of Eastern Europe into France?

Their off-screen ideal is also governed by principles of order and teamwork. Their mentor for the production of film was a Russian, Vertov, chief theoretician of the Kino-Eye school:

> We observe the remarkable precision and complexity in the organization of Soviet cinema, and, at the same time, its great unity. The state cinema works for the state. It is not astonishing that the films produced are stamped with the purest spirit of propaganda. In our aged Occident, which no longer believes in itself, what we cannot understand is that such constraint is not felt as constraint, at least not in its initial impulse. Eisenstein may not be a member of the Party, but he knows that he is expressing his era and that this era is a revolutionary one. Even if he is hampered in a few details, he is profoundly in agreement with revolutionary demands and necessities. The whole organization of the Soviet film industry, still alive and supple, serves as the framework for a faith. The excessive amount of propaganda, the stupidity of certain themes, the low intellectual level and even the lies which shock us so are all part of this faith. We can criticize it and condemn it, but it would be foolish to believe that so formal an organization can be purely mechanical, or that it has suppressed inspiration [*l'élan*]. Whether we like it or not, this inspiration [*l'élan*] exists. (1935, pp. 278–79; 1943, pp. 208–09; Barry, p. 269)

The 1943 edition deletes the phrase "In our aged Occident, which no longer believes in itself" and adds:

> In the interest of good politics (and good film) we can transpose it following a different ideology to give birth to a fascist cinema. (p. 209)

A familiar Bergsonian vocabulary of pure energy and life force is used to transcend mere political differences in the interests of fascist aestheticism. At the center of the new aesthetic is the group. Film aesthetics offers, above all, an alteration of the individually centered worldview, since on screen, it is in the crowd, not against it, that the individual finds meaning. The worst kind of film is one that uses stage technique and stage actors: plays are for and about individuals, movies for and about groups, and the attempt to film theater is a gross misunderstanding of the form. Crowds watching films learn from the screen to know themselves as a crowd: moviegoing becomes a group rite, or a place where strangers gather to dream together. The crowd comes to know itself as film. Subjects knowing themselves as film—that is, internalizing the aesthetic criteria offered in film—have a radically different experience, than if they knew themselves through film. In the film experience the spectators do not merely control a model that remains exterior to their untouched subjectivity; rather, their subjectivity is altered and enlarged by the film—just as Hitler was altered and enlarged for the journalist in *Les Sept Couleurs* when he first saw him on screen.

The following passage of *Histoire du cinéma* sets out to explain the situation:

> In our memory it is all strangely mixed together: the shams of the Popular Front of 1936 and the elections of Mr. Roosevelt; Léon Blum and Daladier in procession to the Place de la Nation; the Italians in the savannas of Abyssinia and the measured conferences at Geneva; the *dinamiteros* of Irun [Spain] and the parades of the phalangists. And always—setting the rhythm of this scattered imagery—the powerful march of the German Empire, Adolf Hitler in front of the brownshirts and the gargantuan ceremonies of national-socialism. And especially, as we look back at our thoughts throughout those fleeting evenings, we're haunted by our growing uneasiness. This ought to furnish the material for an extraordinary film composition: a film where one could feel *the war mounting* [*où l'on sentirait monter la guerre;* their emphasis]. For in these ephemeral visions, it was certainly the War that one saw mounting, just as urea accumulates in an organism. Little by little, during summit talks, semi-mobilisations, minor civil or foreign wars where war seemed to be showing her hand, a total Planetary War appeared and spread before us its illusory images. The film projectionists of the entire universe have thus collaborated on a kind of unique film, which needs only to be re-assembled. Theirs is the most astonishing accomplishment of those deadly years. (1943, p. 336)

So it is not—as in Kracauer's famous analysis of German expressionism, *From Caligari to Hitler*—that certain films reveal the weakness of a nation about to succumb to an authoritarian menace but rather that the film experience (presumably any film experience but most obviously that of documentaries) offers the spectators a chance for their *own* spectacle.[21] The film viewer is

From *Potemkin*: the Odessa step sequence. Photo The Museum of Modern Art/Film Stills Archive.

moved by his or her accumulated film memory to invent a unique film, and every filmgoer becomes director, producer, and editor of war.

The aestheticization of the crowd itself makes the powerful political aspect of film its capacity for effacing, before the crowd, the distinction between their experience of history and their experience of history as it is represented in film. Instead of having a cathartic effect as a work of art (as in the Aristotelian model of Greek tragedy where the audience responds through art), films encourage seasoned viewers to experience catharsis in the real world, as though the world were a film. The problem is no longer one of moral example in art (the identification of the spectator with a hero, for instance) but one of an artistic conception of morality.

Unlike the First World War, whose threat to nationalist values was repressed and projected onto the Jews, the Second World War is understood, while it is happening, as an event conceived and *monté* (note that the authors italicize the word, as though to insist on its double meaning in and out of film vocabulary) within the filmic imagination of the post-World War I generation. The observer

*Triumph of the Will*: filming soldiers' steps. Photo The Museum of Modern Art/Film Stills Archive.

becomes the creator of history, the ultimate film is a montage, by a collective imagination, of a total, planetary war. "On voyait monter la Guerre" – in French grammar, this construction is known as a "voir causatif" – in this case, too, seeing is not merely believing: seeing itself is creating. Disparate current events, much like the disparate voices of the talking screen that need to be controlled with an overvoice, are rhymed by the essential cohering events connected with the rise of nazism.

This reference to the "powerful steps of the German Empire" takes us back to the authors' aesthetic admiration of the soldiers' steps in *Potemkin* and their desire to transpose Soviet cinema into a fascist cinema. But what has been transposed between these two fragments of text is not one cinema into another; instead, the film scene (from *Potemkin*) has been applied as a standard by which to judge real-life events. The mimetic hierarchy tumbles, and cinema becomes "source" material (a "voir causatif") for history. Thus, Brasillach and Bardèche call their war film a "unique film"; although the reproducibility of film has taken away its aura (in Benjamin's historic sense), that aura, that uniqueness, is recuperated in the collective imagination of the spectators by means of the aestheticization of the real war.

The basic underlying message here, however, is still that Brasillach and Bardèche are pacifists: they dread the war that they watch being mounted. But at the same time, their pacifism is encouraged by their pleasure in watching the march of the German Empire organize the disparate little wars into a big one, much as they had taken pleasure in watching the marching soldiers in *Potemkin* restore order to the disparate crowds. They protested the coming of the Second World War because they saw the German Reich not as a threat but as the cure to other threats and a model for an imaginary French empire. Their intolerance of multiplicity, accompanied by their idealization of unity and identity—that is, their fascism as a *totalitarianism*—is complicated by what seems to be an aesthetic celebration of what could prove to be their own destruction at the hands of Hitler. We saw how Marinetti saved the day in just this situation (albeit in the eminently controllable arena of his novel) by inventing a superhuman character, Gazouramah, who could enjoy the crumbling world from on high. Brasillach and Bardèche reinvent the same deus ex machina as moviegoers; like Drieu, who can't resist making his battle-worn narrator wish he were at the movies, they teach us some of the things that are easier from the safety of a theater seat: projecting a community and an enemy, becoming nostalgic about destruction, mastering "the end."

## Notes

1. This is counter to a trend in recent critical studies, in which ideology is approached at the generic level. See, for example, Marc Angenot, *La Parole pamphlétaire*; Susan Suleiman, *Authoritarian Fictions*.

2. *Histoire du cinéma* (1935).

3. Forward by John E. Abbott to Bardèche and Brasillach, *The History of Motion Pictures*, trans. and ed. Barry.

4. Bardèche and Brasillach, *Histoire du cinéma* (1943).

5. Robert Brasillach, "Lettres écrites en prison," pp. 205, 235; discussed by Bardèche in his introduction to the reprint of *Histoire du cinéma* for Brasillach's *Oeuvres complètes*, vol. 10, p. 7.

"The Jews—Masters of French Cinema," display in the 1941–1942 Palais Berlitz Exposition, "Le Juif et la France." Photo courtesy Centre de Documentation Juive Contemporaine.

Barry, it should be noted, was responsible for bringing a number of filmmakers and scholars threatened by fascism to New York from occupied France; it is not likely she would have been well disposed toward Brasillach had she been familiar with his violent stance against immigrants and against the French resistance. (The French government made her a "Chevalier de la Légion d'honneur" in 1949.) For further information about Barry, see Akermark, "Remembering Iris Barry," available through the Museum of Modern Art, New York City.

6. Bardèche and Brasillach, *Histoire du cinéma*: 1948; 1954 (2 volumes); 1964 (2 volumes).

7. Rehrauer, *Cinema Booklist*; Bukalsi, *Film Research*.

8. Georges Sadoul's *Histoire générale du cinéma* is France's best-known marxist film history. References to *Histoire du cinéma* appear in it in vol. 2, pp. 509–10; vol. 3, p. 212; vol. 4, p. 134. The remark cited is in vol. 2, p. 510.

9. 1935, p. 200; Barry, p. 190. I have used Barry's elegant translation whenever possible, but I have had to add ideological elements from the 1935 French edition that had been edited out. An occasional French word from the original text will be noted in brackets. I will also refer in parentheses in the body of the text to the 1935 and 1943 editions and to the 1938 translation, which I'll name "Barry," although I will not note or analyze the variants in that translation.

10. Céline, *Journey to the End of the Night*, trans. Manheim, pp. 172–173.

11. The past participle for *thrown* (*rués*) is the same verb used in French to translate Chaplin's *Gold Rush* into *La Ruée vers l'or*.

12. This description of Chaplin as the bitter loser is really more reminiscent of the Hitler who reacted vindictively to Germany's defeat in World War I—a defeat that he had come to impute to the German Jews. Here, it seems, the authors have unknowingly anticipated Chaplin's aptitude for a 1947 role as the "Great Dictator."

13. Rebatet gives a far less metaphysical version of the same argument in his *Les Tribus du cinéma et du théâtre* (the tribes of cinema and theater), p. 51. Substitute "national film crews" for "soil": "We would be making a big mistake, were we to miss them [the Jews who emigrated to the United States]. With the exception of Fritz Lang, born to a Christian mother, and so in whom the Jewish heredity may not dominate after all, these Jews—preceded by a renown more earth-shattering than all the trumpets of Jericho—necessarily produced complete fiascos once they were separated

from their former film crews. Pommer made a truly boring sort of pseudo-historical rag; Leontine Sagan a bland soap opera. The much celebrated imagination of Charell reveals itself in America to be flat-footed as a rabbi."

14. I thought often of the following passage from Karsten Harries, *The Meaning of Modern Art*, as I formulated my argument: "Hitler still speaks the language of the Platonic tradition when he opposes the flux of appearances to true being. But to identify this being with the pseudo-biological conception of race or people is to put the finite in the place of the transcendent. This shift is not acknowledged. Rather it is veiled by using a language which speaks of the finite as if it were the transcendent. The finite and the transcendent are collapsed, thrown together in a muddle of words and thoughts which speak now prophetically, now with the voice of science" (p. 150).

15. André Bazin, *Qu'est-ce que le cinéma?*, p. 131.

16. For another analysis of racial exotica and fascist ideology, see Sontag's analysis of Leni Riefenstahl's publication *Last of the Nuba* in "Fascinating Fascism," pp. 73–108. Bardèche and Brasillach's comments on Riefenstahl's film portrait of Jessie Owens winning the 1936 Olympics are as revealing of Riefenstahl's vision as of their own: "An extraordinary spectacle: the black man, Owens, distances his followers by two seconds. He's a thing running, rather than a running man. He's the incarnation of the track, inhuman, easy — winning with such simplicity that one isn't in the least surprised" (1943, p. 358).

17. Brasillach, *Les Sept Couleurs*, pp. 160–161.

18. Barry, too, felt this frustration when she expressed regret in a footnote to *The History of Motion Pictures* that the French understood neither the titles nor the dialogue of Marx Brothers films (p. 321). In fact, Brasillach and Bardèche found the addition of verbal to visual slapstick difficult to accept. Harpo was their favorite Marx Brother because he didn't talk—"All that talking adds is idiocies" (1943, p. 260). Given their political seriousness about sound, it is conceivable that they might perceive comedy as an essentially silent art.

19. The words in italics are taken from the closing sentence of Morand's *France la dolce*, p. 218: "France, M. le President, is the Good Lord's veritable concentration camp." I've used Barry's translation except for the last sentence, which in her text reads simply "the concentration camp of the world."

20. According to the entry "concentration camp" in the *Oxford English Dictionary Supplement* (1933), p. 224.

21. Siegfried Kracauer's *From Caligari to Hitler* was the first postwar study to explore the relationship between fascism and film culture (the "other side," if you will, of Brasillach and Bardèche's picture). Kracauer was Barry's colleague at the Museum of Modern Art film library. He writes in a preface that his book was written upon her suggestion and with her inspiration.

# Chapter 7
# The Late Show:
# Conversations with Maurice Bardèche

It is pointless to interview them. Corrupting, too. A former Nazi, or a French Fascist, come to that, can perhaps provide firm facts or testimony, but they find it too hard to face their own reality. All, down to the humblest, who participated in genocide share the same psychological impulse to use an interview to explain away their responsibilities, dodging off beside someone else. An interviewer therefore is invited to accept being the mechanism for certifying those lies which these men need to believe in if they are not to find themselves alone with the dreadful facts.

> — David Pryce-Jones, *Paris under the Third Reich*,
> 1981

There is a fascist *esprit* and above all, there are thousands of people who are fascists without knowing it, fascists under whatever other hat they're wearing. . . . People for whom fascism as *we* conceive of it, and not as it is described, would be their great hope if one explained to them what it is. These people are the mirror in which we see our hearts reflected: I want them to recognize themselves. . . . Even our enemies ought to know what makes them enemies. . . . One must no longer be afraid of words.

> — Maurice Bardèche, *Qu'est-ce que le fascisme?*,
> 1961

Maurice Bardèche makes it clear to me that he is *not* a surviving fascist activist from the 1930s. From the first, he explains, his political writings per se are radically outside any signifying context: he declares himself against the Resistance in 1947, and against the Jews in 1948. Finally, in 1961, he writes, as the opening sentence of a book entitled *Qu'est-ce que le fascisme?*, "I am a fascist writer."[1] He thus establishes himself as the enduring spokesman for the memory and lost ideals of Robert Brasillach, his brother-in-law, and as the willful scapegoat of the new France that executed Brasillach in 1945 for "intelligence with the enemy" and for "intellectual crime."[2] Bardèche lost his university chair in literature after the war; he was, for a time, evicted from his apartment; and he was imprisoned on two occasions.

Bardèche's political eccentricity, his untimeliness, is so important to him that he writes me about it the spring before we meet: "You might as well know that I took no political position, either before or during the War, and that my political activism began in 1947, in reaction to the events taking place at that time in France and in Europe. Until that time my career had been solely academic; I was neither a journalist nor an adherent to any political party."[3]

Explaining the extremity of his reaction, he credits writing itself: "When you construct a sentence, you do it *just so*—with a crack of the whip. You say, 'I am a fascist writer,' or you say nothing at all." (Political pronouncements, in other words, don't work if they are halfhearted.) As a writer and as a thinker, Bardèche believes in closure, in certainty of style—the very opposite, he will imply in our conversations, of Célinian prose with its open-ended punctuation, its infinite suspension points, and its hypertropisms. Stylistic closure and cultural identity: the two appear intimately linked in what Bardèche himself will call "absolute" sentences; a rhetoric that speaks of cleanliness and of order, of what for him is "proper" to a European tradition. Yet, what for him is proper to that tradition is not entirely predictable according to the commonplaces of a moral majority. He confesses to admiring most recently the countercultural energy of the hippies from the 1960s—"the very opposite of what you would think I stand for." He's nostalgic for a pre-Haussmannian Paris, including the Jewish quarter, which brings back for him "the charm of an eighteenth-century village." Bardèche shares with the French New Right an affection, and an identification, with heretic sects like the Languedoc *cathares* who once held out at Montségur and Queribus against the Christians. There are accounts of a Brasillach ancestor martyred in such a fortress near Canet, where I came to find Maurice and Suzanne Bardèche at their summer cottage.

Walter Benjamin's connection between fascism and the aestheticization of politics struck Bardèche as remarkably correct. Like many intellectuals, Bardèche did not see himself as "political" in the 1930s but rather as "attracted" to what he understood as a new fascist culture. The delight with which he accepted Benjamin's thesis suggests his aestheticism as *the* point of access to his attraction *from the inside*—the symptom of fascism, as it were. We hear in his voice the strains of a cultural protectionism common to intellectuals on the right and the left during the 1930s. Benjamin recognized the symptom, although he was too early to see it through. Bardèche has spent his postpurge academic exile defending the symptom and attempting to remain authentic to it, although he is too late.

To interview Bardèche is, thus, to listen not just to the voice of a certain political reaction but to that of a would-be professor or colleague. Bardèche is still, at age 75, very much the *ancien normalien* and literary critic, best-known for his work on Balzac, and known, too, as an editor of Flaubert and Proust, of Brasillach's complete works, as the author of a book on the history of women, as a long-time *habitué* of the Bibliothèque nationale. Bardèche appears to divide his time rather successfully between his purely literary activities and his political ones (including the direction of his own extreme-right review, *Défense de l'Occident*). It is very easy *not* to connect the two, as he often doesn't; to separate, as he does, his aesthetic admiration for the street life of the Jewish ghetto from his official anti-Semitic posturing.

I was struck by the arbitrariness of Bardèche's attraction to the right and, finally, to fascism. It began, by his own account, as a naive "elective affinity" at the rue d'Ulm and kept up with him through his friendship with Brasillach and his marriage to Brasillach's sister. After Brasillach's death, mourning became political. Maurice Bardèche found himself the keeper of the archives, choosing to honor a dishonored past with his personal best. Fascism—what was at first only a vague sympathy—turned out to be a label, and a career. "Are you still a fascist writer—or what?" This is the inevitable opening remark, he reminds me, of all his television appearances, all his interviews.

Serge Toubiana, writing about a pseudodocumentary film based on interviews called, after the Bernanos text, *Français, si vous saviez*, argues quite convincingly that the interview alone is a poor historic indicator.[4] Not that the interview is apolitical, but rather that its politics is one of avoidance. *Français, si vous saviez*, a film about the world wars and about Algeria (admired, we will note, by Bardèche himself), assumes that once projected or transcribed, the discourse of reaction—the logic, for example, of a Vichy apologist like Bardèche—will simply cancel itself out by its own contradictions, or even by its own self-evident stupidity. Is this what results from a certain reading of Arendt: the thought that twentieth century evil can *simply* be banal? History can simply be quoted to be correctly understood? And who would appear more transparently and simply evil, more able to be televised, than a fascist?

To properly analyze our own naive—and specifically American—reliance on the interview as a form of knowledge about history, we would have to go back to the moment when television news began to replace the movie hall newsreel and to promote the idea that events and their meanings are effortlessly accessible from the home. One interesting landmark in television's own metadiscourse was the young Walter Cronkite's *You Are There* series during the 1950s. In such episodes as "You Are There at the Death of Socrates" or that of Caesar, and "You Are There at the Liberation of Paris," the *You Are There* show equated the daily news format with monumental history. Its idea was to demystify history by translating it into local news: "Oh, oh, I see Caesar about to enter the senate," says Cronkite to his television audience. "Mr. Caesar, I wonder if we could get a word. . . ." After the television series ended, tapes of each episode were distributed to school and state film archives for use in history courses and have become part of an American institutional discourse about history: part of what we might self-consciously call the American "coverage"—in the double sense, then, of hiding or covering up history and accounting for or covering history's ground.

It is no wonder that the first generation of American intellectuals socialized on television news should be fascinated by a film like Marcel Ophuls's *Le Chagrin et la pitié*. Here (even the harsh critic of *Français, si vous saviez* acknowledges it) is a film where the interview is at its best: clarifying; unveiling; revealing contradictions at a specific, and therefore manageable, historic moment, the Occupation and Resistance at Clermont-Ferrand.

I remembered the film en route to Bardèche's and, along with it, I suddenly remembered *Annie Hall* as a movie about wanting to go see *Le Chagrin et la pitié* all the time, and dragging along one's friends. "Oh, come on, we've seen it. I'm not in the mood to see a four-hour documentary on Nazis," says Annie to Alvy. But they see it twice in the course of the movie. And in *Annie Hall's* last scene, when Alvy describes running into Annie, his long since "ex," "she is, of all things, dragging some guy in to see *Le Chagrin et la pitié*." "Which," he concludes, "I counted as a personal triumph."

What does this say, I wonder, about the translation of *Le Chagrin et la pitié* into *The Sorrow and the Pity*; about the fascination of the Francophiliac American intellectual—and, perhaps, the moviegoing, television-watching American public in general—with the Occupation, with fascism, with the Holocaust?

Inasmuch as it can be considered representative, Woody Allen's love for the Ophuls film seems to me to be about the ideal of a projected talking cure, globalized to include political discourse. By merely listening and watching collaborators and resisters, by broadcasting their tics, their clothes, their obsessions, one might get a "full picture" of an event that seems still unresolved, that continues to cast its spell on French public life, but that is farther along the road to articulation than, say, our own war in Vietnam. Ophuls goes to work on the Occupation like an analysand on bad memories: they're hard to remember, but harder to forget. And to its credit, perhaps, *Le Chagrin et la pitié* was refused by the ORTF (the Office de radiodiffusion-télévision française, or national radio-television network). It failed to be televisable, and Ophuls was forced to distribute it as a film. This led to its being known by at least as many people in America as in France.

Ophuls, off-camera, confirms our idea of America as the ultimate refuge from fascism, the ultimate free workplace. He is a second-generation *cinéaste* whose German-Jewish father fled first to France (where he became the butt of anti-Semitic diatribes in books like Rebatet's *Les Tribus du cinéma*) and then to the United States. The Clermont-Ferrand schoolteacher in *Le Chagrin et la pitié*, who professes to never having asked why certain of his students simply stopped showing up at school, might—in how nearly identical a world—have been referring to the deportation of a young Marcel Ophuls. A might-have-been victim then who, by the force of geotemporal displacement and his profession, has reversed his status as victim and has become instead the camera eye, the interventionist, the interpreter and maker of historic hindsight: suddenly an analyst, instead of an analysand. Allen imagines Ophuls *free* because he makes history offstage, untouched, in the safety of the analytic editing room. "That movie makes me feel guilty," says Annie to Alvy. "Yeah," replies Alvy, " 'cause it's supposed to."

A cure by guilt, through identification: identification *not*, finally, with Ophuls or with the resisters but with the collaborators themselves, with the "bad guys."

I wonder, then, if the political interview at its best doesn't involve this sort of dialectic—questioning its own susceptibility to the errors it records, acknowledging its own susceptibility to collaboration with the subject?

Talking to Bardèche was disturbing, perhaps because I didn't have a video crew to help me anticipate the distance of the finished product. The meeting put me rather too comfortably, too interpersonally, in the position of the American student of France making her pilgrimage to the family of the author. Received with great warmth, generosity, and patience, I found myself thus living an episode fit for the memoirs of a young Wallace Fowlie, or of any of the critics of his generation whose work was concerned with the author and took into account personal and biographical implications. And then my own training had so carefully avoided the biographical and anecdotal frames of literature that to interview any writer at all seemed to me something like a scandalous act.

Of all the French fascists I've studied, Bardèche is the only one still alive. I had written to him asking for information about the *Histoire du cinéma*. I didn't need to meet him, I had thought, but I did need some information on some of the textual variants that had fascinated me. Perhaps the German censors had written the variants I had found. If so, my analysis of film as *the* obsessional site of the fascist ideologue would look diffferent. My work on *Histoire du cinéma* turned out to be the kind of project with which the interdisciplinary grant committee at my technically oriented university could sympathize: I needed specific data, and I knew where to find it. I received a grant including funds for the interview.

So, although I went to Canet to talk to Bardèche about the history of the movies, the talk soon turned to his own history and his reactions to his times. We seemed to share, in fact, an inability to talk just about films and an ambivalence about the ubiquity of politics in our lives.

As I was to calculate for the nth time the necessity of analyzing even the conditions of such an interview, I returned again and again to my own sincere affection for Bardèche the *littéraire*, the storyteller; to my genuine admiration for the easy bohemian atmosphere of the cottage and the endless hospitality of the entire family to their latest guest. What could be more in keeping, I concluded, with the errors made again and again in analyzing fascism than my own inability to distinguish the personal from the political, family language from polemic, charm from error? I had been working on fascist texts for seven years. The pedagogical structure of the situation was so powerful that, sitting in my own sweat in Bardèche's sun-drenched study, I felt the old pull of the American listening to war stories, the American at the movies—student of Marcel Ophuls, Woody Allen, and Bardèche all at once. Later, I was told by a Bardèche family friend that students at Lille used to jam the amphitheaters for each of Bardèche's lectures; how sad, he remarked, that politics had ruined it all. Still later, in my confusion over the ethics of the situation I had created by seeking to talk to a man whose work I work *against*, I turned to his political writings: easier to read, perhaps, than the man himself?

Bardèche "came out" in print against the Nuremberg War Crimes Trials, and against the Allies who directed them, as soon as he read the transcripts (*Nuremberg ou la terre promise*, 1948). These included endless stories of Nazi torture and genocide (so endless, tells Ophuls in *Memories of Justice*, that the prosecutors had constantly to fight the horror—not at hearing the stories but at becoming bored by them). Bardèche was jailed for his book.

In it, he argues that an American ideological state apparatus used the holocaust *après coup* both to justify and to cover up American war crimes such as the civilian bombings of Dresden. And we have since learned that "backstage" from Nuremberg, American intelligence was ready to harbor Nazi war criminals like Klaus Barbie as tools in the newest ideological war against the Soviet Union. It would be wrong to ignore the fact that Bardèche's attention to the self-righteousness and moral hypocrisy of the Americans has been to some extent justified, most recently by the Barbie revelations. Yet, his reading becomes frightening with a second step: he sees the *representation* of nazism by the Allies at Nuremberg as totally unfaithful to the fascist Germany that he and Brasillach so admired. From 1945 on, political reality becomes for Bardèche a bad antifascist film: an American-made horror film full of special effects. In his most passionate anti-Nuremberg invective, the charming *normalien* is suddenly a crazed victim of the media, a Norma Desmond on the *Sunset Boulevard* of political theory. On the Allied discovery of the concentration camps, he writes:

> They photographed them, they filmed them, they published them, they made them known by a gargantuan publicity campaign, like for some new brand of pen. The moral war was won. . . . After having presented our most sincere compliments to the technicians, mostly Jewish, who orchestrated this program, we now want to see clearly . . .[5]

Truth for Bardèche is spontaneous (the "improvised bonhomie" of Hitler's rallies, for example, makes them *true*); ruse is planned. Even more deceptive in his mind than the liberation photographs of the camps is their postwar transformation into Holocaust museums, described by him as being "decorated" with

> reconstituted torture chambers in places where they never existed . . . like for a film set. . . . And in the pious intention of making them more realistic, supplementary crematory ovens were constructed at Auschwitz and Dachau to appease any scruples which might have been born in the minds of certain mathematicians.[6]

With the critique that the Holocaust circulates inappropriately as a commodity, the six million dead are made to recede from the "picture." The Holocaust is repressed in Bardèche's writing at the same time as it is described as a *mise en scène*, an "admirable montage technique": because the Americans filmed the camps, they might as well have done it in Hollywood — such camps didn't actually exist. Thus, the true signifiers of the Holocaust — the six million dead — are once again murdered and lost from within a critique of their representation.

Later in *Nuremberg*, Bardèche writes that he simply *read* the transcripts of the trials and wrote his reaction by the methods he had learned as a critic; the very same methods of his former learned colleagues in the literature faculties of the French universities. In his exegesis, the trial simply didn't hold up as a text *representing* history. It was impossible to distinguish vengeance from fact and hatred from report in the various testimonies given. Robert Faurisson's polemic, thirty years later, shares with Bardèche's this fundamental frustration with the lack of discrete documents, each corresponding perfectly to every committed horror: frustration, finally, not at the technical mastery of the Allied judges but at all that was hasty and last minute, all that was — in the words of one prosecutor — "snafu"; all that was *un*rehearsed at Nuremberg.[7] Hence, in a bizarre conflation of the insufficiency of the Allied law with the nature of the Nazi crimes, genocide is not so much denied as *dismissed*.

Never having read Faurisson and never wanting to do so, Noam Chomsky will plead in 1978 for the publication of Faurisson's book on purely civil libertarian grounds.[8] When attacked as a neo-Nazi sympathizer, he will argue as follows: the revision of the Holocaust by Faurisson is marginal and will never be supported by major French institutions. We should ask, he then says, why the *Affaire Faurisson* elicits a kind of hysteria on the part of French intellectuals. Do they lash out at the insignificant individual Faurisson (or at Bardèche) as a displacement of their own inability to understand *new* outbursts of racial terrorism on French soil?

Indeed, it seems baffling that when the incoming immigrant population in France has long since shifted from Eastern European—and Jewish—to African—and Arab—the privileged targets of racial terrorism in France are, as I write, still the synagogue and the Jewish quarter: reflections from Israel, like a boomerang effect of the Holocaust. And how inevitable—yet grotesque—are the new analogies coming out of the angry opposition in Israel (as well as, I imagine, out of the mouth of Bardèche) of Israeli terrorism in Beirut with Gestapo terrorism. The generations echo there where they should *not*. The symmetries are atrocious. As is the conflation of a certain Zionism with Jewish cultural identity itself, and the resulting bracketing of the all-important question: *Where are people being murdered, and why?* The question is much harder to ask than it might seem.[9]

When Bardèche, and Faurisson after him, attack what they call a misrepresentation of the Holocaust in history, they are speaking—from however wrong a side—about our inability to remember history, about the failure of an authentic and lasting antifascism in the Society of the Spectacle. The very possibility of an attack on the images of the Holocaust, the possibility of *doubting* the six million dead after seeing those images, suggests that something is insufficient, either in the images themselves or in their production and distribution and in the words that accompany them. John Berger has written of the spectacle that it "creates an eternal present of immediate explanation: memory ceases to be necessary or desirable. With the loss of memory the continuities of meaning are also lost to us. The camera relieves us of the burden of memory . . . the camera records in order to forget."[10] The entertainment value of bad news, of negative spectacle, is widely acknowledged and criticized, but nowhere is what Sontag calls the "anesthetizing image" more scandalous than when set against the imperative to remember the Holocaust and thus to "keep it in the news." If the Holocaust can only be "consumed" within a system of commercial images, to remember it is inevitably to trivialize it. The question is posed brutally by the scandalous writings of Bardèche and Faurisson: how can we criticize the insufficiency of those images without forgetting?

Choice lies rather in the narrative that must surround these images of the holocaust, in the juxtaposition of the images with new ones, in accounts of anti-Semitism no longer "frozen" and isolated from considerations of new forms of racism in our own times. "There is never a single approach to something remembered," writes Berger.[11] We must constantly rehistoricize the past—from all sides—and measure its effect, no matter how indirect, on the present. Bardèche becomes important as a reminder of the *desire* to forget, as an articulate receiver and critic of the image at its most "anesthetized," at the same time that he is its cruelest dupe, incapable of seeing anything but images in the mementos of the six million dead. Might his aestheticism, his own ways of seeing and reading and their institutional genesis, lead us toward some alternative intellectual practice?

We also turn to the sunset fascism of Maurice Bardèche in view of the dawning political aesthetics of a French New Right. Already in the 1960s, Bardèche was defending a purified cultural fascism as a possible third alternative to the "sterile affronts of liberal democracies and communism."[12] In the early 1980s, a brilliant new magazine called *Eléments* takes the alternative a step further, reminding France of its "natural solidarity" with a heterogeneous, independent world falsely labeled "Third": thus, a new political language appears to replace the old. "It is certainly no accident that the most honest—if not the most exact—attempt to analyse our positions has appeared in *Libération*," reads the inside cover of a 1979 issue:

> Between the "new right" and the "new left" there are as many immediate convergences—refusal of totalitarianism, critique of the society of the spectacle, questioning of the hegemony of the superpowers, recourse to popular cultures, desire for roots—as real or possible divergences.

Spokesman Alain de Benoist repeats the position in an April 1982 interview:

> The struggle against intolerance and totalitarian liberalism, against the multinationals and for cultural identity, and for the cause of *peoples* (in opposition to the ideology of the Rights of Man), etc., is taking place today on the left and the right. . . . For me, any conservative is revolutionary: since what must we conserve if not the very possibility of a revolution? And what revolution is worth the trouble of being waged if it doesn't conserve what's worthwhile?[13]

By its combination of elitism with an admiration for third-world nationalisms and by its call for racial segregation in support of cultural "difference," the New Right is truly "neither right nor left."[14] Its cultural heroes are, like Bardèche's, "strange bedfellows": Céline, Jack Lang, Godard, Napoléon, pagans. The New Right delights in embracing unexpected allies, highbrow and lowbrow, postmodern and ancient at once. It reads as new and daring, yet it is undeniably similar in spirit and approach to the antibourgeois fascist avant-garde of the 1930s. Moreover, the signs of its racism are hidden inside a sophisticated rhetoric of "difference"; its politics deflected by layers and layers of appropriated cultures. Never, since Brasillach starred in the press of the 1930s, has reaction been more acceptably intellectual—has ideology been more poetic, and harder to read. It is too early to gauge the effect of the New Right—it appears, as I write (in 1982), to be waning—but not too late to remember its ancestors. Stunned by the horrors of the established Nazi state, we forget that fascism took hold in Europe partly as "radical chic," that it was gaily disseminated by poets and critics. The middle-class intellectuals of my own generation rushed to identify with the victims of fascism. "Nous sommes tous des juifs allemands" (we are all German Jews) went a favorite slogan in May 1968. But the Holocaust cannot be sloganized, especially since the aestheticization of revolt and the marketing of ideology as slogan are the very characteristics of the fascist modernity of the 1930s. They are its legacy.

Thus, it is, ironically, not only in acknowledged totalitarian regimes, but in the media-sophisticated antifascist democratic states where the aestheticization and mass marketing of ideology bear to fascist-form production a most stringent family resemblance. The struggle against totalitarianism is no more transparent than the thing in itself; while we find fascist "content" in oppressive regimes, we don't think to look for it as "form," and, hence, in the very places where it is least expected.

As readers of fascism, as antifascist intellectuals, we need to examine our unconscious political complicity with the errors we denounce: what, for example, are the conditions today for an uncompromised use of the pronoun *we* in mechanically reproduced political discourse? Or, conversely, at what risk its absence? These are the uncomfortable questions that haunt my conversations with Bardèche.

Note: My visits with Bardèche took place over three or four days beginning July 13, 1982. I decided to reproduce here the entirety of the first conversation only, since I read in it a tension and a narrative structure that dissipated with further talk and familiarity. I have transcribed the conversations from tape, and translated the transcription from the original French. In one instance, I have inserted pieces of dialogue from July 14 and 15; this manipulation may be interpreted as formal *parti pris* against Bardèche's views.

## Canet Plage: July 13, 1982

**Kaplan**: I was interested in the politically motivated "corrections" you made in the different editions of *Histoire du cinéma*, because I think that, when juxtaposed, they show a burgeoning fascist perspective on film. You yourself justify the rather strange variants between the 1935 and 1964 editions as inevitable: "We might ask if it's not the same in film history as in the history of certain recent events. After the belated publication of archives we grasp so much more thoroughly events we only thought we'd understood; as though we'd been to a recent showing of some film we'd forgotten."[15] The different editions of *Histoire du cinéma* tell us as much about the history of your own interpretations as about the history of film.

**Bardèche**: Yes, but that history is almost completely indifferent to political conditions, since, contrary to what you might think, the German censor during the war was more or less nonexistent. The Germans held the French intellectuals in the greatest disdain and let whatever we wanted be printed.

**Kaplan**: So it's you who made the corrections, and not the Germans?

**Bardèche**: It's not the Germans who asked for them. We're the ones who made them simply because . . . for example, there are some changes about Chaplin, I think. Simply because our opinion on Chaplin had changed, you understand?

**Kaplan**: Yes, that's what I want to hear about.

**Bardèche**: The Chaplin of the first films is not the same as the Chaplin of the *cinéma engagé* he created afterward. We were irritated by films like *The Dictator*, later films where there is idiocy and side-taking. As early, in fact, as *Modern Times*, we started to say that, yes, he's playing politics, and he's wrong to do it.

**Kaplan**: So you changed your mind?

**Bardèche**: That's not where Chaplin's genius lies. But on the other hand, those later films signaled to us certain aspects of Chaplin's genius, and we said to ourselves that, well, Chaplin isn't as simple as we thought, even in the films of his first phase there are tendencies that are, if you like, unveiled by the political films he made later. Hence these corrections that were not at all made to please the German or to displease them—we didn't care.[16]

**Kaplan**: So you felt independent in the early forties?

**Bardèche**: We felt absolutely independent. Take our attitude on Chaplin. Chaplin came to France at some point—I wasn't around, but Robert [Brasillach] went to see him and Chaplin ran to embrace him—jumped all over him—was extremely nice to him and drew him a little sketch of the tramp.[17] We have it at home in the first edition of [Brasillach's] *Complete Works*—the little man, his shoes, his cane, etc., and the signature of Chaplin. At that point, anyway, there was no hostility toward Chaplin, only some rectifications that we introduced to say that the story of Chaplin isn't as simple as it seems. As for the Germans, there was one thing that displeased them in our edition. The photographs. [The earlier edition contains no photographs.] The censor probably wanted to show his zeal, so he lit on a photo of Chaplin and said, "Not possible, this is a Jewish filmmaker and you can't use this picture."

**Kaplan**: Was it by any chance a photo of Chaplin as the dictator? [My mistake, *The Great Dictator* was first shown in France in 1947.]

**Bardèche**: No, not at all—a photo of Chaplin, in one of his first films, perhaps, I don't even remember.

**Kaplan**: Is it the only photo they touched?

**Bardèche**: I think there are one or two others, some of Soviet films. They didn't ask us—they said to our editor, "If you want the authorization to publish . . ." They had refused it at first because our book seemed to them, unlike what it seems to you, overly favorable with respect to the Jews. You musn't forget that the great man of the cinema, for us, in that first edition, is Eisenstein. Well, Eisenstein is a Jew; however much he's Soviet, he's still a Jew. So, the Germans weren't so taken with *Histoire du cinéma*, and they told the editors, if you want to reprint it, get rid of at least these photos. There are a few preliminary copies of the first edition of 1943—collector's items— which still contain the censored photos.

## On Anti-Semitism

**Bardèche**: Anyway, to finish with these variants, there are also a series of posterior corrections that have nothing to do with the political situation. These are the ones I added in rereading the text in 1948 and again in 1954. But the editions following the war are, in my opinion, *more* anti-Semitic than the rest. More anti-Semitic, because they come out of the position that I, personally, had taken and that was much more aggressive after 1945 than before.

**Kaplan**: Because you were reacting to a political situation intolerable to you, and intolerant of you?

**Bardèche**: Because I reacted, oh, not only to that situation alone. There is one thing you don't understand at all in the United States; it's a problem that escapes you completely. That is—I'd better begin at the beginning. There are two sorts of anti-Semitism for the French. There's an anti-Semitism "under the skin," if you like—they can't stand Jews, "those dirty Jews" etc., whatever—what you find in Céline and Rebatet. That kind of furor you find the minute it's a question of a Jew, etc. This kind of anti-Semitism was completely foreign to Robert, as well as to me. And then a political anti-Semitism whose roots are in the work of Maurras. Robert very quickly became a sympathizer of the Action Française—not an adherent but a sympathizer. He worked for the paper and lived in an Action Française milieu.[18] An anti-Semitic milieu, consequently—but a rational one.[19]

**Kaplan**: Which means?

**Bardèche**: Which means nationalist, if you like. The opinion of the French people who found that the Jews occupied in intellectual and political French life a role disproportionate to their number. And especially that one *heard them* too much.[20] This, at bottom, is the reaction against the Jews that the Jews don't understand and against which they are almost unable to defend themselves [*impropre à se défendre*]. . . . It's the same situation that created anti-Semitism in Germany.

**Kaplan**: Aren't you talking about a reaction to immigration?

**Bardèche**: The Germans were exasperated by the fact that almost the entirety of the German press; a part of the great German businesses; eventually, the whole intellectual program of German life was in the hands of German Jews. Which provoked a sort of—there's a word to express this now . . . it's used with regard to Arabs and things like that . . . a . . . I don't know, the word escapes me, but anyway, when there are *too many* of them, you understand?

**Kaplan**: Mm.

**Bardèche**: And so, in France, the situation was much less serious than in Germany, but just the same we found that the Jewish influence was too great. The anti-Semitism of Robert, and of a great part of the French, was an anti-Semitism of reason that wanted to limit the Jewish influence in France— which is very difficult. The Jews are in France, not by tactics or with a project for conquering influence in France, but for a very simple reason that anti-Semites understand very badly. This is that a Jew finds a Jewish writer talented simply because he discovers his own sensibility in that writer. So, he finds that some Jew is a great writer not because that writer is a Jew, but that because of being Jewish, that writer sees things a bit like he does. The same goes for Jewish actors and actresses. A Jew sees an actor who expresses the things that he feels and who expresses them better than others, and he applauds him, he supports his career, not because the actor is Jewish or so that Jewish actors can have a brilliant future, but because they feel things similarly. The Jew can better represent the Jewish sensibility. Do you see what I mean?

[July 14: I ask Bardèche about the idea of a Jewish "race": "I don't believe in race itself," he answers. "The Jewish race is an invention; even at its origin it's a mix of Cannanites and Jews—just look at the Bible." And later he will argue, "It's absurd to say that there is a Jewish race, but it certainly doesn't prevent there being a Jewish racism."

I suppose that it is because his definition of Jewish identity is untroubled by the memory of the Holocaust that Bardèche does not find Jewish racism at all ironic, as I do. He understands it rather as a *natural* side effect, characteristic of any nationalism regardless of specific historic experience. "The Jews feel like Jews, either because of their condition in life, or for other reasons: they have a sentiment of belonging to Judaism, as they say. Consequently, they ought not to be fundamentally opposed to racists."

I ask Bardèche if one couldn't then attack Zionism in terms of its proto-racism, but he is uninterested in such an attack:

The Zionists are racists, but I don't reproach them for it. They're racists, they ought to say so—everyone would understand. I reproach them for many other things besides being racist. My point of view on the Jews is peculiar—I think that they're making a mistake in wanting to acquire, especially in the diaspora and in focusing on Israel, an influence in the political and intellectual world that their number doesn't justify.

The Jews in the 1930s acquired too much influence after resettling in France and Germany; today, it is after regrouping in Israel that they are "too loudly heard." In both cases, it is the idea of unsuccessfully grounded Jewish refugees which appears to create a threat to the "centuries of geographic immobility" that Bardèche described in *Qu'est-ce que le fascisme?* as a condition for true historic wisdom.[21]

## Tourist of the Shtetl

"The great error of the Jews," he concludes, "is to have left the Jewish communities. I have always been a passionate admirer of the Jewish communities— I've visited all the European ghettos I could. Nothing used to amuse me as much as that, when I was young." I answer that the Jews were deported, that they were murdered, that they were taken from their communities.

Without responding to my remark (without hearing me?), Bardèche continues his reverie:

No, even after the war, when I was most under attack as a racist and as an anti-Semite—*which I am not*—my greatest pleasure was to go down to the Jewish quarter, to walk around when the synagogues were letting out and talk to the little Jewish girls I found so cute. I was really attracted, in a way, to these little Jewish girls; sometimes they had freckles or they weren't pretty but they amused me the way they were. And then, they were . . . charming.

The postwar Jewish quarter struck Bardèche as a place where people still talked to one another, as a place where he, too, found acceptance:

They spoke to you and everyone had the right to speak to everyone else after synagogue got out. It was so *nice*. The girls would invite me home and I didn't want to go, because I told myself that it wouldn't be correct—I liked talking to them but I didn't want them to think they could present me to Papa, and especially that I could become their fiancé [laughing].

The Jewish women he met used to ask Bardèche if he were pious—he still remembers the Yiddish word as *foum* [*frum*?], and he teaches it to me. He describes spending hours in the synagogues, "watching them parading their flowers and extravagant fruits on holy days." Nothing pleases him more, he tells me, than watching "rabbis with great beards" leading their children by the hand. "This is what remains of the family. . . . We don't even know what the French family is anymore, but the Jewish family is solid." Later in the week, Bardèche will take me to visit the port town of Collioure. We will stand briefly at the gravestone of the republican poet Antonio Machado. Speaking to me of his family, as we walk along the port, he remarks that his eldest son was sometimes mistaken for a Jew and remembers someone once yelling "youppins" at the two of them as they crossed a street. From me, he wants to hear about hippies, about LSD, about the hallucinogenic revolution. I talk.

I ask Bardèche if he isn't attracted to a notion of "community" in general: "Yes," he says, "but particularly to Jewish ones, to the Jewish quarter."]

**Kaplan**: Go on.

**Bardèche**: The anti-Semites have the impression, from the outside, that there is a sort of conspiracy to take hold of all the intellectual and sentimental power in the country, whereas it's not that at all—there is simply the fact that the Jews, by their situation, by their personal taste, occupy numerous strategic intellectual positions, and that consequently they help each other—not by a preconceived plan but because it's like that, because it's their sensibility that speaks [*qui parle*] in that manner. So, these two anti-Semitisms, which are absolutely not at all the same, must not be confused. [Bardèche argues that the special issue of *Je Suis Partout* in 1938 was Rebatet's doing. I tell him I've read it. He remarks that Brasillach contributed to the issue but that at *Je Suis Partout* it was always a total editorial anarchy. When I point out that Brasillach ended up severing his ties with *Je Suis Partout*, Bardèche reminds me that the break had nothing to do with anti-Semitism.[22]]

**Bardèche**: The roots of anti-Semitism during the war, and of my anti-Semitism in particular, after the war, go back to what happened in France in 1939–40: a very violent war of religion between the people who wanted the war and the people who didn't want it. We fought absolutely with all our strength, trying to convince the French people that they would be beaten and that it would probably mean the end of French hegemony in Europe—or anyway, of what remained of it. That they would be courting an inevitable catastrophe. And against our point of view we found—in France as well as in Germany—the entire Jewish intelligentsia, which wanted, for reasons of antifascism, to land us in the war.[23] This created a completely different state of mind with respect to the Jews, because from that point on, we considered them responsible for the situation that they had created, for the war that they had wanted. It is very understandable on the part of the Jews against the Germans, given the anti-Semitic politics of Germany. But for us, it seemed to be a veritable national catastrophe. Unhappily, events have proven us abundantly correct.

**Kaplan**: So, you would have called yourself a pacifist during the war—at least, with respect to that particular war?

**Bardèche**: With respect to that particular war, we were absolutely opposed. This is why, in the collaboration, you will find, or we found, in the same ranks and involved in the same political movement, some of the same boys with whom we had fought constantly at the Ecole Normale, since they were on the left and even the extreme left, and we were on the right and even the extreme right. Only they had become, like we were, resolute adversaries of this war. Not for the same reasons—simply by pacifism, by socialism, by hatred of war.

**Kaplan**: Yes, there's an expression in English—we call it "strange bedfellows": people who find themselves in bed together, and shouldn't be there . . .

**Bardèche**: [laughing] Yes, that's what it was all right. There was a completely unexpected meeting of minds [*réunion*] at that moment.[24] Naturally, in 1945, the events of the Purge only confirmed our initial point of view. I've told you in that letter I sent you what is typical about your misunderstanding of me, and what most of the Jews I know and I spend time with don't seem to be able to understand. I didn't do anything before the war.

## Against the Purge

**Kaplan**: You do talk about this in your book on Nuremberg.

**Bardèche**: All of a sudden, after the war. . . . The book you should have read before reading *Nuremberg*, the most characteristic one, is *Lettre à François Mauriac*.[25] It's very important because I found myself right after the war, during the Purge, surrounded by people who had been, who were, admirable patriotic convinced Frenchmen, and who had done their all for their country for years, who were profoundly honest and proper [*propre*] people, who were what is best in the French.[26] And these unhappy people got tossed [*foutu*] into prison—not only did they throw them in prison, they took away their positions, their decorations, and degraded them to the point where they started to say to themselves, "Well, perhaps we were traitors—we didn't realize it, but perhaps we have been traitors." They acted according to their consciences, according to their duty, according to their sense of patriotism, and it was all absolutely overturned. So I was the first to tell them, "You are in the right. When one obeys one's government, one cannot be in the wrong. You were in a dramatic situation. You had a chief of state who had been chosen by plebiscite by the entire French nation, not by 55% but by 90%.[27] All of France was behind him and you have not committed any fault by obeying him. And, on the contrary, it's the people who told you that under such circumstances you ought to have disobeyed who truly carry the responsibility for treason, and especially for all the treason that will be perpetuated in the future, because what you are organizing is a future of treason in which every nation will succumb. It is the end, not only of France, but it will be the end of Europe if your point of view triumphs." That, then, was my first outburst—which had nothing anti-Semitic about it. *Lettre à François Mauriac* is not anti-Semitic. It's against deceit and against the Resistance. In saying the Pétainists were loyal, they were irreproachable, they're the ones who should be holding their heads high. In any case, they should not feel condemned by their conscience. Now this book was an enormous success. It made me famous overnight. This was my first political book. I hadn't done anything political either before the war or during it.

**Kaplan**: Were you a literary critic?

**Bardèche**: Not even that—I was a professor. I was a professor at the Sorbonne at a very young age and, after that, a professor at the University of Lille. Being a professor at the University of Lille during the war was no piece of cake, you know. It was a five-hour train ride, eight hours at the end. There were, at that time, three chairs at Lille, I was carrying all three, and now there are five, or maybe six—it's one of the biggest French universities. I had an enormous amount of work; I had no time to busy myself with politics even if I had wanted to. And so this book transformed me completely. It gave me a format as a political writer that I had not previously possessed, and then *Nuremberg* was born out of that. My reasoning went like this: I reproach the Resistance for creating the state of mind that provoked the Purge in France. The Germans were in the same situation as we were. What were the German generals supposed to do? The German government was the government of Hitler. One had to obey the orders of the government, one had to fight loyally, not for the regime but for the German nation [*patrie*]—and they were sending people to the gallows who had done what any general, what any responsible politician, would have done. Hence, the violence of my polemic against Nuremberg, much more anti-Semitic this time around, because the basic philosophy of Nuremberg was "This is a triumph for Jewish politics, this is the vengeance on all that there was of the best and the most courageous in the German nation." Afterwards, I abandoned all that, or at least I turned to writing political tracts, that are much less interesting—systematic books which wouldn't be of any interest to you.

**Kaplan**: More polemics?

**Bardèche**: I'm only describing all this to show you how there came, in my own thinking, a kind of crystallization, where I considered that all the excesses that came with the victory in 1945 were excesses of Jewish inspiration, and that it was because of that that there was a vengeance disproportionate to the stakes in that war, and which leads us to the current catastrophe — that is to say, the destruction of Europe. So, this book had a very great success.

**Kaplan**: *Nuremberg* or *François Mauriac*?

**Bardèche**: Both. *Mauriac* in France. *Nuremberg* made me known in a number of foreign countries — there were seven or eight translations and then it merited me a trial.

**Kaplan**: Oh?

**Bardèche**: I was thrown into prison under unbelievable conditions. It was the first time in forty years that a writer had been put in prison because of his ideas. Not because of his political actions but because of his ideas. But this is all anecdotal.

## The Literary Republic

**Kaplan**: Did you have the impression after the war that literary history was being rewritten to focus on the writers who had been in the Resistance, writers grouped around Sartre and Camus, and that the rest were thought better off forgotten?

**Bardèche**: Yes, that's it exactly. A phenomenon occurred that is exactly analogous to the one produced in communist parties. A phenomenon of self-censorship by terror. The resisters declared that since all the French newspapers had committed treason during the Occupation, they were the masters of all the newspapers. So they took charge of all of them — and the presses, too. Consequently, absolutely all opinion — not only the mass media but the whole press, was in their hands. They controlled the publishing houses, too. People who had produced works construed as having aided the German propaganda or as having tended in the direction of fascist ideas were ostracized.[28] New directors were named for the publishing houses; there was a sort of intellectual *coup d'état* that put in place solely antifascists.

**Kaplan**: Yes, of course.

**Bardèche**: So these new people declared everyone they wanted to be great writers, and unhappily, they started by burning at the stake all the French writers who had any talent.

**Kaplan**: For example?

**Bardèche**: They banned Montherlant, Marcel Aymé . . .

**Kaplan**: Did Morand suffer from all this?

**Bardèche**: Paul Morand, yes, he suffered horribly. It took him twenty years to regain his footing. He remade his reputation thanks to the cleverness of his wife, a charming woman. You may not be familiar with her; she was a princess who had inherited an enormous fortune in Romania and who had been the great friend of Marcel Proust. So through all that, through his worldly connections, Morand came back into print. Among the foremost banned writers of 1945 there were some absolutely splendid ones—there was Montherland, Marcel Aymé, Anouilh, Paul Morand; there was, in fact, absolutely all that counted in French literature.

**Kaplan**: Was the ban literal?

**Bardèche**: No, it wasn't a judicial ban; they had said that they didn't want those writers getting published, that they would not review their books, that they would be outlawed from the literary republic, if you like. . . . And since *they were* the literary republic . . . Well, for a writer, when nobody wants to talk about him, it's a sort of living death—when his books aren't reviewed, no one talks about him on the radio, when he has no means of letting people know what he's doing, it's total suffocation.

**Kaplan**: And yet, now we end up fascinated by Céline.

**Bardèche**: Yes, but not I—I'm not at all fascinated by Céline.[29]

**Kaplan**: And Rebatet?

**Bardèche**: Rebatet, he's more interesting than Céline. Except that Rebatet was killed as a writer by those politics. Rebatet first spent five years in prison, during which time he wrote *Les Deux Etendards*, a magnificent novel. Then he left prison but no one wanted anything to do with him, and it was years before he could get an editor. And since he had no money at all of his own, he wrote anything at all, pharmaceutical catalogues—*anything*—and he had no time to work. He was an extraordinary man, by his culture, the accuracy of his judgment, his verve, his talent; admirably learned about both painting and music. He wrote a history of music that is a masterpiece.[30] If he had had the time, he would have written a history of painting which would have been a marvel, which would have been one of the great histories of painting in Europe, a magnificent book. And, for all practical purposes, Rebatet was prohibited from writing it.

**Kaplan**: And what of his *Tribus du cinéma*?

**Bardèche**: It's an idiocy.

**Kaplan**: Yes, I know, but idiocy interests me!

[Bardèche had written in his introduction to *Histoire du cinéma* for Brasillach's *Complete Works* that the "air du temps" of the 1930s would scarcely be sensed in the book but for its two-page quotation from Rebatet. In fact, I don't find any mention of Rebatet's *Tribus du cinéma* until the 1943 and 1948 editions. There, it is quoted in italics as estimating the number of Jews, illegal immigrants, masons and marxists in the French film industry between 1936 and 1940 at 100%.[31] The same quote appears in 1954, though no longer in italics, and it disappears from the 1964 edition.[32]]

**Bardèche**: Historic anti-Semitism?

**Kaplan**: Yes.

**Bardèche**: Well, then, let me get back to this 1935 edition of *Histoire du cinéma*. The part that is the most vulnerable in terms of anti-Semitism was written by me. I wasn't especially anti-Semitic at that point, in 1935. And I wrote it because, well, because it's true. I practically copied it — it's the section on the beginnings of American film. I used a book that you can find — in fact, I admitted doing it, I wasn't hiding it — the book by Hampton.[33] I didn't invent the fact that Zukor and all those guys were Jews. It came from Hampton's book. I found it very amusing, this idea of Jewish furriers going into film.

**Kaplan**: And you actually copied all this from an American film history?

**Bardèche**: I simply presented it in an amusing manner, because it seemed funny to me, this flight of Jews descending on the cinema and saying, "Well, here's where the money is," as if they were talking about ready-to-wear, you know? That's what they were selling, and that's where the fast buck could be found; and it's very amusing because you end up with a lot of picturesque characters.[34] It's completely characteristic of American cinema. And this does not in any way mean that I hated the Jews. No, it was simply something picturesque in the birth of American film, that's all.

**Kaplan**: In 1943 you add a chapter to your film book "Rêveries sur un cinéma futur."[35] It seems to me quite important for understanding the ideology of the period. Anyway, I wondered which of you wrote it — your style and Brasillach's correspond rather well, and it's hard to tell.

**Bardèche**: Yes, but still. Once you're in the habit, you can sense the difference. Robert [Brasillach's] style is more fluid, more poetic, richer in images — you feel you're reading someone with a true writer's gift, whereas with me, it's more intellectual. It doesn't happen, if you like, with the same kind of *esprit*, even though I, too, often think in images. It gives more or less the same result, only much more *manufactured*; whereas in Robert's writing, it's *spontaneous*. Let me take a look at this section . . . yes, yes, that's me [reading]: "In 10 years, neither has talking cinema been able to impose a character nor has it strongly depicted a single sentiment." Yes, yes, that's precisely the genre of absolute sentences I'm in the habit of writing [we both laugh].

**Kaplan**: I'd like to hear you talk about a passage from this section that I quote at length in my study, where you say that the Second World War was created in the imagination of film spectators in the 1930s. You say that it's as if the war had already been produced, had been prepared by and at the movies.

**Bardèche**: Yes, that corresponds to my notions. For me, cinema is above all an art to conduct the thought and the sensibilities of people: they can be made to believe anything with cinema; they can be prepared for anything. Cinema is thus a terribly dangerous art. An art for manipulating crowds. Evidently, the cinema of the years preceding the war is, for the most part, an antifascist one.

**Kaplan**: Oh?

**Bardèche**: There is another thing that I'm obligated to tell you, which is important for you in understanding the state of mind during these years. The great break does not take place, as most people think it does, in 1940. It took place in 1936 with the civil war in Spain. Before 1936, the French literary world is (with a few nuances introduced by the surrealists, who were passionate communists) exactly the same literary world as under the symbolists. One took part in a literary world. When one wrote, and when one was what used to be called in those days "a young poet." I heard Supervielle called a "young poet" at age 65, and in all seriousness [laughter]. Anyway, when one was a young poet, one was part of the literary milieu – one of its hopes. And everyone knew one another. There was even a certain etiquette for receiving a book, for calling on someone, like before 1914, in the days of Barrès, when one would write asking to visit an author. "I so admired your book, I would be happy were we able to meet one another," etc. . . . . All of which has totally disappeared. On all sides. In those days there was no sort of antipathy based on political positions, except for the surrealists who were, in general, virulent communists and who wanted to stay apart from all the rest. The others all knew one another, and it never would have occurred to anyone to reproach you your political options or even consider that they were an obstacle to amicable relations. This changed after the war in Spain, when suddenly all of Europe was separated into two camps – fascist and antifascist. Two presses, two groups of publishers. And it was at that moment, in reality, that World War II began. If you like, this was what I was trying to say in another way using films. The psychological preparation of the war started July 18, [1936] I think.

**Kaplan**: [reads the passage] You start with "In our memory it's all strangely mixed up [the phalanges, Roosevelt, Hitler, and so on]. We are haunted by a growing uneasiness which ought to furnish the material for an extraordinary film composition. . . ."

**Bardèche**: [finishing the sentence] Yes, ". . . a film where one could feel the war mounting" [*où l'on sentirait monter la guerre*].[36] It's true, the film was made finally; it's the film *Français si vous saviez*, by Harris and Sedouy.[37] It was a big hit in France. Today, Harris is the head of one of the large French television networks, and Sedouy is a very well-known writer. They made an extremely clever film with bits of documentary footage. That's it – one felt the war mounting, that exact phrase. It isn't at all polemical, it's that one felt the war mount physically, because one felt passions discharging – the nationalists becoming more and more nationalist, the antifascist becoming more and more violent and aggressive on his side. One felt that it would all inevitably end dramatically.

**Kaplan**: But what interests me in that sentence – and indeed, in the film metaphors that run through your polemics after the war as well—is that one can no longer—as of, say, 1939, or maybe even 1915—one can no longer talk politics without talking film. I mean that political ideas or that our images of life come to us quite "naturally" as images from some film. That we no longer have other images.[38]

**Bardèche**: Yes, I'd say rather that they're enhanced or enlivened in film. The images of events given to us by the press and the radio at that moment were *dead* images, as it were. They raised an enthusiasm that had to be provoked and nourished; while the cinema addressed itself directly to the nerves. And consequently, it was our enervation, our nervous tension that we felt to be admirably translated by cinema—as much by the newsreels, in fact, as by narrative films.

*The Talkies—Homage to Benjamin*

**Kaplan**: How do you look back on your reaction to the transition from silent films to the talkies?

**Bardèche**: We felt terribly deceived by the talkies, especially since the first productions were merely reproductions of theater. And we had the impression that the cinema had abruptly ceased to exist—because film had been a language of images, and the minute you start trying to photograph the theater, you're no longer creating the art that we loved. Of course, a certain number of limits were imposed by the privation of speech, but the art came from the suggestion and direction [*gestion*] *by* the image. Whereas we saw no possibility of an art of suggestion in talking films—the few exceptions were the films that showed things that aren't speech but rather *noises* and sensual elements.[39]

**Kaplan**: A cinematic music?

**Bardèche**: A cinematic music, yes, a kind of music of images; images made of sound, if you will. Like the poetry of images, and equally capable of enriching the cinematographic vocabulary. It took us a long time to get used to the new possibilities of sound films. We only discovered them little by little. Even today I have to write a new conclusion to *Histoire du cinéma*. A new edition is supposed to come out next year, but I'm having the updated chapters done by Charles Ford, since it's been years since I've been in touch with films. [The project in question was never completed.][40]

**Kaplan**: Ford—Frenchman with an American name . . .

**Bardèche**: An American movie actor's name, yet [laughter], or an industrialist's name, or whatever! Only I'm the one who has to write the conclusion. And what bothers me the most, what I see as the worst thing about sound film, is that it is always taking on the kind of philosophic problem it can't possibly resolve—the same goes for psychological problems. Cinema does not have the possibility of creating memorable characters: characters by which one remains haunted. Nor can it show what exactly happens within a given sensibility or within someone's mind. That is reserved for the writer. The cinema gives *results*; if you wish, it gives brute results, it gives violent scenes; it shows what happens. But when it wants to give explanations, it gives elementary ones. It falls into didacticism, into all kinds of philosophical stupidities — Freudianism, feminism, tomfoolery — and never is any of it unforgettable. But now I've become a bad judge because I go to the movies rather rarely. I've been deceived so often. Still, there have been some admirable directors, the Italians in particular. Fellini has completely renewed the cinema with what corresponds musically to the invention of jazz or of rock — a sort of syncopated cinema — and he's the only one who has done that.

**Kaplan**: It's interesting that your writing, and even today your conversation about film, keeps coming back to these musical metaphors despite your initial suspicion of sound films. For you and Brasillach, wasn't the *ultimate* film a kind of music?

**Bardèche**: Finally, it isn't purely visual — or the visual must be organized so as to give birth to emotion. Cinema is dangerous precisely because it gives birth to emotion, it directs it; and it can *obtain* anything, you see?

**Kaplan**: What was it, then, that Hitler did in Germany? At Nuremberg? Syberberg has gone so far as to suggest that he "produced and directed" national socialism.[41]

**Bardèche**: Hitler was an ingenious producer of reality: the Nuremberg rallies, even those Olympics. . . . Brasillach's *Notre Avant-Guerre* shows you what Nuremberg was like. We see all that from the outside — we have an idea of what it must have been like, but it's completely wrong. We see this formidable ceremony, and then we don't see all that was improvised, the German bonhomie. There's something meridional about the south of Germany. About Nuremberg — a magnificent prodigious city, straight out of the Middle Ages. They did things at Nuremberg that neither the French nor the Americans would ever have thought of doing. To think that Brasillach and his comrades were only second-rate little journalists. . . . Brasillach was at Nuremberg, and Weimar. And at Nuremberg there was Brasillach, Rebatet, and two or three people from *Je Suis Partout*. Georges Blond, too, I think. The Germans didn't know quite where to put them to show them the parades preceding the rally, so they stuck them in a hotel room reserved for Goering [laughter]. They were in Goering's room. . . . They said that Hitler had marvelous eyes when he looked at you — that it was extraordinary. It's funny.

**Kaplan**: Yes, but it doesn't show in the photos, or in the films.

**Bardèche**: The films don't show the hypnotic Hitler. No one had the power to affect crowds anywhere near the way that he could all alone, speaking into the microphones. He absolutely enthralled [*empoignait*] them. It was even more impressive than all those flags. In 1942, Brasillach was invited to the

Weimar Congress as the representative of *Je Suis Partout*. All the big French papers and important writers were there—Drieu la Rochelle, Bonnard. You've probably seen the photos.

[We talk about *Potemkin*. Bardèche calls it *the* great film of his youth. I bring up its conceivable influence on Hitler and Goebbels.[42]]

**Bardèche**: You reminded me in your letter of something Robert wrote, which seems so true [*juste*] to me; his remark about the *two* poetries of the twentieth century.

**Kaplan**: Yes, communism and fascism.[43]

**Bardèche**: Yes, well, I'm going to add a third that is going to surprise you. When we were about twenty years old, say around 1932, when we were at the Ecole Normale, there was a journal run by Philippe Lamour—I've forgotten its title for the moment—not *Bifur*? [I guess he means *Plans*.[44]] Anyway, we liked it a lot, and it corresponded to a kind of sensibility of all young people at that moment. It consisted of (1) admiration for the construction of a great country in Soviet Russia, and admiration for the same phenomenon in fascist Italy; (2) enthusiasm for national socialism and for the prodigious rise of Hitler; and (3) Roosevelt.

**Kaplan**: [misunderstanding his pronunciation] What's that?

**Bardèche**: Tennessee Valley Authority.

**Kaplan**: [laughing] Roosevelt—the New Deal!

**Bardèche**: [misunderstanding my pronunciation] What?

**Kaplan**: [slowly] The New Deal.

**Bardèche**: The New Deal, yes, that's it! [laughter] From the outside, you understand, crudely informed as we were about America, we saw a renewal, a sort of American fascism; a transformation of America that seemed to us of precisely the same order as what excited us about Soviet Russia, or about Italy or Germany.

**Kaplan**: You saw everything aesthetically, rather than politically.

**Bardèche**: Ah, there you are completely right—aesthetically, and *not* politically, with the contradictions of the aesthetic. There is, if you like, a link between aestheticism and fascism. We were probably mistaken to connect aesthetics and politics, which are not the same thing.

**Kaplan**: It turned out to be a dangerous link.

**Bardèche**: Yes, your diagnosis is exact.

**Kaplan**: It's not mine—Walter Benjamin wrote it up in 1932.

**Bardèche**: Who?

**Kaplan**: Walter Benjamin, the critic. The name doesn't mean anything to you?

**Bardèche**: No, nothing.

**Kaplan**: He died during the war. . . .[45]

**Bardèche**: Well, yes, it is an excellent diagnosis for you; and I see, then, how *Histoire du cinéma* becomes a point of departure: a significant proof of what was, perhaps, the malady of our generation. Our aesthetics were mobilized by the intermediary of the Spanish Civil War to the profit of fascism. If another event had been generated in the U.S., we might have been mobilized in favor of the U.S., although . . .

**Kaplan**: There have been quasi-fascist movements in the U.S.

**Bardèche**: Oh, there certainly are—for years I've received through the mails the [newsletter] "Common Sense" from some old [American] lady [laughter] telling me that everything I've ever said about the Jews is nothing but kind and affectionate bantering.

**Kaplan**: You get fascist fan mail?

**Bardèche**: Oh yes, for a long time I've received letters from nuts, even these days I get abundant mail: look at all these letters and reviews in today's delivery alone. . . . There is a much more virulent fascism in the U.S. than there ever was in Europe. To think that in the United States there is a fascist party, iron crosses, the whole bit.

[We talk about the neo-Nazis in Chicago and in North Carolina.]

**Bardèche**: In general, they're pathetic types. But notice that in America they are tolerated, whereas someone analogous would be completely unthinkable in Europe. In the United States, everyone has the right to express his own opinion.

**Kaplan**: Yes, well, apparently. We call that civil liberties.

**Bardèche**: Does the Faurisson controversy mean anything to you?

**Kaplan**: Yes—the person who said . . .

**Bardèche**: Who said there were never any gas chambers.

*The Faurisson Controversy*

**Bardèche**: There are two arguments. One goes way back, to 1960. Someone name Broszat gave a paper; he was the director of the Institute of Contemporary History in Munich, where you find only resolute anti-Hitlerians, university professors, etc. This man was the first to investigate the camps and to say, wait a minute, contrary to popular belief there were never any camps—I mean any gas chambers—in any of the concentration camps where we were able to verify the accounts, the construction, etc. That means in all of Germany, in all the territory of the former Reich. It was understood that we don't have the possibility of any such confirmation for the camps in Poland—notably Auschwitz. Now this raised no problems—because of the personality of the professor who did the research.[46] And then two years ago, there was this Englishman named Faurisson.

**Kaplan**: I thought he was French.

**Bardèche**: He's French but of English origins. He had always been anti-German, a 40- or 50-year-old man who hadn't been involved in the events of the war. He was a professor at the University of Lyon, a specialist in archival research, who all of a sudden declared to his students, "Look here, I've studied an enormous number of documents and I've looked carefully at all the transcripts from the Nuremberg trials, at everything written on the camps, and I've arrived at the conclusion that no one has ever been able to prove the existence of any gas chamber nor come up with a witness of a gas chamber."

This same argument had already been made by an old friend of mine — a professor who had been in the Resistance and who had been deported, spent two years in a German camp, came back weighing forty kilos, and was elected deputy of Belfort. A socialist with a brilliant political career before him. But he published a book — it was called *Le Mensonge d'Ulysse* [Ulysse's lie] — where he said that "the camps weren't what people thought, I was there and most of what people say about them amounts to a lot of ridiculous propaganda."

**Kaplan**: But just the same, he did come home weighing forty kilos.

**Bardèche**: That he didn't hide; he was badly fed. I'm the one who published his books for him. People struck out against him. No one wanted to talk about his books; he was persecuted in every way. He died miserable. A good person; his name was Paul Rassinier. And no one would believe him.[47]

**Kaplan**: [too quietly] The camps are impossible merely to "tell" about. . . .

**Bardèche**: [not hearing, or not understanding] And now Faurisson, from an entirely different generation, is taking up this investigation once again and has come to this conclusion that there were no concentration camps — I mean, that there were no gas chambers. And when he said so to his students, it didn't cause any uproar. Then one day, he published it in my little review, *Défense de l'Occident*.[48] He wasn't at all right wing — he's a leftist. He came to see me one day, saying, "Look here, I'm bringing you an article. I'm not at all in agreement with your political ideas. I've nothing in common with you politically. I'm on the left, but I can't place this article anywhere — no one will touch it; it's been refused by the entire press, and people say 'There's only one man who would publish this.' "

It would have passed by unnoticed, like everything I publish in my little review, where I can grow hoarse talking about whatever I like and no one picks up on it . . . but by chance, this particular article came to the attention and received the full indignation of the great socialist paper *Le Matin de Paris*, which published an article saying, "It's atrocious, the Nazis are raising their ugly heads. Not only is there this Nazi that you all know, whose sad reputation is no longer in the making [laughs]—what is more, this brute has disciples, a wretched one named Faurisson who has dared to say. . . . It is madness that such things can be written!" And that unleashed the Affaire Faurisson.[49] The entire press, the Jews in particular, screamed about Faurisson. There were serious incidents on the campus at Lyon where he was teaching. He was accosted; he was forbidden to meet his classes.

**Kaplan:** Was he dismissed?

**Bardèche:** He lost his position, and it has now been two years that he's been fighting against an extremely violent opposition. One curious thing is that he's supported in France, on the one hand, by me—by a group on the extreme right—and, on the other hand, by the extreme left. He had the nerve to seek out the ultraleftists.

**Kaplan:** Who?

**Bardèche:** A paper you must know of, if you're at all in on the Paris scene. It's *Libération*. *Libération* is a paper read by all the young people, started by the May '68 crowd, you know, the people who were behind the barricades. *Libération* represents what is farthest to the left in the French press.

**Kaplan:** And they're in agreement with him?

**Bardèche:** Faurisson went to see them. They had been writing furious articles against him saying Faurisson is insane, Faurisson is a criminal, and so on; he should be assassinated; it's intolerable that people like this can even breathe. And Faurisson sought them out and said, "Listen, look at everything you've said about me—couldn't we explain ourselves just the same?" And he told them everything he had done, the verification of the facts, all his work—and the people at *Libération* were extremely surprised. And little by little, a group there took charge of his discoveries and published his books, his documents. They are presently the most active group supporting him.[50] As for me, I'm outside all political action . . . whereas they're at the political forefront. . . .

My own contention is that the so-called gas chambers were constructed for the first time in 1945, for the Allied propaganda effort after the war. That's Faurisson's conclusion, and I think he is right.

**Kaplan:** Putting this contention aside for the moment: there were enough atrocities committed by the Nazis without having to fabricate an additional one. Why on earth would anyone feel the need?

**Bardèche:** Because *this* one was the most convincing atrocity of all. And there they are right. They are right.

**Kaplan:** Can you give me the reference for the Faurisson article? [We are both drained and exhausted.]

**Bardèche:** Yes, and one more thing, in terms of the U.S.. The only man who protested against the Faurisson trial, curiously, is an American professor, a world-renowned linguist whom you must know—Noam Chomsky. And

188 □ THE LATE SHOW

Noam Chomsky created quite a sensation in France; he provoked a serious controversy, and all the intellectuals were indignant that he dared to write what he did.

**Kaplan**: Chomsky is an independent.

**Bardèche**: "The liberty of the press consists precisely in writing things that shock people. If you conceive of the liberty of the press as the liberty to write what everyone already thinks, it's not worth it — don't talk about the liberty of the press. [laughter] The liberty of the press consists in shocking," he said, "I am on the side of Faurisson."[51]

[Suzanne Bardèche interrupts our silence following this remark to announce that one of the grandchildren has returned from the beach, bitten by a jellyfish. After the wound has been tended, we sit on the porch drinking tea. I head back to my hotel in the dusk.]

## Notes

1. Maurice Bardèche, *Lettre à François Mauriac* (1947); *Nuremberg ou la terre promise* (1948); *Qu'est-ce que le fascisme?* (1961).

2. Events and anecdotes surrounding Brasillach's trial and execution are discussed in Robert Aron, *Histoire de l'épuration*, vol. 2, pp. 322–54.

3. Letter received from Maurice Bardèche, dated May 28, 1982. Pierre-Marie Dioudonnat's painstakingly documented *Je Suis Partout* lists Bardèche's publications in this biographical appendix, p. 443:

> Bardèche (Maurice). Born October 1, 1907 at Dun-le-Roi, near Bourges. Secondary studies at the Bourges lycée, then at Louis-le-Grand in Paris where he meets and befriends R. Brasillach, whose sister he marries in July 1934. Admitted to the Ecole Normale Supérieure in 1928. Receives his "agrégation" in literature in 1932. Doctoral thesis on the art of the novel in Balzac. Professor at the Sorbonne on a temporary appointment, then professor of French literature at Lille (1942–1944).
>
> Writes for the *Revue française*. Film critic at *1933* then at *L'Assaut* in 1936–37. Writes with Robert Brasillach a *History of Motion Pictures* (1935), then a *History of the War in Spain* (1939). Contributes two articles to *Je Suis Partout* on Spain: "L'auxilio social, oeuvre du christianisme fasciste" (15 July 1938); "Petit croquis de la vie espagnole" (5 August 1938), and several essays on film [these are all excerpts from what will be the 1943 edition of *Histoire du cinéma*]. . . . Alone: "Rêveries sur un cinéma futur" (7 August 1942) [this appears in the 1943 edition under both signatures; see discussion above] and two literary articles: "Balzac stendahlien" (21 March 1942) and "Stendahl journaliste" (30 April 1943).
>
> Arrested during the Liberation and imprisoned at Drancy.
>
> Since the war, author of numerous political essays and critical studies. *Grand prix de la critique littéraire* in 1971 for his *Marcel Proust, romancier*.

4. Serge Daney and Serge Toubiana, reviewing *Français, si vous saviez*, by Harris and Sedouy, pp. 54–62.

5. Bardèche, *Nuremberg*, pp. 23–24.

6. *Ibid.*, p. 146.

7. In the words of one American trial counsel, "Here we are on the eve of the opening of the second most important trial in the world (no. 1: the trial of Jesus Christ). Tomorrow morning the trial opens. And believe me, the prosecution is utterly, completely, hopelessly unprepared. Jackson will deliver a sensational opening statement—and from that point on we're in the soup." Unpublished correspondence dated Nuremberg, November 19, 1945, property of the author.

8. For an account of Chomsky's role in the Faurisson controversy, see *Le Monde*, December 20, 1980; December 24, 1980. The most thorough analysis of Faurisson's complete works (including his literary criticism on Rimbaud and Lautréamont) is in Nadine Fresco, "Les redresseurs de morts," pp. 2150–2211.

9. On opposing reactions to the war in Lebanon within the French Jewish community, see Walker, "Divided They Stand," pp. 8 - 17.

10. John Berger, *About Looking*, p. 59.

11. *Ibid., p. 60*

12. Bardèche, *Qu'est-ce que le fascisme?*, p. 177.

13. Alain de Benoist, quoted in "L'Intellectuel et le pouvoir," p. 48.

14. Remember that this same rhetoric of neither/nor-ness furnished Sternhell with a title for his book on fascist ideology in France (*Ni droite ni gauche*).

15. Maurice Bardèche, introduction to the reprint of *Histoire du cinéma* in Brasillach, *Oeuvres complètes*, vol. 10, p. 8.

16. The 1943 edition mentioned Chaplin's "strangely Hebraic" persona (see p. 146 above). *The Great Dictator* was not shown in France until after the war, and thus after Brasillach's execution. Bardèche writes alone in the 1948 edition:

> *The Great Dictator* is a polemical Chaplin. Let's not hold him responsible even for that ridiculous ending where Charlie gives a great speech to the public in which he lets all of his messianic spirit, all the clichés of propaganda show. It was the end of the pacifist of *Shoulder Arms*, the end of the inspired poet of the primitive era, it was an entry into fake glory, fake values, it was a talking Charlie, it was no longer Charlie. (p. 440)

Bardèche, who had considered himself a pro-Hitlerian pacifist in the 1930s, blamed both the outbreak of war in France and the violence of the postwar purges on an uncontrollable Jewish lust for vengeance. For him, then, the Jewish ghetto barber turned dictator must have seemed a literal portrait of the Jew as warmonger, the Jew as messianic polemicist, the Jew as the true embodiment of the evil "misattributed" to Hitler. Yet, later in the same passage, Bardèche lauds the film's scenes of the Jewish ghetto, reminiscent for him of the forgotten greatness of the European Yiddish theaters.

17. The date of the visit isn't clear to me. Chaplin came to France in 1931 and 1932 after the European release of *City Lights*, thus before the making of the more polemical *Modern Times*. Brasillach was then 22 years old and had just become the literary critic for *Action Française*. The first edition of *Histoire du cinéma*, which would have made him known to Chaplin, wasn't to appear until 1935.

18. He describes his decision to join the milieu in *Notre Avant-Guerre*, p. 86: "I don't think there exists a single big paper outside of *Action Française*, which would have given as important a literary page to a 22-year-old boy."

19. The distinction between a rational and an instinctive racism is traditional on the racist right. See Brasillach's "rational" version outlined in "La Question Juive," an April 15, 1938, editorial in *Je Suis Partout*. His context is a special issue of that newspaper entitled "Les Juifs dans le monde," directed by Rebatet. Rebatet will edit another special issue, "Les Juifs et la France," appearing February 17, 1939: racism is nearing closer to home.

20. See my discussion of French anti-Semitism as telephonocentricism, pp. 133–39 above.

21. *Qu'est-ce que le fascisme?*, p. 165. The literary echo here is obviously Barrès, *Les Déracinés*.

22. By 1943, Brasillach realized that the journal's policy of advocating a German victory was foolhardy. He resigned as editor in chief of *Je Suis Partout* on August 15, 1943.

23. Marrus and Paxton, *Vichy France and the Jews*, give an important sense of the pervasiveness of intellectual anti-Semitism in the 1930s, as apparent in the antiparliamentarianism of Giraudoux's *Pleins Pouvoirs* as in the "outer limits of acceptable discourse set by the Céline's, the Brasillach's, and the Drieu's." Marrus and Paxton link the anti-Semitism to the protective xenophobia created by the massive numbers of political refugees coming into France between 1931 and 1940: "One would have to have been, simultaneously, an advocate of war, a Keynesian, and a cultural pluralist to make a frontal attack on xenophobia and anti-semitism in the France of the 1930's. . . . There remained only the moral argument in favor of the immigrants" (p. 49).

24. Marrus and Paxton mention the French Jewish writer Emmanuel Berl as a most incongruous supporter of Munich and of Pétain (Berl's work had been favorably reviewed by Brasillach, and he was a personal friend of Drieu, portrayed by him as the character Preuss in *Gilles*). Of the left-wing pacifists, the best known is perhaps Simone Weil. According to Simone Petrément, Weil writes Gaston Bergery in 1938 that she "preferred German hegemony to war, even though it would mean 'certain laws of exclusion against communists and Jews' " (*La Vie de Simone Weil*, vol. II, p. 187, quoted in Marrus and Paxton, p. 39).

25. See Robert Aron, *Histoire de l'épuration*, vol. 1, for an account of Mauriac's postwar attempt to act as a moral conciliator between Vichy and Resistance intellectuals.

26. Paxton's oft-quoted remark corresponds to Bardèche's: "to judge Vichy is to judge the French elite," *Vichy France*, p. 228. But note Bardèche's strategy: Brasillach, Drieu, and Rebatet were self-proclaimed Parisian collaborators, often critical of Vichy intellectuals for their lack of gumption; it is in the name of the Vichy writers, not the Parisian ones, that Bardèche launches his defense.

27. The use of percentages is misleading. On June 16, 1940, Pétain replaced Reynaud as Président du Conseil. On July 10, the National Assembly voted constituent powers to Pétain by 569 votes to 80 (a number of assembly members who had fled for safety were unable to vote). Pétain was charged with the task of creating a new constitution, which was to have been approved by a plebiscite—but this never took place. See Novick, *The Resistance versus Vichy*, p. 5. Paxton (*Vichy France*, p. 234) states that Pétain was probably as universally accepted by the French public in June 1940 as was de Gaulle in August 1944: his observation is widely accepted.

28. See Robert Aron, *Histoire de l'épuration*, vol. 3. The literary purge came from within the literary community. On September 6, 1944, a group of Resistance intellectuals (*Le Comité national des écrivains*) signed a pledge not to publish with any press that published certain renowned collaborators. Among the collaborators listed were Brasillach, Céline, Alphonse de Chateaubriant, and Giono. Three subsequent lists were drawn up in September and October. Morand was dropped from the blacklist on October 21.

29. In a letter to me dated October 29, 1985, Bardèche writes in response to my manuscript that he has since undertaken a study of Céline (forthcoming in spring or summer of 1986). The point of view expressed in the study is completely different from that expressed here.

30. Rebatet's *Une Histoire de la musique* has most recently been favorably reviewed in *Eléments*, February-March 1980, no. 33, though its pro-Wagnerian "obsession" was criticized in an ensuing letter to the editor of that journal, summer 1980, no. 35, p. 52. See my note on the reedition of Rebatet's "fascist memoirs," p. 139–40 (Note 1) above.

31. Bardèche and Brasillach, *Histoire du cinéma* (1943), pp. 350–51, (1948), pp. 410–11.

32. *Histoire du cinéma* (1954), vol. 2, p. 170.

33. Benjamin B. Hampton, *A History of the Movies*, reprinted as *History of the American Film Industry from its Beginning to 1931*.

34. Hampton, a former American Tobacco executive who, along with Paramount head Hodkin-

son, was financially defeated in the film business by mastermind Adolph Zukor, actually wrote his film history in defense of Zukor's methods and of what he understood as film's contribution to American democracy (Hampton even baptizes the American filmgoer "Demos"). Hampton is an American populist. It's the "just plain folk," he argues, who, much more than the businessmen and the producers, control the film industry and who choose its stars as expressions of their own desires for entertainment. And he argues that this unprecedented measure of consumer control in the film industry dictated an unprecedented business practice. Hampton is thus fascinated and impressed by the upset of the "blue-blooded" Wall Street set by the "east side upstarts" of the film industry, "ambitious young Jews . . . restlessly searching for access to the sources of wealth and power" (p. 26). He mocks racially motivated myths of Zukor's "Oriental [read Semitic] subtlety" by lauding his entrepreneurial insight: "While others [ostensibly Hampton himself] were debating the wisdom of established customs, Zukor would quietly change his opinions and move swiftly along new and apparently dangerous lines to deal with crises" (pp. 183–84).

Bardèche's rewrite of this assessment puts the emphasis back onto Zukor's Judaism and his connection to "his coreligionist bankers at Kuhn, Loeb, and Company." Zukor's maneuvers are, in Bardèche's text, "underhanded [*sournois*] and complex." Zukor succeeds in eliminating Hodkinson from Paramount and takes advantage of the latter's difficulties to negotiate exclusive rights to Mary Pickford. "And American film," Bardèche concludes, "the 'third industry of the world,' woke up one fine morning in the hands of the patient little Jewish furrier" (1954, p. 42).

35. Bardèche and Brasillach, *Histoire du cinéma* (1943), pp. 401–4.

36. Ibid., p. 336.

37. See my discussion of the film above, p. 163.

38. The most extreme metaphoric reaction comes in Bardèche's anti-Semitic prose in *Nuremberg*, in which he describes the camps as a "media scam" perpetrated by the Allies after the war.

39. Bardèche and Brasillach's favorite early sound films were *Hallelujah*, for its "black baptismal hysteria," and *Eskimo*, shot entirely in the Eskimo language, with subtitles (*Histoire du cinéma*, 1943, p. 248). See my discussion of sound film, pp. 147–53 above.

40. See Charles Ford, "Cinéma et propagande," pp. 49–50.

41. Hans-Jürgen Syberberg, *Our Hitler*; or *Hitler—A Film from Germany*, 1977.

42. The anecdote we discuss is treated by Charles Ford in "Cinéma et propagande." Apparently, it was Goebbels who called for the creation of a film that would be for national socialism what *Potemkin* was for communism. Ford argues that cinema is *not* directly effective as a propaganda tool, since, for example, *Potemkin* has been shown again and again in capitalist countries without inciting revolution. My own response to Ford would be that the political effect of a film on its viewers may very well be completely unrelated to that film's "theme" or "intentions"—for example, *Potemkin* itself was for national socialism what it was for communism—or maybe *more*.

43. Robert Brasillach, "Lettre à un soldat de la classe 60," pp. 140–41: "fascism has been the very poetry of the 20th century (alongside communism). . . . Perhaps in a thousand years, people will mix up the two revolutions of the 20th century."

44. Sternhell discusses the fascist modernism of *Plans* in *Ni droite ni gauche*, p. 222. Brasillach and Bardèche quote from the 1930's magazine *Bifur* in *Histoire du cinéma* (1943, p. 248; Barry, p. 311).

45. September 26, 1940. Walter Benjamin, en route to America at the Franco-Spanish border, committed suicide after learning of a sudden embargo on visas. The embargo was to be lifted several weeks later.

46. Bardèche refers to a footnote in Faurisson's article, citing a letter written by Martin Broszat, director of the Institute of Contemporary History at Munich, to *Die Zeit* (August 19, 1960). The purpose of Broszat's letter to the editor was simply to point out an error in an earlier article in *Die Zeit* in which the author had referred to "gas chambers at Dachau"—one of the camps where there were no gas chambers. Broszat underlined the importance of historical accuracy and the danger of

using information out of context. Faurisson, in turn, uses Broszat's letter completely out of context as though it contained some kind of revelation. (See Fresco's biting analysis of Faurisson's pseudo-evidence in "Les Redresseurs de morts," p. 2177.) On the basis of this misreading, Bardèche can tell the story of Faurisson's "truth" as though it originated with Broszat.

In a letter to me dated October 29, 1985, in response to the manuscript of this interview, Bardèche asks that I note a "rectification by Broszat" published in *Le Monde*, May 23, 1967, p. 4. The article he refers to, entitled "Camps de concentration avec et sans chambre à gaz," is more precisely the rectification of a May 10, 1967, article (p. 1) in which *Le Monde* had quoted a neo-Nazi politico in Germany, stating that neither camps nor gas chambers existed on Third Reich territory. The article then refers to the Munich Institute of Contemporary History's August 19, 1960, finding that the Nazi gas chambers were located in the occupied territories of the Third Reich, rather than within the Third Reich proper. *Le Monde* concludes bitterly "Certain German neo-Nazis have attempted to make this *distinguo* serve to demonstrate their thesis on the 'exaggeration' of the accusations made against the Third Reich." Indeed! Obviously the scare quotes and bitter sarcasm of *Le Monde*'s final sentence are not enough to prevent Bardèche from believing that the article, if quoted or described out of context, might somehow serve his purposes. Again, see Fresco's analysis ("Les redresseurs de morts," pp. 2150–2211) of these same slippery tactics of misquotation and misappropriation of empirical research in the writings of Faurisson.

47. Paul Rassinier, *Le Mensonge d'Ulysse*, 4th edition. This edition contains two books. *Passage de la ligne* (originally published in 1948 by the Editions Bressanes) is an account of the author's experiences at Dora and Buchenwald. *Le Mensonge d'Ulysse* (originally published by the same editors in 1950) is a critical review of literature about the camps—and especially David Rousset's *L'Univers concentrationnaire*. Rassinier attacks the "cover-up" of non-Nazi camps in the U.S.S.R. and the U.S., and he attacks the behavior of the detainee "*Kapos*" within the camps. He argues that the horror of the camps was exaggerated and that there were no gas chambers at Buchenwald or Dora. Like Bardèche he is scandalized by the "mentality of the purge" but does not appear to consider himself an apologist for fascism. Rassinier will appear as a martyr figure in the writings of Faurisson.

48. Robert Faurisson, "Le 'Problème' des chambres à gaz," pp. 32–40. Faurisson's work might serve as a bizarre and disturbing appendix to George Mosse's *Toward the Final Solution*, which tracks the Holocaust from its eighteenth-century foundations. Here, it is the very denial of that trajectory that is in question.

49. The story "broke" in *Le Matin* on November 9, 1978.

50. Bardèche confuses the editors of *Libération* with the members of an extreme-left anarchist publishing house, La Vieille Taupe, whose members have what might be called "historic ties" with *Libération* from earlier days. La Vieille Taupe reprinted work by Faurisson and Rassinier in the name of an obscure libertarian-anarchist position, using their work as part of a strategy for attacking others' use of Holocaust memories to justify certain present-day forms of imperialism. Among the more vocal members of La Vieille Taupe are Serge Thion and Pierre Guillaume. *Libération* was highly criticized for publishing an editorial column by Guillaume (March 8, 1979). The paper did not support the position of La Vieille Taupe and, according to Fresco, refused to print at least one letter by Guillaume endorsing Faurisson.

51. According to accounts in *Le Monde*, it was finally Jean-Pierre Faye, author of *Langages totalitaires*, who dissuaded Chomsky from pursuing his civil-liberties stand with respect to Faurisson. Faye's thesis is that fascism was legitimized by the spread, or slippage, of certain messages from text to text—the more "innocent" the author and intentions, the swifter the passage.

# References

# References

All page numbers in the footnotes correspond to the editions cited below. I refer the reader to published English language translations whenever possible.

Adorno, Theodor W., in collaboration with Betty Aron, Maria Hertz Levinson, and William Morow. *The Authoritarian Personality.* New York: Norton, 1969.

Akermark, Margareta, ed. "Remembering Iris Barry" (brochure). New York: The Museum of Modern Art, 1980.

*Almanach de la T.S.F.* Paris: Editions de "Tout," 1934; 1937.

Althusser, Louis. "Ideology and Ideological State Apparatuses (Notes Towards an Investigation)." In *Lenin and Philosophy and Other Essays*, trans. Ben Brewster, pp. 127-86. London: New Left Books, 1971.

Andreu, Pierre. *Drieu, témoin et visionnaire.* Preface by Daniel Halévy. Paris: Grasset, 1952.

Andreu, Pierre, and Frédéric Grover. *Drieu la Rochelle.* Paris: Hachette, 1979.

Angenot, Marc. *La Parole pamphlétaire: Contribution à la typologie des discours modernes.* Paris: Payot, 1982.

Arendt, Hannah. *Eichmann in Jerusalem: A Report on the Banality of Evil.* New York: Penguin Books, 1964.

Arendt, Hannah. "From the Dreyfus Affair to France Today." In *Essays on Antisemitism*, ed. Koppel S. Pinson. pp. 173-217. New York: Conference on Jewish Relations, 1946.

Arendt, Hannah. *The Origins of Totalitarianism: Antisemitism, Imperialism, Totalitarianism.* New York: Harcourt Brace, 1966.

Aron, Robert. *Histoire de l'épuration.* 3 vols. in 4. Paris: Fayard, 1969.

Bakhtin, Mikhail. *Rabelais and His World.* Cambridge, Mass: MIT Press, 1968.

Banham, Reyner. *Theory and Design in the First Machine Age.* Cambridge, Mass.: MIT Press, 1981.

Bardèche, Maurice. *Lettre à François Mauriac.* Paris: La Pensée Libre, 1947.

Bardèche, Maurice. *Nuremberg ou la terre promise.* Paris: Les Sept Couleurs, 1948.

Bardèche, Maurice. *Qu'est-ce que le fascisme?* Paris: Les Sept Couleurs, 1961.

Bardèche, Maurice, and Robert Brasillach. *Histoire du cinéma.* Paris: Denoël, 1935.

Bardèche, Maurice, and Robert Brasillach. *Histoire du cinéma: Edition définitive illustrée de soixante et une photographies hors-texte.* Paris: Denoël, 1943.

Bardèche, Maurice, and Robert Brasillach. *Histoire du cinéma.* 3d ed. Givors: André Martel, 1948.

Bardèche, Maurice, and Robert Brasillach. *Histoire du cinéma.* 4th ed. 2 vols. Givors: André Martel, 1954.

Bardèche, Maurice, and Robert Brasillach. *Histoire du cinéma.* 6th ed. 2 vols. Paris: Le Livre de poche, 1964.

Bardèche, Maurice, and Robert Brasillach. *The History of Motion Pictures.* Trans. and ed. Iris Barry, forward by John E. Abbott. New York: Norton and the Museum of Modern Art, 1938. Reprint. New York: Arno Press, 1970.

Baron, Etienne. *La France et ses colonies.* Paris: Magnard, 1936.

Baron, Etienne. *Géographie générale.* Paris: Magnard, 1942.

Baron, Etienne. *Géographie de la France et du monde.* Paris: Magnard, 1943.

Baron, Etienne. *Histoire de la France.* Paris: Magnard, 1941.

Barrès, Maurice. *Les Déracinés* [*Le Roman de l'énergie nationale*, (I)]. 2 vols. Paris: Plon-Nourrit, 1920 [orig. ed., 1897]. [Reprint. Paris: Livre de poche, 1967.]

Barsam, Richard Meran. *Filmguide to Triumph of the Will.* Bloomington: Indiana University Press, 1975.

Bataille, Georges. "Textes se rattachant à 'La Structure psychologique du fascisme'." In *Oeuvres complètes*, vol. 3, pp. 161–65. Paris: Gallimard, 1970.

Bazin, André. *Qu'est-ce que le cinéma?* Paris: Editions du Cerf, 1958.

Bellanger, Claude, et. al. *Histoire générale de la presse française.* Vol. 3 (1871–1940). Paris: Presses Universitaires de France, 1972.

Benjamin, Walter. "André Gide et ses nouveaux adversaires." In *Oeuvres de Walter Benjamin.* Trans. Maurice de Gandillac. Vol. 2, pp. 211–24. Paris: Denoël, 1971. (Originally appeared in *Das Wort*, vol. 1, 1936 as "Letter from Paris".)

Benjamin, Walter. *Briefe.* Letter to Gerhard Scholem, July 2, 1937, and to Max Horkheimer, April 16, 1938. Ed. Gershom Scholem and Theodor W. Adorno. Frankfurt am Maim: Suhrkamp Verlag, 1966, pp. 730–31 and 750–54. (Available in French as: *Correspondance.* Ed. Gershom Scholem and Théodor W. Adorno. Trans. Guy Petitdemange. Paris: Aubier Montaigne, 1978.)

Benjamin, Walter. "Theories of German Fascism: On the Collection of Essays War and Warrior, edited by Ernst Jünger." Trans. Jerolf Wikoff. *New German Critique* 17 (Spring 1979):120–128.

Benjamin, Walter. "The Work of Art in the Age of Mechanical Reproduction." In *Illuminations*, trans. Harry Zohn, pp. 217–52. New York: Schocken Books, 1969.

Benoist-Méchin, Jacques. *La Moisson de quarante; journal d'un prisonnier de guerre.* Paris: A. Michel, 1941.

Berg, Elizabeth. "The Third Woman" (reviewing work by Luce Irigaray and Sarah Kofman). *Diacritics* 12, no. 2 (Summer 1982):11–20.

Berger, John. *About Looking.* New York: Pantheon Books, 1980.

Bergson, Henri. *An Introduction to Metaphysics.* Trans. T. E. Hulme. New York and London: G.P. Putnam's Sons, 1912 (orig. ed., 1903).

Blos, Peter. "The Second Individuation Process of Adolescence." In *The Psychoanalytic Study of the Child*, vol. 22, pp. 162–86. New York: International Universities Press, 1967.

Bottomore, Tom, ed. *A Dictionary of Marxist Thought.* Cambridge, Mass.: Harvard University Press, 1983.

Brasillach, Robert. "Cent heures chez Hitler." *La Revue Universelle* (October 1937): 55–73.

Brasillach, Robert. Reviewing Rebatet, *Les Décombres.* "Espoir ou colère." *Je Suis Partout.* April 11, 1942. Reprint. *Oeuvres complètes*, vol. 12, pp. 610–14.

Brasillach, Robert. "Lettre à quelques jeunes gens." *Révolution Nationale* (February 19, 1943). Reprint. *Oeuvres complètes*, vol. 12, pp. 610–14 .

Brasillach, Robert. "Lettre à un soldat de la classe '60." In *Ecrit à Fresnes*, pp 127–50. Paris: Plon, 1967.

Brasillach, Robert. *Lettres écrites en prison*. In *Ecrit à Fresnes*, pp. 151–268 and 431–67. Paris: Plon, 1967.

Brasillach, Robert. *Notre Avant-Guerre* (1941). Reprint in *Une Génération dans l'orage*. Paris: Plon, 1968.

Brasillach, Robert. *Oeuvres complètes*. Ed. and annotated Maurice Bardèche. 12 vols. Paris: Club de l'honnête homme, 1963–64.

Brasillach, Robert. "Pour un fascisme français." *Je Suis Partout*, November 6, 1942. Reprint. *Oeuvres complètes*, vol. 12, pp. 499–500.

Brasillach, Robert. "La Question juive." Editorial in "Les Juifs." Special issue, *Je Suis Partout*, April 15, 1938, p. 1.

Brasillach, Robert. Reviewing Céline, *L'Ecole des cadavres*. "Les Juifs et la France." Special issue, *Je Suis Partout*, February 17, 1939, p. 8.

Brasillach, Robert. *Les Sept Couleurs* (orig. ed., 1939) and *Le Marchand d'oiseaux*. Paris: Plon, 1970.

Bukalsi, Peter J., ed. *Film Research*. Boston: G. K. Hall, 1972.

Cantimori, Delio. *Conversandi di storia*. Bari: Editori Laterza, 1967.

Cazeneuve, Jean. *La Société de l'ubiquité: Communication et diffusion*. Paris: Denoël, 1972.

Céline, Louis-Ferdinand. *Bagatelles pour un massacre*. Paris: Denoël, 1937.

Céline, Louis-Ferdinand. *Bagatelles pour un massacre*. (New illustrated edition). Paris: Denoël, 1943.

Céline, Louis-Ferdinand. *Death on the Installment Plan*. Trans. Ralph Manheim. New York: New Directions, 1966. (Originally published as *Mort à crédit*. Paris: Denoël, 1936.)

Céline, Louis-Ferdinand. *Journey to the End of the Night*. Trans. Ralph Manheim. New York: New Directions, 1983. (Originally published as *Voyage au bout de la nuit*. Paris: Denoël, 1932.)

Céline, Louis-Ferdinand. "L.-F. Céline vous parle." In *Céline*, Pléiade edition, vol. 2, p. 934. Paris: Gallimard, 1974.

Céline, Louis-Ferdinand. "Morceaux Choisis: *Bagatelles pour un massacre* (Le Livre de la semaine)." *Je Suis Partout*, March 4, 1938, p. 8.

Céline, Louis-Ferdinand. "Semmelweis et l'infection puerpérale." In *Semmelweis et autres écrits médicaux: Cahiers Céline*, ed. Jean-Pierre Dauphin and Henri Godard, pp. 13–109. Paris: Gallimard, 1977.

Chodorow, Nancy. "Gender, Relation, and Difference in Psychoanalytic Perspective." In *The Future of Difference*, ed. Hester Eisenstein and Alice Jardine, pp. 3–19. New York: Barnard College Women's Center, 1980.

Clark, Timothy J. *Image of the People: Gustave Courbet and the Second French Republic 1848–1851*. Greenwich, Conn.: New York Graphic Society, 1973.

Cobb, Richard. *French and Germans/ Germans and French: A Personal Interpretation of France under Two Occupations, 1914–1918/1940–1944*. Hanover and London: University Press of New England, Brandeis University Press, 1983.

Cobb, Richard. *A Second Identity*. Oxford: Oxford University Press, 1969.

Curtis, Michael. *Three against the Third Republic: Sorel, Barrès, and Maurras*. Princeton, N.J.: Princeton University Press, 1979.

Curtius, Ernst Robert. *Essai sur la France*. Trans. Jacques Benoist-Méchin. Paris: Grasset, 1932 (orig. German ed., 1930).

Daney, Serge, and Serge Toubiana. Reviewing *Français, si vous saviez* [filmmakers: André Harris and Alain de Sedouy]. *Cahiers du Cinéma* 246 (April–June, 1973):54–62.

Daudet, Léon. "Un livre symptomatique, *Bagatelles pour un massacre*." *L'Action Française*. February 10, 1938, p. 1.

Dauphin, Jean-Pierre, and Jacques Boudillet, eds. *Album Céline*. Paris: Gallimard, 1977.

de Beauvoir, Simone. *La Force de l'âge*. Paris: Gallimard, 1960.

de Beauvoir, Simone. "Oeil pour oeil." *Les Temps Modernes* 1, no. 5 (Feb. 1946):813–30.

de Benoist, Alain. Interviewed in "L'Intellectuel et le pouvoir: De Platon à Glucksman." *Magazine Littéraire* 183 (April 1982):48.

De Felice, Renzo. *Fascism: An Informal Introduction to Its Theory and Practice* (an interview with Michael A. Leeden). New Brunswick, N.J.: Transaction Books, 1976.

de Györy, Tiberius. Letter to *La Presse Médicale* (September 10, 1924). Reprinted in *Cahiers Céline*, vol. 3. Ed. Jean-Pierre Dauphin and Henri Godard, pp. 94–95. Paris: Gallimard, 1977.

Deleuze, Gilles, and Félix Guattari. *Anti-Oedipus: Capitalism and Schizophrenia*. Trans. Robert Hurley, Mark Seem, and Helen R. Lane. New York: Viking Press, 1977.

Derrida, Jacques. *Grammatology*. Trans. Gayatri Chakravorty Spivak. Baltimore: Johns Hopkins University Press, 1976.

Desanti, Dominique. *Drieu La Rochelle: Le Séducteur mystifié*. Paris: Flammarion, 1978.

Dinnerstein, Dorothy. *The Mermaid and the Minotaur: Sexual Arrangements and Human Malaise*. New York: Harper, 1976.

Dioudonnat, P.-M. *Je Suis Partout: Les Maurrassiens devant la tentation fasciste*. Paris: La Table Ronde, 1973.

Drieu la Rochelle, Pierre. *Chronique politique, 1934–1942*. Paris: Gallimard/Nouvelle Revue Française, 1943.

Drieu la Rochelle, Pierre. "Ecrit en Juin 1940." In *Notes pour comprendre le siècle*, pp. 171–86. Paris: Gallimard, 1941.

Drieu la Rochelle, Pierre. *Etat civil*. Paris: Gallimard, 1921. Reprint. Gallimard: L'Imaginaire, 1980.

Drieu la Rochelle, Pierre. *Gilles*. Paris: Gallimard, 1939.

Drieu la Rochelle, Pierre. *Interrogation*. Paris: Gallimard, 1917.

Drieu la Rochelle, Pierre. *Mesure de la France* [orig. ed. 1922]: *Suivi de Ecrits, 1939–1940*. Paris: Grasset, 1964.

Drieu la Rochelle, Pierre. *Socialisme fasciste*. Paris: Gallimard, 1934.

Duval, René. *Histoire de la radio en France*. Paris: A. Moreau, 1980.

*Eléments pour la civilisation européenne*. "Une Histoire de la musique" [editor's review of Lucien Rebatet, *Histoire de la musique* (Paris: Laffont, 1969)] 33 (Feb.–Mar. 1980), p. 69; "Pas d'accord avec Lucien Rebatet" [letter to editors from Anne and Pierre Jobert, Grenoble, France, followed by editors' response] 35 (Summer 1980), p. 52.

Ellul, Jacques. *De la révolution aux révoltes*. Paris: Calmann-Lévy, 1972.

Exposition "Le Juif et la France." Paris, Palais Berlitz, 1941. Centre de Documentation Juive et Contemporaine, Archives of the Institut d'Etudes des Questions Juives, XIg-119, 30.

Fabre-Luce, Alfred. *Journal de la France, 1939–1944*. 2 vol. Geneva: Les Éditions du cheval ailé, 1946.

Fanon, Frantz. *Wretched of the Earth*. Trans. Constance Farrington. (*Les Damnés de la terre*. Paris: Maspero, 1961.) New York: Grove Press, 1963.

Faurisson, Robert. "Le 'Problème' des chambres à gaz." *Défense de l'Occident* (June 1978):32–40.

Faye, Jean-Pierre. *Théorie du récit: Introduction aux "Langages totalitaires."* Paris: Hermann, 1972.

Field, Frank. "Drieu la Rochelle and Fascism." In *Three French Writers and the Great War*, pp. 81–138. Cambridge: Cambridge University Press, 1975.

Flax, Jane. "Mother-Daughter Relationships: Psychodynamics, Politics, and Philosophy." In *The Future of Difference*, ed. Hester Eisenstein and Alice Jardine, pp. 20–40. New York: Barnard College Women's Center, 1980.

Fleischauer, Oberst. Letter to Georges Montandon, January 2, 1939. Centre de Documentation Juive Contemporaine, Montandon Archives, document no. XCV, 47.

Fleischauer, Oberst. Letter to Georges Montandon, February 16, 1939. Centre de Documentation Juive Contemporaine, Montandon Archives, document no. XCV, 72.

Fónagy, Ivan. *La Vive Voix: Esais de psycho-phonétique*. Paris: Payot, 1983.

Ford, Charles. "Cinéma et propagande." *Eléments* 43 (Oct.-Nov. 1982):49-50.

Fresco, Nadine. "Les redresseurs de morts. Chambres à gaz: la bonne nouvelle. Comment on révise l'histoire." *Les Temps Modernes* 407 (June 1980):2150-2211.

Freud, Sigmund. "Childhood and Screen Memories." In *The Psychopathology of Everyday Life* (1901B). *The Standard Edition*, trans. and ed. James Strachey with Anna Freud, assisted by Alix Strachey and Alan Tyson, vol. 6, pp. 43-52.

Freud, Sigmund. *Civilization and Its Discontents*. *The Standard Edition*. trans. and ed. James Strachey with Anna Freud, assisted by Alix Strachey and Alan Tyson, vol. 21, pp. 64-145.

Freud, Sigmund. "The Relation of the Poet to DayDreaming (1908)." In *On Creativity and the Unconscious*, pp. 44-54. New York: Harper and Row, 1958.

Freud, Sigmund. "Remembering, Repeating and Working Through (1914g)." *The Standard Edition*, trans. and ed. James Strachey with Anna Freud, assisted by Alix Strachey and Alan Tyson, vol. 12, pp. 147-56.

Freud, Sigmund. "Screen Memories (1899a)." *The Standard Edition*, trans. and ed. James Strachey with Anna Freud, assisted by Alix Strachey and Alan Tyson, vol. 3, pp. 303-22.

Freud, Sigmund. "The Uncanny" ("Das Unheimliche," originally published 1919). In *On Creativity and the Unconscious*, pp. 122-61. New York: Harper and Row, 1958.

Fromm, Eric. *Escape from Freedom*. New York: Holt, Rinehart, and Winston, 1941.

Fussell, Paul. *The Great War and Modern Memory*. London: Oxford University Press, 1975.

Gallo, Max. *L'Italie de Mussolini; vingt ans d'ère fasciste*. Paris: Libraire Académique Perrin, 1964.

Gaultier, Paul. *L'Ame française*. Paris: Flammarion, 1936.

Gide, André. "Les Juifs, Céline et Maritain." *Nouvelle Revue Française*, April 1, 1938, pp. 630-36.

Girardet, R. "Notes sur l'esprit d'un fascisme français 1934-1948." *Revue Française de Science Politique* 3, no. 3 (July-Sept. 1955):529-46.

Giraudoux, Jean. *Pleins Pouvoirs*. Paris: Gallimard, 1939.

Gramsci, Antonio. "Caesarism." In *Selections from the Prison Notebooks*, trans. and ed. Quintin Hoare and Geoffrey Nowell Smith, pp. 219-23. London: Lawrence and Wishart, 1971.

Grover, Frédéric J. *Drieu la Rochelle and the Fiction of Testimony*. Berkeley: University of California Press, 1958.

Hamilton, Alistair. *The Appeal of Fascism: A Study of Intellectuals and Fascism, 1919-1945*. New York: Macmillan, 1971.

Hampton, Benjamin B. *A History of the Movies*. New York: Covici, Friede, 1931. Reprinted as *History of the American Film Industry from Its Beginning to 1931*. Introduction by Richard Griffith. New York: Dover, 1970.

Hanrez, Marc, ed. "Drieu la Rochelle." *Cahiers de l'Herne*. Paris: Editions de l'Herne, 1982.

Hansen, Miriam. "T. E. Hulme, Mercenary of Modernism, or, Fragments of Avantgarde Sensibility in Pre-World War I Britain." *Journal of English Literary History* 47 (1980):355-85.

Hardy, Georges. *La Géographie psychologique*. Paris: Gallimard/Nouvelle Revue Française, 1939.

Harries, Karsten. *The Meaning of Modern Art*. Chicago: Northwestern University Press, 1965.

Hempel, Carl G. "Scientific Inquiry: Invention and Test." In *Philosophy of Natural Science*, pp. 3-18. Englewood Cliffs, N.J.: Prentice-Hall, Inc., 1966.

Hoffmann, Stanley. "The Fall." Part 1 of *Decline or Renewal? France since the 1930's*, pp. 1-62. New York: Viking Press, 1974.

Howe, Irving. "Céline: The Sod beneath the Skin." In *Decline of the New*, pp. 54-66. New York: Harcourt, Brace, and World, 1963.

Huth, Arno. *La Radiodiffusion*. Paris: Gallimard, 1937.

Isorni, Jacques. *Le Procès de Robert Brasillach*. Paris: Flammarion, 1946. Reprint, 1956.

Jameson, Fredric. *Fables of Agression: The Modernist as Fascist*. Berkeley: University of California Press, 1979.

Jameson, Fredric. *The Political Unconscious: Narrative as a Socially Symbolic Act*. Ithaca: Cornell University Press, 1981.

Jardine, Alice. "Ideology and Writing Couples." Lecture at the 1983 Columbia University Colloquium on the Poetics of Ideology. Published as "Death Sentences. Writing Couples and Ideology" in *The Female Body in Western Culture: Semiotic Perspectives* [special issue] *Poetics Today*, ed. Susan Rubin Suleiman, vol, 6, nos. 1-2 (1985):119-31.

Joll, James. "F. T. Marinetti: Futurism and Fascism." In *Three Intellectuals in Politics*, pp. 133–84. New York: Harper and Row, 1960.

Jünger, Ernst. *Premier Journal parisien: Journal II, 1941-1943*. Ed. Henri Plard. Paris: Christian Bourgois, 1980.

Kaplan, Alice, and Kristin Ross, eds. "Everyday Life." Forthcoming, Spring 1987. *Yale French Studies*.

Kitchen, Martin. *Fascism*. London: Macmillan, 1976.

Klein, Melanie. "Mourning and Its Relation to Manic-Depressive States (1940)." *Love, Guilt, and Reparation and Other Works 1921-1945*, pp. 344-69. New York: Dell Publishing Company, 1975.

Kracauer, Siegfried. *From Caligari to Hitler: A Psychological History of the German Film*. New York: Princeton University Press, 1947.

Kristeva, Julia. *Desire in Language: A Semiotic Approach to Literature and Art*. Trans. Thomas Gora, Alice Jardine and Leon S. Roudiez. (Includes essays from *Polylogue*. Paris: Seuil/"Tel Quel," 1977.) New York: Columbia University Press, 1980.

Kristeva, Julia. *Powers of Horror: An Essay on Abjection*. Trans. Leon Roudiez. (Originally published as *Pouvoirs de l'horreur: Essai sur l'abjection*. Paris: Seuil/"Tel Quel," 1980.) New York: Columbia University Press, 1982.

Kunnas, Tarmo. *Drieu la Rochelle, Céline, Brasillach et la tentation fasciste*. Paris: Les Sept Couleurs, 1972.

Lacan, Jacques. "The Insistence of the Letter in the Unconscious." Trans. Jan Miel. *Yale French Studies*. No. 36-37 (Oct. 1966): 112-47.

Laclau, Ernesto. *Politics and Ideology in Marxist Theory*. London: New Left Books, 1977.

Laplanche, Jean, and J. B. Pontalis. *The Language of Psycho-Analysis*. Trans. Donald Nicholson-Smith. New York: Norton, 1973.

Laprade, Albert. "La Trop Belle Exposition." Introduction to *L'Exposition de Paris*. Ed. A. Calavas. Paris: Librairie des Arts Décoratifs, 1937.

Lefebvre, Henri. *Critique de la vie quotidienne*. 2 vols. Paris: L'Arche, 1958-62.

Leiris, Michel. *L'Age d'homme*. Paris: Gallimard, 1946. (Translated as *Manhood* by Richard Howard. London: Cape, 1968.)

Le Roux, Dominique, ed. "Louis-Ferdinand Céline." *Cahiers de l'Herne*, No. 3. Paris: Editions de l'Herne, 1963.

Lévy, Bernard-Henri. *L'Idéologie française*. Paris: Grasset, 1981.

*Libération*. Press file on the Affaire Faurisson. Nov. 11, 1978 to Feb. 11, 1981.

Lista, Giovanni. *Marinetti et le futurisme*. Lausanne: L'Age d'homme, 1977.

Mahler, Margaret S. "On Human Symbiosis and the Vicissitudes of Individuation." *Infantile Psychosis*. Vol. 1. New York: International Universities Press, 1968.

Mandel, Ernest. *Late Capitalism*. Trans. Joris De Bres. London: Verso, 1978.

Marinetti Archives. Beinecke Rare Book and Manuscript Library, New Haven, Conn.

Marinetti, F. T. "The Founding and Manifesto of Futurism," "Against Amore and Parliamentarianism," "Electric War," "Multiplied Man and the Reign of the Machine" (from *War, the World's*

*Only Hygiene*), "The Futurist Cinema." In *Marinetti: Selected Writings*. Preface R. W. Flint. Ed. Flint. Trans. R. W. Flint and Arthur A. Coppotelli. New York: Farrar, Strauss, and Giroux, 1972.

Marinetti, F. T. *Les Mots en liberté futuristes* (1919). Reprint. Philadelphia: Albert Saifer, 1970.

Marinetti, F. T. *Mafarka le futuriste, roman africain*. Paris: E. Sansot et Cie, 1909.

Marrus, Michael R., and Robert O. Paxton. *Vichy France and the Jews*. New York: Schocken Books, 1981.

Mehlman, Jeffrey. *Legacies of Anti-Semitism in France*. Minneapolis: University of Minnesota Press, 1983.

Michaud, Regis. *Ce qu'il faut connaître de l'âme américaine*. Paris: Boivin and Cie, 1929.

Miller, Gérard. *Les Pousse-au-Jouir du Maréchal Pétain*. Paris: Seuil, 1975.

Modiano, Patrick. *La Place de l'Etoile*. Paris: Gallimard, 1968.

Montandon, Georges. *Comment reconnaître le Juif? Suivi d'un Portrait moral du juif selon les livres de[ . . . ]L. F. Céline[ . . . ]*. Paris: Nouvelles editions françaises, 1940. Signed Dr. Montandon.

Montandon, Georges. Letter to Oberst Fleischauer, February 20, 1939. Centre de Documentation Juive Contemporaine, Montandon Archives, document no. XCVk-72.

Moore, Marianne. *Futurist Art and Theory, 1909-1915*. New York: Hacket Art Books, 1978.

Morand, Paul. *France la dolce*. Paris: Gallimard, 1934.

Mosse, George L. *Toward the Final Solution: A History of European Racism*. New York: Harper and Row, 1978.

Mussolini, Benito. "Fascismo." In *Enciclopedia Italiana*, ed. G. Treccani, vol. 14, pp. 847-84. Milan: Rizzoli and Co., 1932. (Generally acknowledged author is Giovanni Gentile.)

Nesbit, Margaret Spence. "Atget's Seven Albums: In Practice." Ph.D. diss., Yale University, 1983.

Novick, Peter. *The Resistance versus Vichy*. New York: Columbia University Press, 1968.

Ory, Pascal. "Apologie pour un meurtre." *Le Monde*, February 6, 1975, p. 10.

Ory, Pascal. *Les Collaborateurs, 1940-1945*. Paris: Seuil, 1976, Reedited, Paris: Collection Points-Histoire, 1980.

Pagès, Pierre. "Un Jeune Ménage s'installe" (water color with text). *Marie Claire* 232 (January 10, 1942): back cover.

Paxton, Robert. *Vichy France: Old Guard and New Order*. New York: Norton, 1972.

Payne, Stanley. *Fascism: Comparison and Definition*. Madison: University of Wisconsin Press, 1980.

Pelassy, Dominique. *Le Signe nazi: L'Univers symbolique d'une dictature*. Paris: Fayard, 1983.

Petrément, Simone. *La Vie de Simone Weil*. 2 vols. Paris: Fayard, 1973.

Plumyène, Jean, and Raymond Lasierra. *Les Fascismes français: 1923-1963*. Paris: Seuil, 1963.

Portnoy, Harold. "Entretien avec Louis Magnard. Les Editions en question. Première partie: des origines à l'expansion." *Préparons l'Avenir* 100 (May 1984):31-44.

Postone, Moishe. "Anti-Semitism and National Socialism: Notes on the German Reaction to 'Holocaust.' " *New German Critique* 19 (Winter 1980):97-117.

Poulantzas, Nicos. *Fascism and Dictatorship: The Third International and the Problem of Fascism*. Trans. Judith White. London: New Left Books, 1974.

Pound, Ezra. *"Ezra Pound Speaking": Radio Speeches of World War II*. Ed. Leonard W. Doob. Contributions in American Studies, no. 37. Westport, Conn.: Greenwood Press, 1978.

Pryce-Jones, David, and Michael Rand (picture editor). *Paris under the Third Reich: A History of the German Occupation, 1940-1944*. New York: Holt, Rinehart and Winston, 1981.

Rassinier, Paul. *Le Mensonge d'Ulysse*. 4th ed. Paris: La Librairie française, 1955.

Rebatet, Lucien. *Les Décombres*. Paris: Denoël, 1942.

Rebatet, Lucien. *Les Mémoires d'un fasçiste I: Les Décombres, 1938-1940*. Paris: Pauvert, 1976.

Rebatet, Lucien. *Les Mémoires d'un fasçiste II: 1941-1947*. Paris: Pauvert, 1976.

Rebatet, Lucien. Reviewing Céline, *Bagatelles pour un massacre*. *Je Suis Partout*, January 21, 1938, p. 8.

Rebatet, Lucien. (Signed François Vinneuil.) Reviewing *Triumph of the Will*. *Je Suis Partout*, August 20, 1937, p. 2.

Rebatet, Lucien, ed. Special issues, *Je Suis Partout*. "Les Juifs dans le monde," April 15, 1938; "Les Juifs et la France," February 17, 1939.

Rebatet, Lucien. (Also signed, in parentheses, François Vinneuil.) *Les Tribus du cinéma et du théâtre*. Paris: Nouvelles éditions françaises, 1941, p. 40.

Rehrauer, George, ed. *Cinema Booklist*. Metuchen, N.J.: Scarecrow Press, 1972.

Reich, Wilhelm. *The Mass Psychology of Fascism*. Trans. Vincent R. Carfagno. New York: Simon and Schuster, 1970.

Reif, Adelbert, ed. *Gespräche mit Hannah Arendt*. Munich: Piper and Co., 1976.

Rolo, Charles J. *Radio Goes to War*. New York: Putnam's Sons, 1942.

Ross, Kristin. "Rimbaud and the Transformation of Everyday Life." Forthcoming, Spring 1987. *Yale French Studies*.

Roth, Jack J. *The Cult of Violence: Sorel and the Sorelians*. Berkeley: University of California Press, 1980.

Roudiez, Leon S. "On Several Approaches to Céline." *Romanic Review* 72, no. 1 (Jan. 1981):94–104.

Roué, Paul. "Le Code de la T.S.F.," *Almanach de la T.S.F.* Paris: Editions de "Tout," 1934, pp. 42–50.

Rousset, David. *L'Univers concentrationnaire*. Paris: Editions du Pavois, 1946.

Sadoul, Georges. *Histoire générale du cinéma*. 6 vols. Paris: Denoël, 1973.

Said, Edward W. *The World, the Text, and the Critic*. Cambridge, Mass.: Harvard University Press, 1983.

Sansot, Pierre. *Poétique de la ville*. Paris: Editions Klincksieck, 1971.

Sartre, Jean-Paul. "L'Enfance d'un chef." In *Le Mur*, pp. 151–245. Paris: Gallimard, 1939. (Translated by Lloyd Alexander as "The Childhood of a Leader." In *The Wall*, pp. 84–144. New York: New Directions, 1948.)

Sartre, Jean-Paul. "Qu'est-ce qu'un collaborateur?" In *Situations*. Vol. 3, pp. 43–62. Paris: Gallimard, 1949. (First appeared in *La République Française*. New York: August 1945.)

Schalk, David. "Fascist Engagement." In *The Spectrum of Political Engagement: Mounier, Benda, Nizan, Brasillach, Sartre*, pp. 76–109. Princeton: Princeton University Press, 1979.

Seliger, Martin. *Ideology and Politics*. London: George Allen and Unwin, 1976.

Sérant, Paul. *Le Romantisme fasciste*. Paris: Fasquelle, 1959.

Snell, Andrea Gisela. " 'Die Franzosen' and 'Les Allemands': Cultural Clichés in the Making (1650–1850)." Ph.D. diss., Yale University, 1982.

Somenzi, Mino. "Aerovita." *Futurismo* 2, no. 58 (Nov. 12, 1933):6.

Sontag, Susan. "Fascinating Fascism." In *Under the Sign of Saturn*, pp. 73–108. New York: Farrar, Straus, Giroux, 1980.

Sorel, Georges. *Reflections on Violence*. Trans. T. E. Hulme and J. Roth. New York: Free Press/Macmillan, 1950.

Soucy, Robert. "Drieu la Rochelle and Modernist Anti-Modernism in French Fascism." *Modern Language Notes* 95, no. 4 (1980):922–37.

Soucy, Robert. *Fascism in France: The Case of Maurice Barrès*. University of California, 1972.

Soucy, Robert. *Fascist Intellectual: Drieu la Rochelle*. Berkeley: University of California Press, 1979.

Spackman, Barbara. "Il verbo (e)sangue: Gabriele D'Annunzio and the Ritualization of Violence." *Quaderni D'Italianistica* 4, no. 2 (1983):218–29.

Spitz, René. *No and Yes in the Genesis of Human Communication*. New York: International Universities Press, 1957.

Stanley, John L. *The Sociology of Virtue: The Social and Political Theories of Georges Sorel*. Berkeley: University of California Press, 1981.

Stanley, John L., ed. *From Georges Sorel: Essays in Socialism and Philosophy*. Trans. John and Charlotte Stanley. New York: Oxford University Press, 1976.

Sternhell, Zeev. "Fascist Ideology." In *Fascism: A Reader's Guide*, ed. Walter Laqueur, pp. 315–78. Berkeley: University of California Press, 1976.

Sternhell, Zeev. *La Droite révolutionnaire, 1885–1914: Les Origines françaises du fascisme*. Paris: Seuil, 1978.

Sternhell, Zeev. *Ni droite ni gauche: Idéologies fascistes en France*. Paris: Seuil, 1983.

Sternhell, Zeev. "Strands of French Fascism." In *Who Were the Fascists*, ed. Stein Ugelvik Larsen, Berrit Hagtvet, Jan Petter Myklebust, and Gerhard Botz, pp. 479–501. Bergen: Universitetsforlaget, 1980.

Suleiman, Susan Rubin. *Authoritarian Fictions: The Ideological Novel as a Literary Genre*. New York: Columbia University Press, 1983.

Suleiman, Susan R. "Ideological Dissent from Works of Fiction: Toward a Rhetoric of the Roman à thèse." *Neophilologus* 60 (1976):162–77.

Talmon, J. L. "The Legacy of Georges Sorel: Marxism, Violence, Fascism." *Encounter* 34 (Jan.–June 1970): 47–60.

Tanda, Anacleto. "Il Duce Aviatore." *Futurismo* no. 60 (Feb. 1, 1934):7.

Tausk, Victor. "On the Origin of the 'Influencing Machine' in Schizophrenia (1919)." In *The Psycho-Analytic Reader*, ed. Robert Fliess, pp. 31–64. London: The Hogarth Press, 1950.

Thalheimer, August. "Über den Faschismus." In *Faschismus und Kapitalismus*, pp. 19–38. Frankfurt: Europäische Verlags-Anstalt, 1967.

Theweleit, Klaus. *Männerphantasien* (forthcoming translation, Minneapolis: University of Minnesota Press).

*Trésor de la langue française: Dictionnaire de la langue du 19ème et du 20ème siècle (1789–1960)*. Paris: Editions du Centre National de la Recherche Scientifique, 1980.

Tucker, Robert. *The Fascist Ego: A Political Biography of Robert Brasillach*. Berkeley: University of California Press, 1975.

Tudesq, André-Jean, and Elizabeth Cazenave. "Radiodiffusion et politique: les élections radiophoniques de 1937." *Revue d'Histoire Moderne et Contemporaine* 23 (1976): 529–55.

Turner, Henry. "Fascism and Modernization." *World Politics* 24 (July 1972):547–64.

Valois, Georges. *Le Fascisme*. Paris: Nouvelles Librairies Nationales, 1927.

Vandromme, Pol. *Louis-Ferdinand Céline*. Paris: Editions Universitaires, 1963.

Vandromme, Pol. *Pierre Drieu la Rochelle*. Paris: Editions Universitaires, 1958.

Vandromme, Pol. *Rebatet*. Paris: Editions Universitaires, 1968.

Veaux, Micheline. "Réflexions vocales dans un miroir et voix mythiques." *Bulletin d'Audiophonologie* 16, no. 4, 435–47.

Walde, Alois, ed. *Vergleichendes Wörterbuch der Indogermanischen Sprachen*. Vol. 2. Ed. Julius Pokorny. Berlin and Leipzig: Walter de Gruyter, 1927. Reprint, 1973.

Walker, Gila. "Divided They Stand." *Jewish Monthly* 97, no. 7 (March 1983):8–17.

Weber, Eugen. *Action Française: Royalism and Reaction in Twentieth-Century France*. Stanford, Calif.: Stanford University Press, 1962.

Wilburn, Josette. "Le Travail de l'inconscient dans la création romanesque chez Robert Brasillach." Ph.D. diss., Ohio State University, 1979.

Winnicott, D. W. *Playing and Reality*. London: Penguin Books, 1971.

Winock, Michel. *Edouard Drumont et Cie: Antisémitisme et fascisme en France*. Paris: Seuil, 1983.

Wohl, Robert. *The Generation of 1914*. Cambridge, Mass.: Harvard University Press, 1979.

Young-Bruehl, Elisabeth. "From the Pariah's Point of View: Reflections on Hannah Arendt's Life and Work." In *Hannah Arendt: The Recovery of the Public World*. Ed. M. A. Hill, pp. 3–26. New York: St. Martin's, 1979.

Young-Bruehl, Elisabeth. *Hannah Arendt: For Love of the World*. New Haven: Yale University Press, 1982.

Zumthor, Paul. *Introduction à la poésie orale*. Paris: Seuil, 1983.

# Index

# Index

Abbott, John, 142, 143
Abortion, 101, 102, 104, 105, 106
Action Française. *See* Nationalism
Adorno, Theodor, xiv
Affaire Faurisson, 42, 185, 187, 191–92 n.46; *See also* Faurisson, Robert
Airplanes, 3–4, 71, 85–92
Allen, Woody, 164, 165, 166
Althusser, Louis, 8, 9, 20, 53
Ambush warfare, Italian, 91
Anouilh, Jean, 179
Antifascism, xi–xv, 6–7, 13, 18–22, 24–25, 34, 43–45, 166, 170, 180
Antiparliamentarianism, xxii, 31, 66, 69, 84, 86–87, 96, 99–101, 150
*Antipatrie*, 129
Anti-Semitism; Maurice Bardèche's, 180, 191 n.38; as caricature, 91, 122 n.21, 130, 131; L.-F. Céline's, 107, 109, 119–20, 127, 129, 130; critical analyses of, 43–44, 48; Pierre Drieu la Rochelle's, 68, 69, 71, 95, 99–100; fear of abstraction in, 27; film and, 146–49, 150, 191 n.38; French varieties of, 18, 153, 172, 190 n.23; German varieties of, xii, xv, xx–xxii, 173, 177; immigration and, 7, 30, 31, 68, 154; nationalism and, 18, 152–53; as philo-Semitism, xix, 162–63, 174; post-

World War II varieties of, 42, 167–69, 170, 175–76, 185; as projection, 6, 24; Lucien Rebatet's, 132–34, 139–40 n.1, 140–41 n.14, 159–60 n.13, 165, 179; voice and, 134
Antisentimentalism, 84
Aphorism, 132, 133
Aragon, Louis, 95
Arendt, Hannah, xv–xviii, xix, 47, 48, 49, 50, 57 n.12, 60, 61, 127, 163
Artaud, Antonin, 108
Auschwitz. *See* Camps, concentration and extermination
Avant-garde, xi, xiv, xx, 4–5, 10, 13, 28, 30, 35 n.2, 75–76, 108, 120, 121 n.1. *See also* Modernism
Aymé, Marcel, 178, 179

Balint, Michael, 12
Banality; as used by Hannah Arendt, xv–xviii, xxiii, 47, 48, 163; as used by Walter Benjamin, 49, 50; defined, 43; in psychoanalysis, 46, 47; George Sorel and, 60
Banham, Reyner, 54, 71
Barbie, Klaus, 42, 166
Bardèche, Maurice, xix, xxii–xxiii, 45, 46, 142, 165, 168, 188 n.3, 189 n.16, 190–91 n.34, 191–92 n.46, 192 n.50; career of, 162–63;

Volksradio, 135

Wagner, Richard, "Judaism in Music" (essay),
xx–xxi, xxii
War, total, 155
Warnod, André, 89
Weber, Max, xiii
Weil, Simone, 190 n.24
Weimar Congress, 183–84
Welt-Dienst (a.k.a. World Service, Service Mon-
dial) xxiii n.1, 131, 140 n.12
*White Shadows in the South Seas. See* Van
Dyke, W. S.

Wilde, Oscar, 28
Wilder, Billy. *See Sunset Boulevard*
Winnicott, D. W., 4, 5, 35–36 n.4
World Service. *See* Welt-Dienst
World War I, xxviii, 104, 145, 156; imagina-
tion and, 4, 96, 144–45; trenches, 94, 96, 97
World War II, xvi, 29, 156, 162, 181
Writing, committed, 95

Zionism, 173–74
Zukor, Adolph, 180, 191 n.34

**Alice Yaeger Kaplan** is associate professor of Romance languages at Duke University. A native of Minneapolis, she earned her Ph.D. in French with a minor in philosophy at Yale University in 1981, and taught French at North Carolina State and Columbia universities for several years. Kaplan edited a special issue of *SubStance* on anti-Semitism (Spring 1986) and co-edited, with Kristin Ross, a forthcoming issue of *Yale French Studies* entitled "Everyday Life." Her book on Céline's pamphlet *Bagatelles pour un massacre* will appear in France in March 1987; her next book-length project will be on the American fascination with French culture.

**Russell Berman** is associate professor of German and co-chairs the Program on Modern Thought and Literature at Stanford University. His latest book is *The Rise of the Modern German Novel*.